Private Enterprise and Public Education

Private Enterprise and Public Education

EDITED BY
Frederick M. Hess
Michael B. Horn

Teachers College
Columbia University
New York and London

Published by Teachers College Press, 1234 Amsterdam Avenue, New York, NY 10027

Library of Congress Cataloging-in-Publication Data

Private enterprise and public education / edited by
Frederick M. Hess and Michael B. Horn.
      pages ; cm
   Includes bibliographical references and index.
   ISBN 978-0-8077-5442-9 (pbk. : alk. paper)
   ISBN 978-0-8077-5443-6 (hardcover : alk. paper)
   1. Public schools—United States. 2. Entrepreneurship—United States.
  3. Educational change—United States. I. Hess, Frederick M. II. Horn, Michael B.
  LA217.2.P69 2013
  371.010973—dc23   2013008315

ISBN 978-0-8077-5442-9 (paperback)
ISBN 978-0-8077-5443-6 (hardcover)

Printed on acid-free paper
Manufactured in the United States of America

20 19 18 17 16 15 14 13   8 7 6 5 4 3 2 1

Contents

Acknowledgments   vii

Introduction   1
      Frederick M. Hess, Michael B. Horn, & Whitney Downs

1.   **More Than Meets the Eye:**
    The Politics of For-Profits in Education   11
      Andrew P. Kelly

2.   **The Costs and Benefits of Nonprofit and For-Profit Status:**
    Perspectives from Executives and Entrepreneurs   33
      Mickey Muldoon

3.   **Crossing to the Dark Side?**
    An Interview-Based Comparison of
    Traditional and For-Profit Higher Education   57
      Ben Wildavsky

4.   **Unequal Access:**
    Hidden Barriers to Achieving Both Quality
    and Profit in Early Care and Education   80
      Todd Grindal

5.   **Beyond Good and Evil:**
    Understanding the Role of For-Profits in Education
    Through the Theories of Disruptive Innovation   100
      Michael B. Horn

6.   **Odd Man Out:**
    How Government Supports Private-Sector
    Innovation, Except in Education   121
      John Bailey

7. **The Role of For-Profits in K–12 Online Learning**   140
       Michael B. Horn

8. **Philanthropic Dollars in Commercial Markets:
    Blessing or Curse?**   154
       Stacey Childress & Tamara Butler Battaglino

9. **Between Efficiency and Effectiveness:
    Evaluation in For-Profit Education Organizations**   173
       Matthew Riggan

10. **Would Steve Jobs Be a Hero if He Had Built an
    Education Company Every Bit as Good as Apple?**   192
       Chris Whittle

Conclusion   204
       Michael B. Horn, Frederick M. Hess, & KC Deane

Notes   211

References   225

About the Contributors   239

Index   245

Acknowledgments

For decades, educators have merely tolerated for-profit educational providers in public education. Even in reform-minded areas, such as charter schooling, for-profits are lambasted and sometimes prohibited—and never spotlighted. The same goes for higher education, where for-profit institutions now enroll millions of nontraditional students, yet still suffer from harsh criticism as media pundits and political wonks call for federal investigations and regulatory action. Without fail—whether the question is online learning, grant eligibility, new charter school legislation, or changes to student lending—there is profound preference for nonprofit or public alternatives. All of this is so familiar as to be unremarkable. Entrenched in rhetoric, critics argue in favor of limiting for-profit operation with onerous rules, if not denying their operation entirely. These questions distract from the primary goal of education: to improve our students' educational experiences, and set the stage for their future success.

American public education struggles to adapt to the changing demographics of today's students. K–12 and higher education are desperately in need of the innovative thinking and nimble adaptation that for-profits can provide. As critics have noted, for-profits do indeed have incentives to cut corners, aggressively pursue customers, and seek profits. But these traits are the flip side of valuable characteristics—the inclination to grow rapidly, maximize cost effectiveness, and accommodate customer needs. For-profits are typically able to tap capital and talent much more easily than nonprofits or public institutions. Alongside nonprofit and public providers, for-profits have a crucial role to play in meeting America's educational challenges cost-effectively and at scale in the 21st century. Indeed, traditional providers may struggle to do so without help from for-profit entrants.

We rarely discuss for-profits, however, with an eye to how they can improve our education system—an unfortunate truth that the authors in our volume seek to change. Without an external impetus to shift the conversation, relevant statutory and regulatory discussion will continue to focus on how to rein in or eliminate for-profit providers. While compiling this volume, we realized that there exists a space in the conversation for a more nuanced examination of what it would take to harness the potential of such providers. This requires erecting the incentives and accountability measures that ensure a level, dynamic, and performance-oriented playing field. Our volume seeks to thoughtfully explore the value of for-profit provision while acknowledging the potential negative consequences. When used to form policy, our analysis can ensure that we take advantage of the benefits while designing incentives that discourage undesirable behavior.

Producing this volume required the devotion of everyone involved. We thank our authors, who researched, revised, and discussed their topics without ever wavering in their engagement with the project. Their presentations, at private meetings meant to encourage fruitful discussion, led to more research and greater insight. We thank the dozens of meeting participants who asked the tough questions and pushed back when they felt it was appropriate. Without their input, this volume would lack invaluable context. With it, our chapters reflect the comments and concerns of numerous constituencies—policymakers, journalists, researchers, and practitioners. This context makes the volume accessible to all types of educators.

We are also indebted to the steadfast support provided by AEI and its president, Arthur Brooks. The Templeton Foundation generously provided financial support for this project, and we are deeply indebted to our program officers for their support and guidance throughout.

We would also like to thank the terrific staff at AEI and Innosight Institute, whose hard work coordinating the research and compiling and editing the contributions herein makes this volume possible. At AEI, we thank Whitney Downs and KC Deane for their efforts managing and overseeing the project, as well as Lauren Aronson, Taryn Hochleitner, Allison Kimmel, Daniel Lautzenheiser, and Chelsea Straus for their vital assistance. At Innosight Institute, we thank Meg Evans, Cathleen Calice, Clayton Christensen, and Gunnar Counselman for their assistance. Finally, we express our gratitude to the Teachers College Press team, in particular our acquisitions editor, Brian Ellerbeck, and our production editor, Aureliano Vazquez, who have demonstrated their skillful and timely guidance throughout the course of this project.

Private Enterprise and Public Education

Introduction

Frederick M. Hess,
Michael B. Horn, & Whitney Downs

For-profits have long been regarded as an evil, if sometimes necessary, imposition in the education sector. Skeptics dismiss for-profits as "seeking to profit on the backs of our children." In more measured terms, they charge that for-profits will cut corners when they can and prioritize acquiring customers over quality at times. Phrases like "privatization" are tossed off as broadly disparaging terms, and used to criticize public policies (like No Child Left Behind or charter schooling) and even nonprofit ventures (like Teach For America or the KIPP Academies).

We tolerate for-profit providers in education today—especially when it comes to buying pencils, buses, textbooks, or assessments—but they are widely imagined by educators, journalists, and many policymakers to have little or no redeeming traits. At the same time, for-profit providers complain about unwarranted persecution and plaintively wail that they "just want to be treated like everybody else."

We think both camps are mistaken. We think the tendency to reflexively dismiss for-profits is misguided. Although cautions are certainly warranted, we think skeptics do a disservice to students and the public when they fail to duly consider the unique strengths that for-profits can bring. In that light, we think it especially misguided for for-profit executives and employees to argue that they're "just like everybody else." For-profits have many similarities to nonprofits and public enterprises, but they also have distinctive traits—for both good and ill. In this volume, we seek to shed some light on those strengths and weaknesses and to argue that we would do well to assess the role of free enterprise in public education in a more nuanced, textured manner.

For-profits in the education sector deserve scrutiny because their corporate mission is—no great secret here—to make money. As in many industries, the incentive to grow rapidly and to squeeze costs can, at times, lead dubious actors to market themselves in deceptive ways or to cut corners when it comes to providing high-quality goods and services. The extent to which people believe for-profits are likely to do so—and whether they believe nonprofits also exhibit these behaviors—is one of the key fault lines that determines whether observers are optimistic or skeptical about the role of for-profits in schooling.

At the same time, investors' watchful eyes can lend for-profits a healthful discipline around performance and productivity. The prospect of returns means that promising profit-seeking ventures can offer terrific employees lucrative long-term opportunities and that they can tap vast sums through the private equity markets. For-profits also have a relentless, selfish imperative to seek out and adopt cost efficiencies where district and nonprofit managers will typically move more gingerly (school systems are typically loath to trim even a single job if they can avoid it). The pressure to increase revenue means that for-profits have cause to expand rapidly. Finally, a focus on the bottom line means for-profits are inclined to move nimbly and reallocate resources when circumstances warrant. Meanwhile, critics rarely acknowledge that, because for-profits are taxpaying ventures, they (unlike nonprofits or public institutions) pay taxes that help underwrite public school systems.

Many readers may balk at the notion that for-profits have a useful role to play in public education. They may find terms like *market shares* and *growth in productivity* to be off-putting and assume that those who believe for-profits have a vital role in education are dismissive of the values of public education. Of course, the record of private ventures in education, as in other sectors, is mixed. It's no wiser to romanticize for-profit providers than to demonize them. There are legitimate concerns about for-profits that demand transparency, oversight, and sensible regulation. But, before dismissing the role for-profits can play, it's at least worth pushing past casual stereotypes or general impressions.

In K–12 education, for-profit institutions have long existed to serve the public education system in a variety of ways—from providing transportation to publishing textbooks. More recently, the advent of charter schools, the founding of Edison Schools in 1992, and for-profit involvement in the school turnaround space have opened pathways for for-profits to do more when it comes to running or managing whole schools. The growth of online learning has also yielded a flurry of new for-profit companies, from full-school providers to upstart curriculum and tutoring corporations.

When it comes to higher education, for-profit institutions have dotted the landscape since at least the 1850s when H. B. Stratton and P. R. Bryant founded a chain of career colleges to teach shorthand, bookkeeping, and how to use the typewriter.[1] Driven by the disruptive innovation of online learning, for-profit universities have grown from bit actors on the outskirts to large-scale players enrolling a tenth of America's higher education population. Between 2000 and 2009, for example, for-profit institutions increased enrollment by 300%, while public colleges and universities grew by only 27%.[2] The University of Phoenix, a for-profit university system, alone now educates more than 300,000 students a year; its MBA program, for example, dwarfs the largest nonprofit MBA program in the United States by several orders of magnitude.

As of late, venture capital and private equity firms have poured more and more dollars into education as well—almost $23 billion was invested in financing and mergers and acquisition activity between 2008 and 2011, though these numbers are still dwarfed by investments in clean tech and other sectors.[3]

POLICIES TARGET FOR-PROFITS

In the K–12 sector, for-profits are often explicitly barred from bidding for or providing educational services. For instance, federal legislation banned for-profit ventures from competing in the U.S. Department of Education's Investing in Innovation Fund (i3) and restricted their participation in the $3 billion federal School Improvement Grant program (SIG). In the case of the "parent trigger," the reform-minded advocacy group Parent Revolution has pushed for legislation that prohibits parents who have pulled the "trigger" from partnering with for-profit charter school operators.

More generally, many states bar for-profits from educational provision. As of 2008, laws in 16 states barred for-profits from opening a charter school. New York's May 2010 charter legislation, for example, lifted the state's "charter cap"— but the key concession made by charter proponents was to prohibit the opening of any new for-profit charter schools.[4] For instance, the New Mexico charter law states, "Municipalities, counties, private post-secondary educational institutions and for-profit business entities are not eligible to apply for or receive a charter."[5]

Reflecting an oft-heard sentiment, prominent education historian Diane Ravitch has said, "I have no problem with businesses making a profit when they offer value for goods and services. But there is something about this for-profit education industry that feels unseemly." She continued: "I find myself uncomfortable about the very idea of making a profit by providing public education."[6] This statement pithily captures the concerns shared by many skeptics.

In higher education, as the for-profit institutions have grown rapidly, they have earned enmity and suspicion. In 2011, congressional hearings on for-profits showcased deep skepticism among key lawmakers.[7] The Department of Education, acting on similar concerns and responding to a Government Accounting Office report that identified several instances of troubling conduct by for-profit college providers, issued "gainful employment" regulations that curtailed for-profit colleges' business models. As a result, student enrollment at many for-profit colleges declined sharply.

It can be easy to overlook how unusual this state of affairs really is. John Bailey, executive director of Digital Learning Now, notes in his chapter that in areas such as health care, clean energy, and space exploration, policymakers spend less time questioning whether for-profit companies should be involved, and more time determining *how* best to involve them. For example, he notes, NASA set aside $6 billion to support private ventures competing to design and operate spacecrafts. SpaceX built its "Dragon" capsule, capable of transporting humans and cargo into space for $800 million—less than a tenth of the $10 billion NASA had spent trying to build its own model.

Indeed, in the case of education, the fervor that attends to labels like "for-profit" and "public education" can stifle more thoughtful conversation about their appropriate role in the sector. And while skeptics fear that for-profits want to treat classrooms and teachers like factory floors and automated workers, a range of for-profits—from Apple to REI to Google to Zappos—are widely thought to be attentive to the needs of workers and customers. Our point? That this stuff is far more complicated than it first seems.

CAN FOR-PROFITS BE AN AGENT OF REFORM?

This tendency of policymakers and the public to cast aside for-profit providers might not be a problem were there agreement that the educational status quo was satisfactory. In such a case, debates about what free enterprise might offer to public education might seem a frivolous luxury. But when one considers the reality of tight budgets, disappointing outcomes, high remediation rates, and rising expectations, it's no surprise that there's widespread agreement that we need to do much better.[8] For-profit enterprises have brought innovative power to an array of sectors. Given sensible policies and quality-control mechanisms, the particular strengths of for-profits can make them an invaluable part of the education tapestry.

Creating this environment, of course, requires transparency, appropriate regulation, sensible policy, and good information on results and performance—all crucial elements of any healthy marketplace. In all of this, though, it's important to recognize that for-profits' inclination to lower costs and prioritize market share can be enormously beneficial, as can the drive to scale rapidly and the ability to tap capital. Meanwhile, for-profits can use their agility and resources to lure impressive talent to tackle vital challenges, while focusing relentlessly on consumer needs. In a healthy marketplace, these traits can yield terrific results.

Yet, in our experience, educators, journalists, scholars, parents, and policymakers rarely consider the more positive half of the for-profit equation. Even the school choice discussion, which purportedly celebrates market-based solutions, has been centered on the opportunity for parents to use vouchers or other forms of choice to send their children to private nonprofit, traditional public, or parochial schools. When the for-profit sector is considered at all, it is generally done so in terms of "good versus evil." To those who regard these providers as unsavory or even exploitative, "making a profit" is often referred to in pejorative terms—not as something that could be consistent with educating students well and for good and noble reasons. As such, most statutory and regulatory discussion focuses on how to rein in for-profit providers.

For-profit proponents, for their part, have done an abysmal job of articulating just why it is that their desire to make a profit ought not be viewed as a dubious, suspect goal, and one innately at odds with the values of public education. Absent such explanations, it's no surprise that educators, policymakers, and scholars rarely discuss the upside of for-profit provision. A productive dialogue would include how best to harness for-profits or what kinds of incentives and accountability measures will ensure a dynamic and performance-oriented marketplace while policing against undesirable behaviors.

Moreover, for-profit proponents have been only too happy to rest on their laurels and take advantage of easy market opportunities. For instance, during the George W. Bush administration, more than a few dubious actors in the for-profit higher education industry showed themselves only too willing to take advantage of a regulatory scheme that had no consequences for poor performance or lousy results. Between 2001 and 2009, the Department of Education—with the enthusiastic support of the for-profit higher education industry—largely turned a blind eye to questions of problematic practices by for-profit colleges or for-profit lending. The resulting outcomes helped validate the concerns raised by those skeptical of for-profits and helped to fuel the ambitious regulatory efforts of the Obama administration's Department of Education.

ACCOUNTS OF FOR-PROFITS ARE TYPICALLY BLACK-AND-WHITE

Accounts exploring the role of for-profits in education are scarce. Those volumes that do highlight for-profit providers tend to either demonize or cheer them. Indeed, the "good versus evil" view of for-profits pervades the policy and scholarly conversation. Most works condemn for-profits for the toll their ruthless pursuit of dollars has taken on the students, teachers, or spirit of K–12 and higher education. Meanwhile, a few offer cheerful images of for-profits and argue that their growing presence in education, especially in postsecondary education, is a force that can fix much that ails the nation's education system.

In K–12, authors argue that the advent of No Child Left Behind—and its focus on high-stakes assessments and provision of supplemental educational services—has created a market where for-profit testing companies, tutoring services, and technology firms can prey upon districts and students. The authors of books like *In Defense of Our Children: When Politics, Profit, and Education Collide* (Garan, 2004), *Reading for Profit: How the Bottom Line Leaves Kids Behind* (Altwerger,

2005), and *Making Failure Pay: For-Profit Tutoring, High-Stakes Testing, and Public Schools* (Koyoma, 2010) suggest that it's not possible to reconcile the profit motive with serving children well. A more measured, but still highly skeptical, approach to for-profits in education was outlined by Larry Cuban in his 2007 book *The Blackboard and the Bottom Line: Why Schools Can't Be Business.* Although more open to the ability of business to play certain kinds of roles in education, Cuban still assumes that there's something about for-profits that renders them unsuitable for the core work of teaching and learning.

In higher education, opponents of for-profit educational providers sound many of the same alarms, as they argue that market principles and corporate models have been a corrupting force in the postsecondary landscape. For-profit university practices, such as the standardization of courses, syllabi, and assessments; data-based evaluation of faculty; and student-centric learning models, are seen as antithetical to the tenants of traditional higher education providers such as faculty autonomy, rigid course schedules, and an emphasis on research. Ellen Schrecker's *The Lost Soul of Higher Education: Corporatization, the Assault on Academic Freedom, and the End of the American University* (2010) and Gaye Tuchman's *Wannabe U: Inside the Corporate University* (2011) are just a few examples of books that cast for-profits in a negative light when it comes to their impact on higher education.

A select number of books come down on the other side of the "good versus evil" debate. These include John Sperling's *Rebel with a Cause: The Entrepreneur Who Created the University of Phoenix and the For-Profit Revolution in Higher Education* (2000) and Kaplan president Andy Rosen's *Change.edu* (2011). Proponents of for-profit educational providers, such as Sperling and Rosen, energetically insist that for-profits have much to offer thanks to their ability to reach nontraditional students and prepare them for the workforce. To these advocates, the problems with the sector can be attributed to a handful of "bad actors," rather than any fundamental flaws in the marketplace that encourage for-profits to sacrifice quality in return for increased market share.

Some authors have attempted to move beyond simply arguing for or against for-profits and instead draw out a more nuanced understanding of the rise and composition of for-profits, specifically in postsecondary education. Others have focused on the lessons traditional institutions can learn from the private sector, such as utilizing online technology, but have not really sought to study the private sector itself. Still others, such as those writing about disruptive innovation or the role of educational technology, have sought to understand the changes for-profit corporations have caused in both K–12 and postsecondary education without dismissing these developments as "good" or "evil."

Perhaps the two books that come closest to what we attempt here are *For-Profit Colleges and Universities: Their Markets, Regulation, Performance, and Place in Higher Education* (2010) by Guilbert C. Hentschke, Vicente M. Lechuga, and

William G. Tierney and *New Players, Different Game: Understanding the Rise of For-Profit Colleges and Universities* (2007) by William G. Tierney and Guilbert C. Hentschke. In each work, the authors take a balanced and detailed look at all facets of for-profit postsecondary providers, including their history, business and management practices, their place within today's marketplace and regulatory landscape, and the role they can play in expanding access to nontraditional students. Stephen Ball's *Education plc: Understanding Private Sector Participation in Public Sector Education* (2007) also warrants mention in this category. Unfortunately, such balanced analysis is virtually nonexistent when it comes to K–12.

THE BOOK AHEAD

By looking at the for-profit question in a variety of contexts and through a variety of lenses, the contributors to this volume seek to illuminate and explain the status of for-profits in education. None of the authors are hostile to for-profits, but all recognize that whether for-profits serve students effectively and promote social welfare will depend on the rules and policies that shape the educational environment in which they operate. The volume tries to look beyond the familiar myths about for-profits to shed some light on how they actually operate in the worlds of pre-K, K–12, and higher education.

Contributors suggest potentially more useful ways to think about and categorize the merits of providers, other than by focusing on tax status. Other contributors explore how policymakers, foundations, and other key actors can create better incentives for for-profits, increasing the odds that their selfish imperatives will lead them to act in ways that serve the needs of students and promote the common good.

Andrew P. Kelly, a research fellow at the American Enterprise Institute, gets things started by exploring how for-profit educational providers fare in the court of public opinion. By examining voting data, public opinion polling, and what public officials have to say on the matter, Kelly suggests that the politics of for-profit involvement in K–12 and higher education are more nuanced than they seem at first glance. As Kelly writes in his chapter, "The traditional Left–Right ideological continuum fails to capture the ways policymakers and the public confront questions about for-profit involvement in education. Instead, government policy and public opinion are built on an underlying set of distinctions that we might miss if we focus only on the high-profile partisan battles that occupy the headlines." Kelly argues that both policymakers and the public are quite comfortable with for-profit companies providing "peripheral" or supplemental education services, but are uncomfortable with for-profits running and managing schools. He concludes his contribution with a new framework for thinking about the politics of for-profit education.

In the next two chapters, Mickey Muldoon, formerly with the School of One for the New York City Department of Education, and Ben Wildavsky, a senior scholar at the Ewing Marion Kauffman Foundation, explore the unique role and characteristics of for-profits in the K–12 and postsecondary sector, respectively. Using survey data and interviews with prominent nonprofit and for-profit leaders and individuals who have worked for both nonprofit and for-profit organizations, Muldoon and Wildavsky explore the differences between these two types of providers. As people who have worked in both types of organizations, they offer an interesting perspective when it comes to business models, performance evaluations, data collection, and scalability.

If there's one area of education where for-profit provision can be said to have made significant inroads, it's the preschool sector. In his chapter, Todd Grindal, Harvard doctorate student and former executive director of a Montessori preschool in Washington, DC, surveys the landscape of for-profit providers in the pre-K and early childhood space. Drawing on both the author's firsthand experience with these issues and interviews from others in the sector, Grindal examines why the pre-K sector has allowed for-profits to gain a more robust presence than in K–12 or higher education. He also suggests how the practices of for-profit preschools could inform the public pre-K sector.

Michael B. Horn, director of the education division at Innosight Institute, explains why policymakers and reformers who castigate for-profits or nonprofits as inherently bad or good are categorizing the world incorrectly. It is not about whether for-profits are "bad" or "good," he cautions, but about what for-profits are and aren't incentivized to do when it comes to consumer satisfaction, embedded regulatory structures, and shareholder demands. As Horn argues in his chapter, "Government should not discriminate between for-profits and nonprofits as a matter of blanket policy. Instead, it should ask if the company with which it is contracting, for-profit or nonprofit, is delivering on what society is paying it to do, as determined by both the spirit and letter of the law. And policymakers more broadly should consider whether the law is asking these organizations to do the right thing."

John Bailey, director of Whiteboard Advisors and former appointee at the U.S. Department of Education and Department of Commerce, suggests that the exclusion of for-profit educational providers from federal governmental efforts is very different from how Uncle Sam treats for-profits in most other sectors. Bailey notes that policymakers and government officials are comfortable with for-profits routinely playing a substantial role when it comes to addressing pressing social problems in areas such as health care or green energy, but not in education. "When it comes to other crucial challenges our country faces—creating a more reliable health-care system, finding efficient sources of clean energy, or improving space exploration—policymakers do not ask whether they should engage for-profit companies, but how they should," Bailey writes in his chapter, continuing, "It's time for education policymakers to follow suit."

The ever-growing market for online educational provision presents unprecedented opportunities for innovation and for-profit involvement in all levels of education. But Michael B. Horn, coeditor of this volume and director of the Innosight Institute, explains in his second chapter of the volume that the opportunities can only be seized if policy barriers designed to blockade the advancement of for-profit virtual provision remain minimal. For instance, the current regulatory environment for online learning does little to push out for-profit providers; if sentiment toward their tax status continues to decline, however, outcries for regulation may hinder their growth. Horn advocates for smarter, quality-based efforts to control online learning providers and against regulations that artificially cap the demand for services or arbitrarily single out for-profit virtual education providers.

Although many assume that an influx of philanthropic dollars is uniformly "good," Stacey Childress, deputy director of education at the Bill & Melinda Gates Foundation, and Tamara Butler Battaglino, partner and head of public education practice at The Parthenon Group, caution that foundations can actually stifle the marketplace for quality for-profit providers. Childress and Battaglino introduce a framework to evaluate whether philanthropic investments will spark for-profit innovation in a positive way—and offer case studies to help illuminate how the framework should guide foundations.

For-profits pose particular challenges and opportunities when it comes to research and evaluation. In the increased push for "data-driven" accountability, Matt Riggan, a researcher at the University of Pennsylvania Graduate School of Education, notes that for-profits' opportunities for evaluation are unmatched. Riggan elaborates, however, that with this opportunity come significant caveats. Although these data present a virtual treasure trove for researchers, it's often not in the best interest of for-profits to offer themselves up for unfettered evaluation or to share internal research. He goes on to suggest policy remedies that could balance the proprietary interest of for-profits with the need for a transparent, quality-based marketplace.

The final contribution proffers a firsthand account of one for-profit entrepreneur's journey through the education system. Chris Whittle, who has a wealth of experience starting and running for-profit enterprises in education, including most recently as founder and CEO of Avenues: The World School, explores the underlying emotional reasons for the kneejerk discrimination against for-profits. He seeks to explain why the same reaction is not true for other organizations that may also have other interests in play besides serving children. He argues that the topic of for-profits in education is a complicated one, and while there is no single right answer for how they should be addressed in the education sector, there are better ways to approach the subject than solely through the lens of tax status.

The volume closes with a brief conclusion by the editors. Time after time— whether the question is regulating for-profit colleges, eligibility for federal grants, charter school legislation, student lending, online provision, or what have you—there are heated issue-by-issue debates about whether for-profits should even be allowed to operate. We hope the thoughtful contributions to this volume may help fuel more informed and useful conversations about the role of for-profits—hopefully moving us beyond tales of shining knights and menacing villains. Such a shift may allow us to more thoughtfully assess the potential upsides and downsides of for-profit provision and the kinds of policies and practices that can help take advantage of the former while mitigating the latter.

CHAPTER I

More Than Meets the Eye

The Politics of For-Profits in Education

Andrew P. Kelly

In the aftermath of President Barack Obama's "education-obsessed" State of the Union address in February 2011, one savvy education policy observer declared that we are on the verge of a new "Washington consensus."[1] In some ways, it certainly feels like it. A Democratic president has pushed for charter schools, teacher incentives, and innovative models of schooling. The secretary of education has bluntly told educators and established interests that they will have to adapt to a "new normal" by cutting costs and rethinking business as usual. Democratic- and Republican-led states have signed on to the Common Core standards.

At the higher education level, the president and prominent foundations have set ambitious goals to raise college attainment and have focused attention on productivity, cost cutting, and accountability for results. This "college completion agenda" has mobilized Republican and Democratic governors, and states across the country are adopting performance-funding measures that reward campuses for courses and degrees completed rather than enrollment.

Beneath this cheery consensus, however, a serious fissure remains over what role, if any, private, for-profit organizations should play in providing education. Recent policy developments have widened these divisions. At both the K–12 and higher education levels, the Obama administration and congressional Democrats have made it clear in word and deed that they are skeptical of for-profit providers. In K–12, the Democratic majority in Congress explicitly barred for-profit providers from individually applying to the administration's high-profile Investing in Innovation (i3) competition. Eligibility for the administration's Charter Schools Program Grants for Replication and Expansion of High-Quality Charter Schools was also limited to nonprofit charter management organizations.[2] These limits on for-profit involvement have prompted vocal protests from providers and

11

sympathetic observers. In higher education, Democrats have successfully phased out private student lending, pushed for new "gainful employment" regulations that will hold for-profit colleges responsible for the debt-to-income ratios of their graduates, and led a highly visible investigation of recruiting and financial aid abuses at for-profit institutions. Republicans in Congress have criticized the Democrats' single-minded focus on for-profits and have threatened the administration's new regulations through legislation.

This chapter argues that while the current debate about for-profits in education reflects basic philosophical differences between liberals and conservatives— a point driven home by the chapters that follow—there are important nuances that are critical to understanding politics and policy. A closer look reveals that even policymakers and citizens who are skeptical of for-profits in education are not opposed to for-profit involvement across the board, but are quite supportive of for-profits acting in particular roles. At the K–12 level, for instance, while congressional Democrats successfully thwarted Republican attempts to create voucher programs for private schools, they assented to federal Title I dollars flowing to for-profit providers of supplemental education services (SES) under No Child Left Behind. Shortly after Congress barred for-profits from applying to i3, Secretary of Education Arne Duncan urged for-profit providers to join in the turnaround efforts of the School Improvement Grants (SIG) program. And in spite of the recent rhetoric about for-profit colleges and universities, there are significant divisions within the Democratic caucus over the issue, with many Democrats from urban districts voicing serious reservations about the effects that regulating for-profit colleges will have on access to higher education for their constituents.

These crosscutting political dynamics—easily missed in the heated partisan rhetoric that often surrounds the for-profit question—mirror public ambivalence about the role of for-profit providers in education. On the one hand, the public is skeptical of for-profit companies running public K–12 schools. This skepticism is shared by Democrats and Republicans alike. On the other hand, large majorities approve of private contracting with for-profit providers for peripheral services such as transportation, food, and facilities management. Superintendents report a similar position.

Americans are more comfortable with for-profit colleges and universities than they are with for-profit K–12 schools. Overall, data suggest that a majority of the public approves of for-profit colleges and universities and believes they serve an important role in the system. But respondents also see for-profit colleges as lower in quality than public or private nonprofit institutions. Support of for-profits is particularly strong when they are cast as institutions that provide access to traditionally underrepresented groups, and African Americans and Latinos are quite supportive of for-profit colleges.

WASHINGTON POLITICS:
TRADITIONAL DIVISIONS, WITH A TWIST

Recent high-profile debates about for-profit involvement in education have divided liberals and conservatives. The Obama administration and Democrats in Congress ruffled feathers by pursuing education policies that target for-profit providers for additional regulation or limit their ability to participate in new programs. In higher education, the administration and Democratic members of the Senate Committee on Health, Education, Labor, and Pensions (HELP) launched aggressive efforts to investigate and regulate for-profit colleges. These moves prompted conservative critics to argue that Obama had declared a "war on for-profits" in education and to liken the Senate investigation to a "witch hunt."[3]

These fights have garnered the headlines, and they follow the traditional political/ideological script. But I argue below that there is significantly more to these debates than the typical political caricature lets on.

Democratic policymakers often voice concerns about the "privatization" of public education and the inherent tension between profit motive and providing high-quality service. Republicans, meanwhile, typically call for more market competition in public services, which has made them natural proponents of for-profit providers in education.

Many recent policy debates have reflected these traditional divisions. When Congress decided to bar for-profits from being lead applicants in the i3 competition, Jim Shelton, the head of the Department of Education's Office of Innovation and Improvement, explained: "The reason there is an additional caution there is that a for-profit, by definition, has a different part to its mission than just serving the children. . . . Every time there is a competing mission, you have to be sure that it's aligned with the service of the children."[4] When congressional Democrats initiated a series of hearings on for-profit colleges, Senator Dick Durbin (D-IL) told a National Press Club audience, "We need to consider whether it is wise for corporations that are more beholden to their shareholders than to their students to profit so lavishly from taxpayer dollars."[5] Senator Tom Harkin (D-IA), the other prominent Democrat in the for-profit skirmish, struck a similar chord in late December 2010, suggesting that for-profit colleges, by their nature, will put serving investors ahead of serving students:

> The result [of investor ownership] is that the vast majority of for-profit schools have prioritized growth over education in order to satisfy the demands of their investors. In fact, growth and return on investment for shareholders is their legal obligation. So it should not surprise us that educating students is taking a backseat to just getting more bodies in the door.[6]

The assumption underlying these arguments is that any educational organization motivated by profit will have a difficult time pursuing both goals simultaneously. When they conflict, for-profits will privilege profit margins over the interests of their students.

In other words, Democratic skepticism toward for-profit providers goes beyond the "few bad apples" variety. To be sure, this characterization does not apply across the board; in the debate about regulating for-profit colleges, Duncan and others at the Department of Education have been careful to justify gainful employment on the need to root out bad actors. But the congressional debates have rarely been as nuanced. As one journalist argued in the summer of 2010, once the for-profit question was taken up by Congress, the tone of the inquiry changed, with congressional Democrats "[appearing] more willing to question the quality and performance of the entire sector in a dramatic way."[7] According to Harkin, the abuses revealed at his committee hearings are not the result of a few bad actors but are an inherent outgrowth of profit motive. In reference to the Government Accountability Office's (GAO) controversial "secret shopper" study of 15 for-profit colleges, Harkin argued:

> GAO's findings . . . make it disturbingly clear that abuses in for-profit recruiting are not limited to a few rogue recruiters or even a few schools with lax oversight. To the contrary, the evidence points to a problem that is systemic to the for-profit industry: a recruitment process specifically designed to do whatever it takes to drive up enrollment numbers, more often than not to the disadvantage of students.[8]

As I discuss below, not all Democrats agree with this blanket indictment of for-profit providers, or with the administration's aggressive attempts to regulate the sector. But the most prominent voices on the Democratic side have certainly signaled an anti-for-profit position.

Republicans have always been philosophically comfortable with the role private firms play in fostering a market for public goods, and a number of existing education policies reflect this openness to for-profit involvement. The effort to reconfigure the program-integrity regulations (of which gainful employment is a part) is largely a response to the relaxation of many regulations related to for-profit colleges in the late 1990s and early 2000s. As a result, conservative commentators and Republican leaders have bemoaned the administration's efforts in higher education as an ideologically driven strategy to tear down the entire sector. In the first of Harkin's hearings on for-profit colleges, for instance, ranking member Mike Enzi (R-WY) urged federal regulators to use a "scalpel and not a machete" in removing bad actors from the for-profit sector, calling them an "essential part" of preparing our workforce.[9] Enzi and his fellow Republicans have also argued that looking at for-profit performance in a vacuum ignores the problems present across the higher education system. On the House side, Representative John

Kline (R-MN), chair of the House Committee on Education and the Workforce, has made it clear that he will use the legislative tools at his disposal to halt the implementation of the Department of Education's gainful employment regulations. Kline sponsored such an amendment in mid-February, and it passed by an overwhelming margin, garnering almost 60 Democratic votes.[10]

The series of Harkin hearings in the summer and fall of 2010 exacerbated the divisions between Democrats and Republicans. In September, Enzi denounced the for-profit investigation, telling Harkin, "I'll leave you to go ahead and beat up on the for-profit schools" before walking out of the chamber.[11] At the same hearing, Senator John McCain (R-AZ) expressed "regret that this debate has exemplified the sharp division between our two parties and philosophies" and criticized Harkin for focusing on the for-profit college question "ad nauseam."[12] In April 2011, the Republicans on the HELP committee sent a letter to Harkin condemning the "disorganized and prejudicial hearings" on the subject. In May, Enzi urged the Securities and Exchange Commission to review whether there was improper contact between Wall Street "short sellers" and the Department of Education on the gainful employment rule. Enzi and others have alleged that Department of Education regulators were in close contact with investors looking to profit from the negative impact that the new regulations would have on the stock prices of for-profit firms.[13]

MORE THAN JUST "POLITICS AS USUAL"

The highly politicized debate of the past 2 years should not obscure important wrinkles in the Democratic position on for-profits in education. Indeed, at both the K–12 and higher education levels, there are important departures from politics as usual. In elementary and secondary education, Democrats have been much more amenable to for-profit involvement that stops short of traditional school management or is limited to a subset of schools (a pattern also seen among the public). At the higher education level, a surprising coalition of Democrats broke from the rank and file to express concerns about the proposed gainful-employment regulations and the administration's singular focus on for-profits.

The Curious Politics of
Supplemental Services and School Turnarounds

In his study of the birth and implementation of No Child Left Behind's SES provision, Jeffrey R. Henig argues that SES should have fallen directly on the fault lines described above. "In a time when privatization of public services has become the scrimmage line for partisan battles between the right and left," Henig writes, "SES is an apparent endorsement of the notion that for-profit providers may hold answers that direct public provision does not."[14] Given the traditional division between the parties on this issue, it is particularly interesting that Democrats, including the reliably liberal Ted Kennedy, have approved of for-profit eligibility in SES from the start. Indeed, while there was considerable back-and-forth on how money would flow from Title I to tutoring providers, there was not significant debate about whether for-profits should be eligible to participate.[15] Those familiar with the negotiations suggest that Kennedy and other Democrats were not pushed to accept private providers in SES but legitimately believed that SES was a worthwhile alternative to publicly funded vouchers.

Indeed, as Henig points out, Democrats had already signaled their support for public funding of private tutoring for students in failing schools. In 2000, Senator Joe Lieberman (I-CT) proposed an amendment resembling the SES provision that would come later; the proposal would have freed up federal money for tutoring children in failing schools, with for-profit companies eligible to serve as providers. The amendment, tacked to an education bill offered by centrist New Democrats, failed to pass but garnered 13 Democratic votes.[16] Two years before the Lieberman amendment, Republicans and Democrats overwhelmingly passed the Reading Excellence Act of 1998, which set up a program of "tutorial assistance" subgrants that later served as the model for the SES provision.[17] Private, for-profit tutoring providers were eligible to participate, and this participation was not a point of contention. The law passed under suspension of the rules in the House and unanimous consent in the Senate with the support of President Bill Clinton.

More recently, the Obama administration has welcomed for-profit providers in its efforts to turn around failing schools. In a June 2009 speech, Duncan implored a broad array of providers to get involved in the turnaround game: "We need everyone who cares about public education to . . . get in the business of turning around our lowest-performing schools. That includes states, districts, nonprofits, for-profits, universities, unions, and charter organizations."[18] For-profit organizations are eligible to receive federal funds through the SIG program—the administration's turnaround program created as part of the stimulus bill. Under the "restart" turnaround model, districts can contract with for-profit education management organizations (EMOs) to provide "'whole school operation' services."[19] According to the grant's final instructions, for-profit EMOs can also provide "technical assistance" to schools that pursue the "transformation model."[20]

In light of concerns about the tension between profit motive and educational quality, it is interesting that Democrats would be willing to support and create programs that enable private providers to profit from federal education dollars. If Democrats object to the idea of private investors and shareholders earning a "lavish profit" from taxpayer dollars, the idea that firms are earning this money through afterschool tutoring rather than running public schools should be irrelevant. As Henig's analysis suggests, this distinction—between school management and tutoring—is partly rooted in basic interest-group politics. Because supplemental services are, by definition, "add-ons," they do not "present a head-on challenge" to public school jobs and the powerful unions that protect them.[21] A similar logic applies to EMO participation in the SIG program's "restart" model. Unlike the "turnaround model," which explicitly requires schools to fire the principal and replace at least half the staff, the restart model does not require a particular amount of staff turnover.[22]

Whether or not privatization of any support services constitutes a "head-on" challenge, unions are vocally opposed to it.[23] But even if the for-profit role in these peripheral programs ruffled union feathers, it is worth noting that SES and (to a lesser extent) turnaround efforts also pit one traditional Democratic constituency (low-income and minority voters) against another (unions). By limiting for-profit involvement to peripheral services or a small group of schools, Democrats have avoided a direct challenge to the unions while providing extra services to constituents, a net win for Democratic policymakers. Suffice it to say that rather than a kneejerk, ideological aversion to any for-profit involvement in federally funded K–12 education programs, Democratic policymakers are more discerning, assessing the for-profit question according to whether it would threaten the interests of supportive stakeholder groups.

Dissension in the Democratic Ranks

It is no secret that for-profit colleges and universities disproportionately enroll students from underrepresented groups, particularly in urban areas, where demand for community colleges often outstrips capacity. Because they serve traditionally Democratic constituencies—low-income and minority voters—for-profit colleges have become a crosscutting issue for congressional Democrats.

As of fall 2010 (before the midterm election), the Coalition for Educational Success (a for-profit advocacy group) counted 46 Democratic members of Congress who had expressed concerns about the Department of Education's proposed gainful-employment regulations.[24] The opposition was not limited to moderate and conservative Democrats, who are now quite rare in the House. On the contrary, included in that number were 12 of the 39 voting members of the Congressional Black Caucus, three of the four African American members then on the House Committee on Education and Labor, and four members of the Hispanic Caucus.[25] Some of the most liberal Democrats in the House, those from majority-minority districts, have expressed concern that the proposed regulations would lead to a decline in access for students who would not otherwise be enrolled in postsecondary education.

The opposition to gainful employment came to a head in February 2011, when Congressman John Kline (R-MN) proposed an amendment to a spending resolution that would prohibit the Department of Education from using appropriated funds to enforce gainful employment. The amendment passed overwhelmingly,

289–136; 58 Democrats broke rank and voted with Republicans to stop the enforcement of gainful employment. Figure 1.1 illustrates how Democrats from different types of districts voted on the amendment. I divide them according to the Partisan Voting Index of their district: Republican-leaning to evenly split (R + 15 to even), Democratic (D + 1 to D + 10), and heavily Democratic (D + 10 to D + 41).[26] The figure reveals that the small number of moderate Democrats representing Republican districts voted overwhelmingly in favor of the amendment (14 of 19 voted in favor). But even among Democrats from the most liberal districts, 26 members voted in favor of the amendment. The 26 votes included veteran African American Democrats such as Alcee Hastings (FL), Edolphus Towns (NY), and Donald Payne (NJ). Even former speaker Nancy Pelosi (CA), the most steadfast of Democrats, voted in favor of the Kline amendment.

The point is not to overstate the divisions among Democrats, as the majority are certainly skeptical of for-profit colleges. But the Democratic defections on the Kline amendment, along with the vocal opposition of prominent Democrats, reveal that for-profit higher education is a crosscutting issue for the party. Even some of the most progressive interest groups were at odds over the regulation. While the reliably liberal Americans for Democratic Action announced its opposition to the proposed rule in April 2011, other groups like Campus Progress (the student-organizing arm of the Center for American Progress) have consistently argued in favor of tougher regulations.[27]

There is evidence that the administration's push to regulate for-profits is turning off the most steadfast supporters of public and nonprofit higher education. In fall 2010, Representative Tim Bishop (D-NY), a former college provost

Figure 1.1. Democratic Voting on the Gainful-Employment Amendment

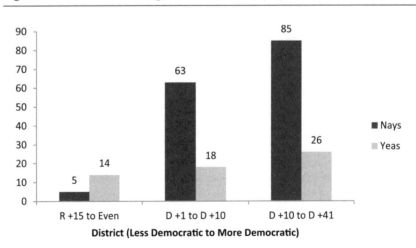

who has urged the GAO to investigate for-profits in the past, suggested that the push to regulate for-profits is too narrow. Asked whether it was right to "single out" for-profits, Bishop responded: "I'm very open-minded on that. I don't necessarily believe that we should be disproportionately targeting the for-profit sector. . . . We all have an obligation to conduct ourselves in a fashion that can withstand any form of scrutiny."[28] Despite these concerns, Bishop voted against the February gainful-employment amendment. But his misgivings about singling out for-profits are apparently shared by a sizable number of Democrats and some of their interest-group allies.

In short, contemporary debates about for-profit colleges have divided the Democratic Party. Electoral concerns and policy preferences shape individual positions on the issue, resulting in considerable heterogeneity within the ranks. Members with an interest in ensuring that their constituents continue to have access to for-profit institutions—many representing urban and majority-minority districts—have an incentive to keep those pathways open, even if it means breaking with the party. Democrats representing purple districts, many of whom lost in November 2010, feel compelled to adopt more centrist positions on divisive questions.[29]

At both the K–12 and higher education levels, the Democratic position on for-profits is much less monolithic than the conventional wisdom might suggest. As we will see below, the public's views are also far from uniform.

REPUBLICAN SUPPORT

Conservative policymakers and advocates have perennially promoted school vouchers and expanded school choice as top education priorities. But Republican leaders have rarely made an explicit, proactive case for allowing and encouraging for-profit providers in K–12 education, choosing instead to focus more broadly on school choice writ large. A look back at the last three Republican Party platforms (2000, 2004, and 2008) shows a heavy emphasis on vouchers for sectarian and other "nonpublic" schools and calls for more charter schools, but no explicit mention of the role private companies could play in fostering an educational market. Republicans have certainly not been hostile toward for-profit schools, but the push for "choice" has rarely translated to calls for more for-profit providers.

Republicans have actively promoted policies favorable to for-profit colleges, however. In 1998, the Republican-controlled Congress relaxed the "85–15 rule," replacing it with the current "90–10 rule," which allows for-profit colleges to receive up to 90% of their revenue from federal student aid. In 2002, George W. Bush's Department of Education softened the rules on incentive compensation for recruiters at for-profit schools, creating a number of "safe harbors" that would allow companies to provide bonuses to employees based on their performance. Bush's choice to head the Office of Postsecondary Education, Sally Stroup, was regarded as an ally of for-profit colleges, having served as a lobbyist for the University of Phoenix.[30]

Republican gains in the 2010 election created a counterpoint to the Democratic push for increased regulation. House Republicans voted overwhelmingly to prevent the Department of Education from spending appropriated funds to enforce the proposed gainful-employment rules. And Representative Virginia Foxx (R-NC), the new chair of the House Subcommittee on Higher Education and Workforce Training, promised to hold hearings on the student-loan reform that phased out private lenders from federal loan programs.[31]

Republicans have also become increasingly proactive in making an economic case for for-profit colleges in their criticism of the regulatory process. In June 2011, Enzi drew a direct link between the administration's efforts to regulate for-profit colleges and the nation's economic and human-capital challenges:

> This entire 436 page rule focuses on the issue of gainful employment, yet this Administration continues to strangle the job creators in this country. The Administration should instead take a closer look at how its burdensome rules and overregulation have hurt our nation's economy and the millions of unemployed Americans. Many of these affected schools provide important training for those who choose to become mechanics, plumbers, and electricians. This rule uses a heavy hand against these schools and makes it more difficult for Americans to access educational opportunities.[32]

Though earlier critiques argued that a focus on for-profits ignores broader issues in postsecondary education and lambasted the investigative hearings and regulatory process, the shifting political tides seem to have emboldened Republicans. For instance, before the November 2010 election, the Coalition for Educational Success listed just 29 Republican House members and five Republican senators as having signaled their opposition to the proposed rule (compared with 46 Democrats).[33] On the Kline amendment 3 months later, Republican opposition to the Department of Education's regulation was nearly unanimous.

Clearly, it would be wrong to suggest that Republicans are skeptical of for-profit involvement in education. When provided with opportunities to encourage for-profits, especially in higher education, Republicans have done so. But in K–12, choice advocates on the right have been so singularly focused on vouchers for sectarian and other nonpublic schools that they have rarely identified the creation and encouragement of for-profit schools and providers as a priority. In the effort to promote choice, advocates have focused on institutions that, because of their long history in American education and considerable goodwill in urban communities, are likely to be more politically palatable than for-profit providers.

PUBLIC OPINION ON FOR-PROFITS

The American public's attitudes toward for-profit involvement in education are mixed. At the K–12 level, Americans are skeptical about for-profit management of public schools, but they support for-profit contracting on noninstructional matters. Data are more limited at the higher education level, but results suggest that the public approves of for-profit colleges and universities, though they consistently see them as lower in quality than public or nonprofit institutions.

K–12: Tough Sell on School Management, Support for Segmented Contracting

Public opinion data over the past 10 to 15 years reveal a relatively consistent picture: Americans are skeptical about for-profit management of K–12 schools. I searched the public opinion database at the Roper Center for Public Opinion Research for surveys that included items about for-profit schools over the past 20 years. The annual Phi Delta Kappa (PDK)/Gallup poll has asked a variety of for-profit questions since the early 1990s, and a handful of other surveys have done the same.

A 2009 CBS News poll asked respondents whether they approve of school districts hiring "private companies that specialize in education" whose goal is to "provide quality education and make a profit." Just 12% reported that they "strongly favor" this idea, while 27% strongly opposed it. When including those who felt less intensely about the issue, the divide narrows somewhat, with 41% somewhat or strongly supporting the idea and 49% somewhat or strongly opposed (about 10% were unsure). When asked whether they would consider sending their children to such a school, 14% of parents said they would "definitely do so," while 18% would "definitely not." Overall, 46% suggested they would seriously consider it, while 49% would not.[34]

The PDK/Gallup poll has regularly asked about the for-profit issue since the mid-1990s, though the question wording has varied. In 1994 and 1999, the poll asked respondents whether they approved of an idea "being tested in a couple of cities" of private contracting with for-profit firms to operate schools. Though more respondents were opposed to the idea, in each year a sizable minority favored it (45% in favor, 54% opposed in 1994; 41% in favor, 47% opposed in 1999).

The public was less enthusiastic when asked about for-profit schools operating in their own community. In 2002, 2006, and 2007, the PDK survey asked whether respondents approved of the school board contracting with "private profit-making corporations" to run "the entire operations of the public schools in [their] community." Table 1.1 reveals that each year, less than one-third of respondents approved of for-profit involvement, while about two-thirds were opposed.[35]

Table 1.1. Public Opinion on Private, For-Profit Firms Managing Local Public Schools

Question: Would you favor or oppose a plan in which your local school board would contract with private profit-making corporations to run the entire operations of the public schools in your community?

Year	Favor	Oppose	Don't Know
2007	31%	66%	3%
2006	24%	69%	7%
2002	31%	65%	4%

Source: Phi Delta Kappa International, n.d.

The differences in support across these two items are probably due to the question wording: In the same way that Americans are more likely to think their local schools are doing a good job while national schools are mediocre, they are more supportive of an idea being tested in a handful of districts than they are of for-profits operating in their own district.[36]

In 2001 and 1996, the PDK poll also asked about for-profit contracting in different segments of schooling, ranging from transportation and food services to whole school management. These questions provide a sense of where the public draws the line on for-profit contracting. The items asked about support for "the school board in your community contracting with local businesses" for transportation, facilities management, food service, and "managing the entire school operation." The results, displayed in Table 1.2, are striking: Americans are extremely supportive of for-profit contracting for peripheral services, but decidedly less comfortable with for-profits running entire schools. In both years, at least 75% of respondents favored contracting with for-profit firms for transportation, food, and facilities management. When it comes to "running the whole school operation," these ratios are essentially reversed, with about 25–35% of respondents supporting the idea.

The public's distinction between peripheral and core services mirrors how school superintendents feel about for-profits. In a 2003 survey of superintendents, Belfield and Wooten found that while 80% of superintendents reported private contracting of some kind, just 17% of districts reported contracting with for-profits on "instructional delivery."[37] In contrast, about 40% reported private contracting on capital improvements, 32% on transportation, and 27% on health and counseling services. Fully 91% of superintendents reported that they had "never considered" contracting with a for-profit entity to "manage an entire school site."

Table 1.2. Public Opinion on Local Business Providing School Services

Question: Are you in favor [of] or opposed to the school board in your community contracting with local businesses to provide the following: school bus and other transportation services, school building and facilities maintenance, food services, running the entire school operation?

	Favor	Oppose	DK
Year: 2001			
School bus and other transportation services	75%	23%	2%
School building and facilities maintenance	75%	23%	2%
Food services	75%	22%	3%
Running the entire school operation	26%	72%	2%
Year: 1996			
School bus and other transportation services	75%	20%	5%
School building and facilities maintenance	79%	17%	4%
Food services	81%	15%	4%
Running the entire school operation	34%	59%	7%

Source: Phi Delta Kappa International, n.d.

Just 2% had given it serious consideration. Urban superintendents and those earlier in their careers were more supportive of for-profit contracting.

Superintendents sense the public's reluctance to embrace for-profit school management, or at least recognize the risk of public opposition. When asked whether particular groups would support or oppose for-profit management of instruction, sizable majorities of superintendents reported that unions, school boards, district personnel, parents, and the local community would all be opposed to the idea. Just 4% of superintendents thought parents and the community would be supportive.

There are some gaps across respondents with different backgrounds and party identification, but they are rarely so large that majority support of for-profit school management emerges. On the 2002 PDK survey, urban respondents and those under age 30 were more supportive of for-profit contracting than their suburban and older peers. However, even among more sympathetic groups, support remained at about 42%—hardly a resounding vote of confidence.[38] The results are similar if we divide respondents according to how they view the quality of their local public schools (see Table 1.3). PDK always asks respondents to assign a letter grade to the public schools in their communities. Among those who gave their local schools a grade of C or worse on the 2001 PDK survey, support for for-profit school management is just below 30%. Not surprisingly, those who gave local schools an A or B are less supportive—just 23% favor for-profit management. But even among respondents who are most dissatisfied with their local public schools, for-profit management is still a tough sell.

Nor does support of for-profit schools reach a majority among self-identified Republicans. In 2001, 21% of Democrats expressed support for for-profit management of schools in the community. A larger proportion of Republicans were in favor of the idea (30%), but support still failed to reach a plurality (see Table 1.3).[39] In the 2009 CBS poll, just 13% of Republicans were strongly in favor of for-profit schools, compared with 11% of Democrats; 27% of Republicans and 29% of Democrats were strongly opposed to the idea. Including the lukewarm responses, 46% of Republicans strongly or somewhat favored for-profit schools, compared with 37% of Democrats. This gap is expected, but it still means that a majority of Republicans were either opposed to or unsure of for-profit school management.

To summarize, the public is generally supportive of for-profit contracting for peripheral services, but much less comfortable with for-profit management of entire school sites and instruction. Public opinion is more evenly divided when the polls ask about testing an idea in a handful of districts than when the polls ask about their own local schools, which dovetails with existing research on how

Table 1.3. Support for For-Profit Firms "Running the Entire School Operation," by Groups, 2001

	Favor	Oppose
Local School Grade		
A or B	23%	75%
C or below	29%	69%
Party Identification		
Democrats	21%	78%
Republicans	30%	68%

Source: Phi Delta Kappa International, n.d.

people feel about local versus national public schools. Although Republicans are somewhat more supportive than Democrats, majorities of both are typically opposed to for-profit management of public schools.

Public Support of For-Profit Colleges

In general, the public is more comfortable with for-profit colleges than with for-profit K–12 schools, though it rates for-profit colleges less favorably than other types of institutions. For example, a September 2010 poll by the Associated Press and Stanford University asked respondents to rate the "quality of education" offered by various types of institutions and found that 66% of respondents rated for-profit colleges and universities excellent or good; just 7% rated them poor or very poor (see Table 1.4). Fifty-eight percent gave positive ratings to for-profit trade schools, and 6% rated them poor or very poor. These ratings lagged behind those for other institutions, but not by a large margin (69% positive rating for public 2-year schools and 74% for public 4-year schools). Moreover, roughly the same percentage of respondents (about 25%) rated for-profits, public 4-years, and nonprofit 4-years as "excellent."

The most in-depth survey of attitudes toward for-profit colleges was, oddly enough, conducted by the Americans for Democratic Action, a liberal advocacy group.[40] The survey was fielded in 2009, largely predating the latest controversy, but the results mirror the Stanford poll. Overall, 58% of respondents had a favorable view of for-profit colleges and universities, while 20% had an unfavorable view. Almost as many had "no opinion" (19%), suggesting that public attitudes toward for-profits are still underdeveloped. This level of public support lagged

Table 1.4. Public Opinion on School Quality

Question: In general, how would you rate the quality of education offered by the following in your state?

Type	Excellent	Good	Fair	Poor	V. Poor
Nonprofit 4-Year	25%	45%	14%	2%	1%
Public 4-Year	22%	52%	19%	3%	1%
Public 2-Year	18%	51%	21%	3%	2%
For-Profit	24%	42%	16%	5%	2%
For-Profit Trade Schools	16%	42%	19%	5%	1%

Source: Associated Press & Stanford University, 2010.

further behind other types of institutions than in the Stanford poll; community colleges and state 4-years topped the list, respectively, with 86% and 84% of respondents having a very favorable or somewhat favorable view. Private nonprofits came in at 75% favorable. Just 49% of respondents felt favorably toward colleges that "only offer online courses."

Respondents recognized differences in quality across different types of institutions; while 62% of respondents reported that "traditional state or private universities" do an excellent or good job of "giving students the knowledge and skills they need to be competitive," 50% said the same about for-profits (18% did not know enough to have an opinion). When asked to directly compare traditional colleges and for-profits, however, respondents were split, with just about half (49%) reporting that the education at for-profits was of higher or about the same quality as that at state or nonprofit colleges and universities.

The study also found that most Americans do not believe that for-profits are "exploiting" their students; when asked to choose which statement came closest to their views, just 22% of respondents chose the statement that "for-profit, accredited universities exploit their students into taking more and more loans, and then never graduate them," while 57% chose "[for-profits] play an important role in higher education and should be encouraged to grow." Six in ten people disagreed with the idea that "for-profit university growth should be stopped."

African Americans and Latinos were somewhat more supportive of for-profits than Whites. For instance, 65% of African Americans and 64% of Latinos had a favorable view of for-profits, compared to just 52% of low-income Whites. The same is true for online colleges: 58% of African Americans and 60% of Latinos felt favorably toward these institutions, while just 40% of low-income Whites did. In terms of party identification, Republicans were about as supportive of for-profit expansion as Democrats (67% of Democrats in favor versus 64% of Republicans).

The picture was not entirely rosy for for-profit colleges. In spite of this generic support, the public was more closely divided on questions about profits versus quality. When asked if "by their very nature, for-profit universities will exploit their students because they will sacrifice quality for increased profits," 42% of respondents disagreed, while 48% agreed. When asked whether these for-profit universities are "'diploma mills' that produce students without real skills," 46% disagreed, while 42% agreed.

In my survey of 1,000 parents of high school–age students in the five most populous states, I found that a majority of respondents supported providing federal student aid to a hypothetical student enrolled in a for-profit university. The survey items asked respondents whether they thought various types of students should be eligible for federal student aid (grants or loans). Table 1.5 displays the results. In general, the public was quite supportive of providing federal aid to "a 25-year-old high school graduate at a for-profit university," as 63% of parents believed such students should be eligible for federal grants, and 75% believed they

Table 1.5. Public Opinion on Federal Grant and Loan Eligibility

Question: Should these students be eligible for federal grants/loans?

Hypothetical Student	Federal Grants		Federal Loans	
	Should be eligible	*Should not be eligible*	*Should be eligible*	*Should not be eligible*
25-year-old high school grad. at for-profit college	63%	36%	75%	23%
Middle-aged housewife	80%	19%	89%	10%
High school dropout with GED	77%	22%	84%	15%

Note: One-half of the sample was asked about grants, and one-half was asked about loans.
   Some percentages do not sum to 100 because some respondents skipped the question.

Source: American Enterprise Institute, 2010.

should be eligible for federal loans. As with the surveys discussed above, these levels of support lag behind those for other types of students, and it is worth noting that more than 35% of parents opposed federal grant aid to students at for-profits. But majorities still believed that a student at a for-profit college should be eligible for both forms of federal aid.

In sum, the public approves of for-profit colleges, especially compared with the meager levels of support for for-profit management of K–12 schools. Support for for-profit colleges stands in stark contrast to the contemporary debate and corresponding media coverage, which has typically focused on for-profit abuses and fraud. Whether the tone of media coverage of for-profits will have a longer-term impact on public opinion is a question I return to below.

IS EDUCATION "DIFFERENT"?

Debates about privatization and the role of for-profits have raged across many different policy areas. A quick look at the libertarian Reason Foundation's exhaustive coverage of privatization efforts or the liberal Privatizationwatch.org reveals that the privatization of everything from trash collection to highways to international armed conflict has been hotly debated in recent years.[41] How does the public feel about for-profit involvement in other areas, and how does that compare with for-profits in public education?

There is a large body of research on American attitudes toward privatization, far too much to summarize here. One issue is that advocacy groups often run their own polls on privatization topics, producing results that are typically in line with their policy goals. Given the source, these polls are less credible than those conducted by independent polling organizations or academic groups.

In general, though, Americans are more comfortable with privatization in other policy areas. In 1996, the General Social Survey asked Americans whether banks, hospitals, and electric power should be provided by the government or private companies. Almost 80% of Americans favored private ownership of both electric power and banks, while 74% favored private ownership of hospitals. When compared with their international peers (the same questions were on the 1996 International Social Survey Programme), Americans are more comfortable with private ownership in these areas.[42] Unfortunately, because the survey did not ask about schools, we cannot directly compare these results.

Hospitals may be the closest analog to schools, and researchers have paid considerable attention to the nonprofit/for-profit divide in health care. A 2004 review of the survey research found that Americans feel that for-profit versus nonprofit ownership of hospitals and insurance companies "matters," and that the sectors have different strengths.[43] During the late 1990s, a plurality of respondents consistently reported that the growth of for-profit involvement was a "bad thing" (ranging from 42 to 54%), while just one in five thought it was a "good thing." The authors found that the public sees nonprofit hospitals and insurance providers as more trustworthy, more humane, and less costly. But respondents also felt that for-profits delivered higher-quality care and were more efficient than nonprofits. As in education, public attitudes toward for-profit hospitals and health insurance plans are clearly mixed and multidimensional. But the perception that for-profit hospitals are of equal or higher quality contrasts with much of the data on for-profits in K–12 and postsecondary education explored above.

WHAT SHOULD WE MAKE OF THESE POLITICS?

The traditional left–right ideological continuum fails to capture the ways policymakers and the public confront questions about for-profit involvement in education. Instead, government policy and public opinion are built on an underlying set of distinctions that we might miss if we focus only on the high-profile partisan battles that occupy the headlines.

At the risk of oversimplifying, the evidence suggests that the politics of for-profits can be summarized using the two-by-two in Figure 1.2. The vertical axis corresponds to the peripheral/core business dimension discussed above—on the bottom are peripheral services such as transportation, facilities, and food services, with tutoring and textbooks in the middle, and management of school operations at the top. The horizontal axis corresponds to the age of those receiving the service—ranging from elementary school students to adult postsecondary learners.

Figure 1.2. Continuum of For-Profit Involvement in Education

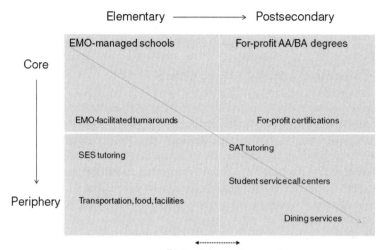

+ Risk - (along diagonal)

The diagonal from the top left to bottom right tracks the degree of risk involved in these services for policymakers and families. The top left corner is where for-profit providers are the most controversial; it involves direct, in loco parentis arrangements between for-profit firms and families and enlists for-profits in providing a distinctly "public" good. As public opinion data suggest, Americans are quite risk-averse to this form of for-profit involvement. Meanwhile, tutoring by private firms such as Sylvan, Kaplan, and Princeton Review has been a distinctly private good available to affluent parents for decades, and SES provides lower-income families with access to these proven providers. In terms of real or perceived social costs, a failed tutoring provider is not as grave as a failed for-profit school.[44]

At the postsecondary level, the participants are adults, and an argument can be made that postsecondary education is a private good. Indeed, a typical defense of the for-profit postsecondary sector is that its customers are adults making rational decisions about their future rather than being duped into a bad investment. In some sense, the public has tolerated, and even encouraged, individuals to take on this personal risk since the country expanded higher education access. Survey data suggest that Americans overwhelmingly blame students for college dropout rates, and they still believe that higher education opportunity should be expanded.[45] Associate's degree completion rates hover around 25–30% and bachelor's degree completion under 60%, but Americans are comfortable with the tradeoff between individual opportunity and risk inherent in investing in higher education. This acceptance of the risk involved in pursuing a college degree seems to shape the way policymakers and the public think about for-profit colleges.

It is reasonable to suggest that we will continue to see more for-profit involvement in education as we move away from the top left corner of Figure 1.2. The figure also suggests that government efforts to prohibit or heavily regulate for-profit providers will resonate more at the K–12 level, where the public is already skeptical, than at the higher education level, where the public is more accepting of risk.

Are the Lines in the Sand Likely to Change?

The interesting policy question is whether the lines in the sand are likely to change as for-profit EMOs become more ubiquitous. In his annual report, noted for-profit critics Alex Molnar, Gary Miron, and Jessica L. Urschel documented the growth of for-profit EMOs over the last 12 years, finding that EMOs have grown in both number and reach (the number of schools operated and students enrolled) since the late 1990s.[46] In spite of this growth (or maybe because of it), the PDK data suggest that public opinion about for-profit school management has not changed much since the mid-1990s.

Part of the explanation may lie in how federal policy incentives shape the supply side. In the same way that the public's and policymakers' opinions have carved out a niche for for-profits in federal programs, some firms have responded to these incentives by developing segments of their business that can benefit from federal funds—tutoring, curriculum, and professional development. Molnar highlights EdisonLearning as one company that has undergone such "diversification" in recent years. The incentive to develop tutoring programs, coupled with the skepticism of school management that is often built into other federal policies, may make SES a more attractive business proposition than managing entire schools. The latter business plan is fraught with political obstacles and lacks the clear-cut incentives that federal and state policies have created in the former. In this way, the growth of for-profit providers in response to incentives (shifting toward peripheral services and away from school management) may reinforce, rather than change, the lines that the public and policymakers have drawn on this question.

We will have to wait and see whether the recent firestorm around for-profit colleges has a long-term effect on public support. The September 2010 Associated Press/Stanford survey suggests that support is still relatively high, but it is still too early to tell.

Asymmetries in the Visibility of Success and Failure

Part of the reason that the risk/reward is skewed against for-profit involvement in any public-service sector is that the visibility of failure is likely to be much higher than the visibility of success. Though I have not collected systematic data on news coverage, anecdotal evidence suggests that stories about for-profit abuses and failed privatization efforts are more likely to make the news than stories about for-profit success.

This has two effects: First, it reinforces public skepticism; and second, it makes policymakers even more gun-shy about pursuing policies that involve for-profit firms. These asymmetries limit for-profit involvement to safe and accepted niches, reinforcing the public's view of where for-profit involvement is appropriate. Future research should test this hypothesis systematically.

Good Idea for Some, But Not for My Kids

Some evidence suggests that Americans are more comfortable with for-profit schools as an experiment in a few districts than they are with for-profits operating in their communities or serving their children. Similarly, the public supports for-profit colleges in the abstract, particularly as an option for underrepresented students. But they readily admit that proprietary colleges are lower in quality and allege that these companies will sacrifice quality to make a profit. In other words, for-profit colleges are a good option for traditionally underrepresented students, but they should not be a mainstream option.

The contours of opinion are likely to cap the potential market for firms, as more sophisticated and affluent customers remain skeptical of for-profits involved in the core business of teaching and learning. Skepticism could in turn limit the extent to which for-profit providers generate competitive pressure in either the K–12 or postsecondary markets. This is particularly true in the case of for-profit colleges: Demographics suggest that proprietary schools are not serving the traditional bachelor's degree–seeking student, and it is unclear whether they are competing with community colleges for the same marginal students. Without a shift in the way the public perceives the quality of these institutions, it is unlikely that for-profit colleges will drive traditional institutions—many of which easily fill their incoming classes—to fundamentally change.

CONCLUSION

These dynamics are linked in what political scientists call "policy feedback," whereby policies shape politics, and political dynamics in turn constrain public policy choices. Public skepticism of for-profit schools leads policymakers to be timid in pushing for policies that encourage for-profit entry, and the limited policies reinforce the public's conception of what constitutes the "appropriate" role of for-profits. In the areas where for-profits are free to operate, instances of abuse often garner significant media coverage, which can sour public opinion, leaving policymakers with little incentive to promote for-profit involvement in education.

The recent opposition to the Democrats' for-profit college agenda may ensure that public approval of these institutions remains relatively buoyant. However, the failure to provide for-profit EMOs with charter school grants or the imprimatur of high-profile programs like i3 will do little to legitimize the role of for-profits in K–12 education reform in the eyes of the public. As long as for-profit schools and colleges remain outside the emerging "Washington consensus," we are unlikely to see a large-scale shift in the prominence of for-profit providers or the way the public feels about them.

CHAPTER 2

The Costs and Benefits of Nonprofit and For-Profit Status

Perspectives from Executives and Entrepreneurs

Mickey Muldoon

Consider a hypothetical example of K–12 education entrepreneurship: An ambitious college graduate is interested in forming a new national organization to teach computer programming as an afterschool academic program. She is passionately interested in the cause of education reform, inspired by organizations such as the Harlem Children's Zone, and would like to reach diverse communities, especially in low-performing urban districts, but imagines that the program would be equally useful in suburban and high-performing settings. She begins the first steps for forming this organization, and very soon encounters a crucial, existential question: Should it be a nonprofit or a for-profit?

On one side, many of the best-known players in America's education entrepreneurship movement—among them, Teach For America, KIPP, The New Teacher Project, and Khan Academy—are nonprofits. Nonprofit status can mean access to the largest philanthropies in the world and, equally as important, can be a powerful demonstration of commitment to social responsibility.[1] On the other side, for-profit status opens the doors to deeper funding from capital markets. How should this hypothetical entrepreneur go about weighing the respective costs and benefits of these two very different options?

In the fall of 2011, I spoke to some of the most prominent players in America's education entrepreneurship movement to answer this question. For a full list of these players, see Table 2.1. To learn about the true costs and benefits of nonprofit and for-profit status in the K–12 education sector, I interviewed the founders and chief executives at acclaimed education nonprofits, including KIPP, Wikipedia, and Harlem Success; and at high-profile education for-profits, including Pearson, 2U, Houghton-Mifflin Harcourt, and Mosaica. I spoke to current and former

Table 2.1. Interviewees

Name	Education Executive Experience (Selected)	Sector	Role
Mawi Asgedom	Mawi Learning (FP) *	Character Development	Founder and CEO
Richard Barth	KIPP Foundation (NP)	School Management	President
	Edison Schools (FP)	School Management	President, District Partnerships
	Carter Research (FP)	Consulting	President/Owner
Samuel Casey Carter	Houghton Mifflin Harcourt (FP)	Publishing & Curriculum	SVP, Global Corp. Social Resp.
	CfBT USA (NP)	School Management	President
	National Heritage Academies (FP)	School Management	President
	New Jersey Department of Education (G)	Government	Acting Commissioner
Chris Cerf	Sangari (FP)	Publishing & Curriculum	President, Sangari USA
	New York City Department of Education (G)	Government	Deputy Chancellor
	Edison (FP)	School Management	President and COO
George Cigale	Tutor.com (FP)	Technology	Founder and CEO
	Princeton Review (FP)	Publishing & Curriculum	General Manager

Name	Education Executive Experience (Selected)	Sector	Role
John Danner	Rocketship Education (NP)	School Management	Founder and CEO
	Tennessee Charter School Association (NP)	Government Affairs	Chairman
	NetGravity (FP)	Technology	Founder and CEO
Rose Else-Mitchell	Scholastic (FP)	Publishing & Curriculum	SVP, Product Development
Kevin Hall	Charter School Growth Fund (NP)	Philanthropy	CEO
	The Broad Foundation (NP)	Philanthropy	COO
	Chancellor Beacon Academies (FP)	School Management	Cofounder and SVP
	Teach For America (NP)	Human Capital Pipeline	Los Angeles Executive Director
Jonathan Harber	Pearson/Schoolnet (FP)	Technology	CEO
	New York City Outward Bound (NP)	School Management	Trustee
	Trail Blazers (NP)	Character Development	Trustee
Peg Hoey	Kunskapsskolan USA (FP)	School Management	President
	Equality Charter School (NP)	School Management	Cofounder and Director
John Katzman	Noodle (FP)	Technology	Founder and Chairman
	2U (FP)	Technology	Founder and Executive Chairman
	Princeton Review (FP)	Publishing & Curriculum	Founder and Chairman

(continued)

Table 2.1: (continued)

Name	Education Executive Experience (Selected)	Sector	Role
Temp Keller	TK Capital (FP)	Investment	Board Member
	Innovations for Learning (NP)	Technology	Managing Director
	Resources for Indispensable Schools and Educators (NP)	Human Capital Pipeline	Founder and President
Bobbi Kurshan	Education Impact (FP)	Consulting	Fellow
	Educorp Consultants Corporation (FP)	Consulting	President
	Curriki (NP)	Publishing & Curriculum	Executive Director
Eva Moskowitz	Success Academy Charter Schools (NP)	School Management	Founder and CEO
	New York City Council (G)	Government	Council Member
	University of Virginia (NP)	Higher Education	Professor
Ron Packard	K12 (FP)	Technology	Founder and CEO
	Knowledge Universe (FP)	School Management	Partner
	Blackboard Solutions (FP)	Consulting	Partner
Ebbie Parsons	Mosaica Education (FP)	School Management	Chief Operating Officer
	Hartford Public Schools (G)	School Management	Chief Operating Officer

Name	Education Executive Experience (Selected)	Sector	Role
Nina Rees	National Alliance for Public Charter Schools (NP)	Policy and Advocacy	CEO
	Knowledge Universe (FP)	School Management	SVP, Strategic Initiatives
	US Department of Education (G)	Government	Assistant Deputy Secretary
Andy Rotherham	Bellwether Education Partners (NP)	Consulting	Cofounder and Partner
	Whiteboard Advisors (FP)	Government Affairs	Senior Advisor
Jennifer Schnidman Medbery	Kickboard (FP)	Technology	Founder and CEO
	New Orleans Charter Science and Math Academy (NP)	School Management	Teacher
Jonathan Schorr	NewSchools Venture Fund (NP)	Philanthropy	Partner
	KIPP Foundation (NP)	School Management	Director of New Initiatives
Jim Shelton	US Department of Education (G)	Government	Assistant Deputy Secretary
	Bill and Melinda Gates Foundation (NP)	Philanthropy	Program Director
	LearnNow (FP)	School Management	Founder & President
Kim Smith	Bellwether Education Partners (NP)	Consulting	Cofounder and CEO
	NewSchools Venture Fund (NP)	Philanthropy	Cofounder and CEO
	Teach for America (NP)	Human Capital Pipeline	Various

(continued)

Table 2.1: (continued)

Name	Education Executive Experience (Selected)	Sector	Role
Tom Vander Ark	Learn Capital (FP)	Venture Capital	Managing Partner
	Bill and Melinda Gates Foundation (NP)	Philanthropy	Executive Director, Education
	Federal Way Public Schools (G)	School Management	Superintendent
David Vinca	eSpark (FP)	Technology	Founder
Mark Vineis	Mondo Publishing (FP)	Publishing & Curriculum	President and Founder
Jimmy Wales	Wikia (FP)	Technology	President
	Wikimedia Foundation (NP)	Publishing & Curriculum	Founder & Chairman
Chris Whittle	Avenues (FP)	School Management	Founder & CEO
	Edison (FP)	School Management	Founder & Chairman
Caprice Young	John and Laura Arnold Foundation (NP)	Philanthropy	VP for Education
	EnCorps (NP)	Human Capital Pipeline	CEO and President
	KC Distance Learning (FP)	Technology	CEO and President
	City of Los Angeles (G)	Government	Assistant Deputy Mayor

* *Key:* FP = For-profit; NP = Nonprofit; G = Government.

executive officers at major philanthropies, such as the Bill and Melinda Gates Foundation and the NewSchools Venture Fund, many of whom had experience in both the for-profit and nonprofit sectors; and I interviewed high-ranking government officials at the U.S. Department of Education and New Jersey Department of Education who oversee education innovation and entrepreneurship. After the interviews, I offered an online survey that covered some politically sensitive topics, so that these same individuals could offer responses in complete anonymity. To be sure, I selected interviewees nonrandomly; my goal was to learn about the strengths and weaknesses of nonprofits and for-profits from those who had been successful on both sides—not to publish a representative survey.

As such, this study is the first of its kind. Generic introductory documents available for individuals interested in forming a nonprofit—for example, *Thinking of Forming A Non-Profit? What to Consider Before You Begin*, from New Jersey's Center for Non-Profits (2010)—commonly enumerate the costs and benefits of nonprofit status.[2] The benefits typically include tax exemption and better public perception, and the costs typically include additional public reporting, and restriction against pursuing private profits. In contrast, the purpose of my interviews was to help the prospective entrepreneur move to the next level of analysis—to strategically weigh the costs and benefits of each model against each other, and to understand how the obvious immediate differences between nonprofits and for-profits lead to less obvious long-term differences.

After completing the interviews and surveys, three simple but powerful themes emerged:

- First, interviewees explained clearly and unambiguously that for-profit status has a number of significant universal advantages: In particular, for-profit organizations tend to raise money more efficiently, grow and innovate more rapidly, and generally draw from a deeper pool of talent compared with nonprofit peers.
- Second, interviewees provided a number of specific scenarios in which nonprofit status can have clear advantages. In particular, it is preferable when entrepreneurial founders have special access to deep philanthropic sources, when organizational outcomes can only be expected after many decades, when for-profit status is disadvantaged politically, when an organization exists primarily to support volunteer work, and when tax-exempt donations are absolutely essential to an organization's business model.
- Third and finally, the interviewees shared the perspective that nonprofits and for-profits should be considered moral equals; neither is fundamentally more virtuous, socially valuable, or "mission-driven." In the conversations and surveys, interviewees explained that nonprofits can be greedy and corrupt, for-profits can serve lofty social aims, and

both deal with temptations to compromise values or quality for the sake of money. This was an interesting contrast to the moralistic language in public commentary that often portrays for-profit schools, for example, as more corruptible than their nonprofit peers and nonprofit schools as more likely to serve social aims.

For our hypothetical entrepreneur, the collective advice of this group suggests that she consider for-profit status the default option for her afterschool program—but then carefully consider the exceptional cases posed above that would favor nonprofit status. If, for example, she had access to a large donor, or intended for the organization to be run primarily by volunteers, or encountered serious political disadvantages to for-profits, she would be better off going the nonprofit route; otherwise, for-profit status would likely be a better long-term bet.

For philanthropies and policymakers, the insights suggest that supporting the nonprofit sector may not necessarily lead to better social outcomes than investing in the private sector. On the contrary, given their significant advantages, for-profits can, in some cases, have *more* social impact than their nonprofit peers.

Additionally, the findings have some obvious implications for the American public charter school movement. If the interviewees' insights are valid, then given a level playing field, for-profit charter schools should be expected to grow more quickly, attract better talent, and innovate more rapidly than their nonprofit peers over the long term and systemwide. This result clearly conflicts with commentary and policy suggesting for-profit charter schools are inherently doomed to mediocrity or worse.

To be sure, these findings would not be of much interest if they represented only the viewpoints of for-profit businesspeople with only their self-interest in mind or right-wing ideologues arguing reflexively for the virtues of free markets and capital. But that was not the case: The interviewees represented a broad spectrum of successful organizations, and they drew upon substantive experience in both the nonprofit and for-profit sectors to make their points. And politically, they were left of center—59% of those surveyed considered themselves Democrats. If the comments below therefore appear slanted in one direction of the nonprofit/for-profit debate, then it is perhaps only in contrast to public commentary and policy slanted in the other.

All of the quotations that follow, unless otherwise noted, are drawn from personal interviews conducted with me, by phone or in person.

THE BENEFITS OF FOR-PROFIT

Interviewees explained that for-profit status comes with some key benefits compared with the nonprofit sector. In particular, investment money is easier to raise, growth and organizational agility are more natural, and there is more flexibility to attract top talent. None of these points is particularly novel or controversial, so rather than re-create the full, familiar arguments made by interviewees, I will simply highlight a few of the more interesting conversations in which these points arose. A sampling of survey results are presented in Figure 2.1 below.

Fundraising Efficiency

When I asked John Katzman, the founder of the Princeton Review, about his views on the relative strengths and weaknesses of nonprofits, he replied that nonprofits ultimately "have more flexibility, more access to capital, and more time to focus on customers rather than fundraising." Many interviewees made a similar point. Several mentioned a 2003 article by McKinsey & Co. executives, which estimated that nonprofits spend 18 cents to raise every dollar, whereas for-profits spend between just 2 and 5 cents to attract the same amount of capital.[3]

Caprice Young—whose resume includes stints on Capitol Hill, in Los Angeles city government, at IBM, on the Los Angeles school board, at a for-profit online learning company, several nonprofits, and currently as the vice president for education at the John and Laura Arnold Foundation—explained a difference between fundraising in the for-profit and nonprofit sectors: "In the private sector, if you have a good idea and it'll make money, you're going to get funding." For all their differences, she explained, investors' interests are ultimately simple: They want to see a healthy financial return on their investment.

On the other hand, philanthropic donors desire a social return on their donations. But social value is not a common currency: A dozen different philanthropists may have a dozen different ways to measure the social values of their grants. And some donors are interested in entirely different outcomes—among them, prestige, relationships, legacy, and pursuing their own agendas. Young explained that it's this potential mismatch between the agendas of grantors and grantees that can create some of the biggest challenges. "There are many cases when the nonprofits spend so much effort chasing the foundations that they forget what their core mission is," she said.

Nonprofit funding doesn't just take more time and effort to obtain, explained interviewees—it is also much scarcer. Discussing the origins of Tutor.com, CEO George Cigale said:

> My assumption was that this venture was going to require a great deal of capital in order to build out the technology primarily but also to figure out the marketplace. We were going to have to fail and learn and iterate. And I could not envision raising the millions of dollars I needed for a concept without a for-profit structure that would allow shareholders to be incentivized by the eventual growth of the company.

Figure 2.1. Selected Anonymous Survey Responses Among Interviewees

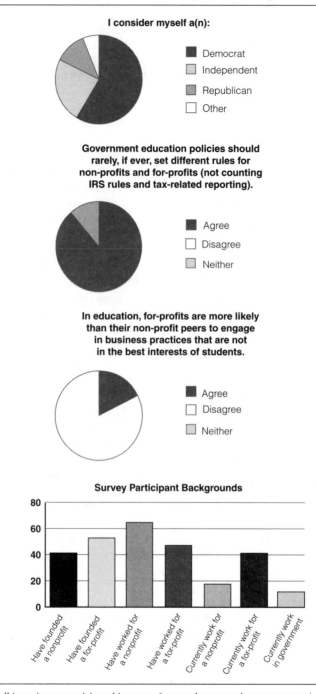

I consider myself a(n):

- Democrat
- Independent
- Republican
- Other

Government education policies should rarely, if ever, set different rules for non-profits and for-profits (not counting IRS rules and tax-related reporting).

- Agree
- Disagree
- Neither

In education, for-profits are more likely than their non-profit peers to engage in business practices that are not in the best interests of students.

- Agree
- Disagree
- Neither

Survey Participant Backgrounds

Note: Not all interviewees participated in survey. It was voluntary and nonrepresentative. *n* = 17.

Along the same lines, Chris Whittle, the CEO of Avenues, a new for-profit private K–12 school in Manhattan with plans to open new campuses in major cities worldwide, remarked, "We just raised $75 million to start our first campus at Avenues in New York City. I couldn't possibly fathom the amount of time it would take to raise that money as a nonprofit. Even more important—what about Campus 2 and 3 and 4?"

Entrepreneurs with significant nonprofit experience agreed with this assessment about the relative ease of fundraising in the for-profit sector. For example, Jim Shelton, who has executive experience in for-profits and philanthropies (and is now a senior official at the U.S. Department of Education), described that when he set out to create a charter school network with ambitious scale-up plans in the late 1990s, the only feasible way to raise enough money quickly was to go the for-profit route. Jimmy Wales, who cofounded both nonprofit Wikipedia and for-profit Wikia, said about the differences between nonprofit and for-profit, "One of the big issues is investment capital—getting the money up front to build something. It's a lot easier if the people providing the capital are expecting to get a return on that capital."

Growing and Staying Nimble

Interviewees explained that the profit motive also pushes for-profits to scale up and to make strategic organizational changes more quickly, in line with previous findings that support the same conclusion.[4] David Vinca, founder of eSpark, a for-profit e-learning company, explained:

> I think we don't have any disadvantage as compared to a nonprofit. We have an advantage in that we can access more capital if we have a scalable business model. What I've heard is that foundations are willing to experiment and it's easy to get a $100,000-type tinkering investment, but it's hard to get a big, $10 million [investment] to scale up.

And Jonathan Harber of Schoolnet explained that he never considered nonprofit as an option because Schoolnet "could never reach the scale, or get the capital, or have a sustainable model" without for-profit status to attract investment.

On the other hand, Jimmy Wales, cofounder of Wikipedia, a nonprofit, explained that there are reverse incentives for nonprofits to waste the money they have rather than to reinvest in growth. He said, "If you're making more money than you spend, the answer you're liable to get from a foundation is, 'Sounds like you've got plenty of money. Why are you talking to us?' There's this perverse incentive to be inefficient."

Indeed, Tom Vander Ark, the former executive director of education for the Bill and Melinda Gates Foundation and a current venture capital investor at Learn Capital, explained that part of the challenge that nonprofits have with scaling up is that nonprofit funders can tend to look backward, where for-profit funders look forward to search for scalable models. With large foundations, he said, "[Grantees] spend so much time trying to prove that they did exactly what you set out to do. It's insanely complicated and detailed." He explained that many foundations have extensive reporting requirements with little flexibility to change direction as an initiative evolves. On the other hand, said Vander Ark, for-profit venture investors are more comfortable giving their grantees flexibility to test different models and strategies until they find one that works, especially in the early stages. "That's the beauty of venture capital," he said. "It just follows a good idea to a better one."

Ron Packard, the CEO of K–12, Inc., summed up his advice to prospective education entrepreneurs as follows: "If you have to grow and innovate quickly, you're much better off as a for-profit."

Attracting Talent

Andy Rotherham—the *TIME* education columnist, former education aide to Bill Clinton, and cofounder and partner at nonprofit Bellwether Education Partners—explained that the tax code in effect forces nonprofits to pay lower salaries. Under IRS "excessive gain" guidelines, he explained, nonprofit employees may be paid no more than the going market rate for similar work in the nonprofit or for-profit sector. But even when they pay market-based salaries, he said, "Nonprofits are still at a disadvantage because many of the best-paying for-profits do not disclose salary information, whereas nonprofits, which generally pay less, are required to disclose salaries. It puts a deflationary pressure on the nonprofit salaries." His comment also lines up with external research: In a 2001 survey of more than 50,000 nonprofits, the Urban Institute found that the median salary of chief executives at educational nonprofits (excluding higher education) was just $40,000.[5] (Despite the overall trend, to be certain, several for-profit leaders did give anecdotal examples of nonprofit executives with outsized salaries and hidden perks.)

Beyond the issue of cash salaries, Rotherham and others explained that nonprofits have a very clear restriction related to compensation: Since nonprofits have no shares or shareholders, they cannot offer stock options as a potential upside for new employees who take a risk in joining the enterprise. Chris Whittle of Avenues explained that at the senior levels, and especially in new and high-growth ventures, equity can be a major part of the total compensation package. When nonprofit organizations cannot offer incentives such as equity, he said, "What it does almost by definition is limit you to that subset of individuals who are prepared to live their lives that way . . . it narrows the field." Rotherham said of his organization: "Bellwether has salaries that are very competitive, but you're not getting equity. That does make it unattractive for some talented people. But it's more of a challenge than an insurmountable obstacle."

FIVE CASES IN WHICH NONPROFIT STATUS IS PREFERABLE

Whereas for-profit status confers a number of powerful universal advantages related to fundraising, scale, and talent, the interviews revealed that nonprofit status can confer narrower, situational advantages. Across the conversations, these situations fell into five categories: (1) when entrepreneurial founders have special access to substantial philanthropic sources, (2) when the organization's primary output can only be delivered over the course of decades, (3) when for-profit status is disadvantaged politically, (4) when tax-exempt donations and philanthropic subsidies are essential to an organization's business model, and (5) when the organization exists primarily to support volunteer work. These cases are nonexclusive; some nonprofit organizations fit into more than one of these categories. Below, I provide examples of each case from the interviews.

Case 1: Easy Access to Deep Philanthropic Money

John Katzman, the founder of the Princeton Review, Noodle, and 2U, explained that he generally advises education entrepreneurs to choose the for-profit option because raising large amounts of money is generally much easier, which in turn gives founders more time to focus on customers rather than funders. But he added a caveat: "There are exceptions—people who are so tuned into the philanthropic world that they can raise almost unlimited funds—and that's a pretty good gig." Free money with no obligation for repayment, he explained, is a nice offer.

I spoke (under anonymity) to one nonprofit executive mentioned by one interviewee as a prodigious fundraiser. When forming a new education organization, the executive said that he investigated both the nonprofit and for-profit options, and received serious interest from both sides. But the philanthropies ultimately offered him even more money than the investors, with the added advantage that the philanthropic money would never need to be repaid, so he went with nonprofit status.

In addition, some interviewees mentioned Khan Academy as one of the select few nonprofits that have captured the intense interest of deep-pocketed donors. Vander Ark, however, said, "Khan Academy is an exception. It's a corner case." Khan received viral Internet attention that led to his funding; unknown entrepreneurs can hardly guarantee the same attention and interest, even if their ideas are promising.

Case 2: Expecting Outcomes Only After Many Decades

Temp Keller, founder of the nonprofit Resources for Indispensable Schools and Educators (RISE), explained that because they do not require repayment, philanthropic donations are "the most patient form of capital." On the other hand, he explained, for-profit investors cannot wait more than about a decade before seeing a return on their initial investments. In cases in which outcomes can only be expected after this period, seeking funding from nonprofit sources is the only alternative.

Along these lines, Salman Khan of Khan Academy said (in a public interview not with the author) that taking a long-time horizon to build an institution for future generations was part of his choice to go the nonprofit route. Discussing his early thinking on this issue, he said:

> In a for-profit, we could be the University of Phoenix for K–12, which is okay, and that has some shady elements to it . . . the other option would be to become an institution, a Stanford, literally an institution for the world. Just as Wikipedia is an encyclopedia for the world, this is another utility for the world, where 30 years from now, 50 years from now, 500 years from now, it will be viewed like clean drinking water—how can a society exist without a free, world-class education for everybody?[6]

In line with his vision of Khan Academy as an institution for the world, Khan has also discussed plans to raise an endowment. Several other interviewees explained that endowments can provide nonprofits financial security and allow the organization to take a very long-term perspective, protected from some of the risks of constant grant-based fundraising.[7]

Case 3: Political Pressure

Interviewees explained that when political conditions are sufficiently skewed, some organizations—though potentially preferable as for-profits—can actually find more success as nonprofits. This was particularly true in the case of charter schools.

Discussing the political side of for-profits in education, Chris Cerf, the former chief operating officer of Edison Schools and current acting commissioner of Education of the state of New Jersey, said, "The political resistance to for-profit is deep." In the case of Edison and for-profit ventures, he said, teacher unions partially succeeded in portraying them as "part of a vast right-wing conspiracy." Other interviewees cited specific legal discrimination: In New York, for example, only nonprofit organizations may run charter schools; in other states, for-profits may only operate charter schools in partnership with nonprofits. And in most places, per-pupil charter school funding is so meager that high-quality management essentially requires philanthropic subsidies.[8]

John Danner, cofounder and CEO of the nonprofit Rocketship charter school network, explained his view on the political benefits of nonprofit status:

> Ultimately when you're trying to get to big scale, the politics are going to be the gating factor. If your goal is to have maximum impact, you want to be structurally best able to win whatever political battles you may have.

Case 4: Supporting Volunteers

Jimmy Wales, the Wikipedia cofounder, is, in some ways, an unlikely nonprofit entrepreneur. He spent part of his career as a professional investor. He is a "center-right" libertarian. Wikipedia itself later grew out of a for-profit online encyclopedia project.[9]

Moreover, Wales understands the limitations of nonprofits: Recall his point about the "perverse incentives" to waste money. But despite all those shortcomings, he explained, for-profit is simply not appropriate for an organization like Wikipedia, built primarily on a community of volunteers. Wales explained:

> [Nonprofit status] is really important in the Wikipedia world . . . so when we're in the trenches at Wikipedia talking about editorial policy, they don't feel like "Why am I making this guy rich? What is his motive?" . . . So I think that the nonprofit structure can help in a real grassroots community-based organization. It's really hard to go from that grassroots community to an ownership model.

Wikipedia's fate powerfully demonstrated that the risk of losing the sense of trust and equality among a volunteer community can outweigh all the potential benefits of for-profit status.

Case 5: Donation Revenue Built into the Business Model

Fifth and finally, interviewees explained that nonprofit status is preferable if the organization exists primarily to offer products or services that must be subsidized by tax-exempt donations. As Nina Rees, the CEO of the National Alliance for Public Charter Schools, explained it, nonprofits can make sense "in inner-city settings where you don't have a lot of money and have a lot of needs, where you need to access to philanthropic sources as an extra support." Temp Keller of RISE explained how this works in practice:

> Where we ended up at our peak was working toward a place where earned income from schools fueled half our operational budget. Suffice it to say that given where we ended up operationally, with individual school partnerships, we relied significantly on philanthropy.

These comments should not be of any surprise. The ability to receive tax-exempt donations is obviously one of the primary attractions of for-profit status.

However, many of the interviewees pointed out the ability to collect free grant money can be both a blessing and a curse. Keller explained that when grants covered costs that would otherwise be paid directly by customers, "You're ultimately 'partnering' with schools, but you can't help but feel that you're one of a myriad of partners." Jonathan Harber, the founder of Schoolnet, explained the dynamics bluntly: "I don't think you get the kind of market validation you need when you have an unsustainable funding source."

Jennifer Medbery, CEO of Kickboard, echoed this point. Explaining her choice of for-profit status, she said:

> It was really important for users to prove their need for the tool by paying for it, and that I wasn't going to have to convince schools to try it, and then also turn around and convince a foundation or some other philanthropic means of fueling our growth. To me the focus has always been, if the users have been willing to pay for it that sends a strong message as to the sustainability of the company.

Given the limitations of philanthropic subsidies and the risk of "partnering" with customers who are not paying full price, for-profit founders found alternative routes to channel donations toward high-need customers. Medbery, for example, said that Kickboard was considering establishing a separate, charitable foundation to receive grants and provide scholarships to low-income schools. George Cigale, the CEO of Tutor.com, said that his company routinely helps clients write grants to foundations to pay for the service. These arrangements allow companies to retain the significant benefits of for-profit status and encourage philanthropic subsidies without becoming directly dependent on them.

MORALS AND MISSION

Finally, interviewees broadly shared the perspective that nonprofits and for-profits should be considered moral equals.

Private and Public Gain

The interviewees' perspective on moral equivalency stands in contrast to plenty of implicit and explicit commentary and policy that suggests otherwise. A commonly assumed distinction between for-profit and nonprofit organizations, for example, is that the former category is concerned primarily with making money, whereas the latter is interested in making the world a better place. For example, the author of a recent book on nonprofit marketing wrote, "For some, money is the bottom line. In nonprofits, the mission is the bottom line."[10]

In the most simplistic analysis, serving a social mission and earning profits are two competing outcomes. Famed urban educator Deborah Meier captured this perspective in a Twitter post from 2011, when she suggested that a for-profit virtual school represented the "sell out of public schools for private gain."[11] Michael

Mulgrew of the United Federation of Teachers described for-profit schools as "making money off the backs of kids."[12] *Washington Post* education columnist Jay Mathews wrote, simply, "I am biased against for-profit schools. . . . Teachers I admired saw education as a public trust. They weren't in it for the money. They wanted to help kids."[13] From this perspective, there is a zero-sum competition between companies and children for limited money and resources in education, where "private gain" is the children's loss.

However, none of the entrepreneurs interviewed for this chapter adopted this perspective. Rather, they often spoke in terms of a potential harmony between profits and mission: Over the long term, companies that succeed in their mission to provide excellent services or products should also become profitable. John Danner said, "You can do good and do well at the same time." Chris Whittle, the one-time chairman of *Esquire* magazine and founder of the for-profit Edison Schools and Avenues projects, said, "All companies are set up to provide a good." Ebbie Parsons, a senior executive at Mosaica, a for-profit charter school network, said, "The better we perform, the more profitable we will become. If we are to be a profitable business, we have to be the best at whatever we do in order to remain competitive. There is no way we could get by with poor results and still grow." When I asked Jonathan Schorr of the nonprofit NewSchools Venture Fund if he agreed that nonprofits are more mission-driven, he replied, "Not at all. It's a potentially more complicated conversation, but for-profits like Better Lesson and Revolution Foods are utterly mission-driven." Caprice Young said, "The most important skill of a nonprofit leader is to manage resources so that they can stay on mission." And when asked if the same could be said of for-profit leaders, she did not hesitate to reply, "Absolutely."

Chris Whittle, echoing the thesis of his chapter in this volume, focused on the complexity of organizations and missions and stakeholders, urging entrepreneurs to avoid simplifying the moral differences between nonprofits and for-profits. He said, "The unions are nonprofits, but to say that their mission is singularly serving students, I'm going to find that hard to believe. In virtually any setting, you are serving a variety of constituents and interests. The purity of single purpose is more elusive than many of us might think." He furthermore explained that there is nothing about their tax status that requires nonprofits to serve needy populations and for-profits to avoid them; elite private K-12 schools for the wealthy, for example, are usually nonprofits.

Cheating and Compromise

Moreover, interviewees challenged the notion that for-profits have more built-in incentives to cheat or sacrifice quality—a notion that is pervasive in public debate about the matter. (Even Rick Hess, of the conservative American Enterprise Institute and coeditor of this volume, wrote, "The incentive to cut costs [at for-profits] can translate into an incentive to cut corners. The urge to grow can lead to unacceptable compromises in quality."[14]) Interviewees explained that nonprofits can face equally powerful incentives to compromise quality or mission. Recall Caprice Young's statement about the temptation for nonprofits to lose their direction to "chase the foundations," and Jimmy Wales's point about the incentives to waste money to appear to be in need. These compromise quality and mission, too. Of course, if a nonprofit seeks to maximize its social impact, then it may want to scale up—and face the exact same compromises in quality that Hess described as accompanying the "urge to grow."

Additionally, George Cigale explained that bad behavior can and does happen in both nonprofit and for-profit settings. He said:

> You can find rogue operators anywhere. I'm sure there are CEOs who start a [for-profit] company who don't care the slightest bit about the student results, and I'm sure there are nonprofit CEOs who take the job just for the huge salary and perks of the nonprofit and don't care about the mission.

Short-Term Profits Versus Long-Term Value

Several interviewees challenged the line of reasoning that suggests that given their investors' demands for speedy returns on their investments, for-profits are necessarily pressured to focus only on short-term results at the expense of long-term value.

Peg Hoey is the president of Kunskapsskolan USA, the American subsidiary of a Swedish company that runs for-profit charter schools in Sweden and internationally. It is the largest nongovernmental public school operator in Sweden, and has delivered stellar academic results; according to its website, 18 of its 20 schools in Sweden are rated best or second-best in their districts.[15] One key to Kunskapsskollan's success, Hoey explained, is that it is privately owned by just a few families, rather than traded on a stock market. Private ownership, she explained, can make it easier for a company to take a long-term view, since there are no public shareholders or quarterly earnings reports.

She also contrasted Kunskapsskolan with nonprofits that are constantly hunting for grant money: "We can have a long-term perspective," she said. "We're not bound by what grantors find the most compelling at a given moment."

Along the same lines, George Cigale of Tutor.com, explained, "My key shareholders say to me very bluntly, when strategic planning time comes around every year, they *don't* want me to generate a profit." Rather, he explained, he is focused on improving the product and serving current customers—and his investors are willing to wait years for more aggressive expansion and profitability.

"A Lot of Different Motivations"

Even the most honest nonprofit employees cannot be singularly dedicated to "mission," explained Jimmy Wales. Even if for-profit employees make more money, he explained, nonprofit employees are also interested in the personal benefits of their work—earning raises, getting promoted, and so on—and that can create some natural tension with the organization's mission.

John Katzman, the Princeton Review founder, argued that for-profits, on the balance, are no less beneficial to education: "There are more people who have become very wealthy at taxpayer expense in the for-profit world than in the nonprofit world. But in terms of working in good faith, or actually benefiting kids at reasonable expense, for-profits have as good a track record as nonprofits. Policymakers shouldn't be suspicious; they should work harder to set incentives for both groups to promote good behavior." Instead of harboring suspicion toward either nonprofits or for-profits, the interviewees were, as Andy Rotherham put it, "strongly nonideological." They viewed both nonprofits and for-profits as equally valuable means to the end of providing quality education.

Caprice Young personified the nonideological perspective of the entrepreneurs. In our conversation, she admitted growing up in a household in which "the people in the private sector were considered thieves, and going to business school was akin to registering for the Republican Party, which was evil." But after her varied experience across sectors, she settled on a deep pragmatism. Now, she says, "All these forms of capital—philanthropic, private, political, and government—are morally neutral until someone puts an intent there."

Finally, in the anonymous survey, participants broadly agreed that neither for-profits nor nonprofits could a priori claim higher ground: of those who responded to the survey, 82% (and 90% of those who had worked at a nonprofit) disagreed with the statement that "In education, for-profits are more likely than their nonprofit peers to engage in business practices that are not in the best interests of students."

SIGNIFICANCE FOR EDUCATION
ENTREPRENEURSHIP AND REFORM

The insights of the preceding sections—about the unique strengths of for-profits, the specific cases in which nonprofit status is preferable, and about the moral equality of both models—suggest a handful of useful lessons and recommendations for entrepreneurs, philanthropies, and education policymakers.

For Philanthropies and Government

Philanthropies are permitted to donate their money and invest in for-profit companies. Although donations to for-profits are not tax-deductible (or for foundations, do not count toward the minimum grant-making level required to maintain tax-exempt status), they are not illegal, either. The interviewees' comments suggest that philanthropies should pursue these vehicles more actively. For all donors—large and small, established and upstart—there are reasons to believe that their money will go further toward their charitable missions if invested in the for-profit sector rather than in nonprofits. In particular, over the long term, for-profit investments in certain fields will grow more naturally, attract better talent, and are no more likely to lead to corruption or compromises to social mission.

Such an approach might be controversial; by engaging in the for-profit marketplace, it can be argued, foundations could undermine it. As Jonathan Schorr of the NewSchools Venture Fund said, "The question of whether [we], by making an investment, are declaring a front-runner in a competitive marketplace on the for-profit side is a really interesting one."

But the potential problem of donors "declaring a front-runner" by investing in the for-profit market must be compared to the alternative: donating to nonprofits, without requiring that any of the money be paid back, let alone seeking a profitable return. This interferes with the competitive marketplace even more. As various interviewees explained, the interests of donors are generally more diverse than the interests of paid customers in the for-profit marketplace, mainly because social aims are difficult to measure. And because social change is so much more complex, the relationships between buyers and sellers in the nonprofit world are less direct. If one's concern is purely about undermining market forces, then supporting the nonprofit sector in the first place is perhaps more problematic than supporting the for-profit sector.

Jonathan Harber, the founder of education data company Schoolnet and, after its acquisition, now a senior executive at Pearson, made this point strongly. He said:

> I'm a big believer in markets—the country's really well set up to have
> markets work to solve complex problems on a long-term sustainable basis. A
> lot of the work foundations do is good in research and publications and stuff
> like that and direct allocations to those that are less privileged. From the
> perspective of market-making or market-choosing, I think that foundations
> can do a lot of damage, they can confuse the market, they can delay the
> market . . . they can sometimes sponsor solutions that are not market-driven
> and they have no accountability to do the proper due diligence and generally
> just assume that the market is broken and can't make those decisions for
> itself. I think they're misguided.

Harber added that tax advantages can also undermine market forces:

> With respect to nonprofit organizations, I'm not sure why foundations and government policy should provide them with market advantages. We now have companies with different tax status competing for the same business in assessment, school improvement, digital content, schools, etc. Nonprofits are being driven by their funders, often foundations, to create sustainable business models. But if there is a market where an organization can reach sustainability through customer demand, why not leave it to the market mechanisms to solve?

And John Katzman, founder of the Princeton Review, made a related point:

> Foundations and government disrupt markets—somebody who is politically connected can simply tap into untold millions of dollars and become a fiercer competitor. In one sense, that's just part of the game, but it's a tough part of the game. There are two markets—one of them servicing kids and schools, and the other servicing foundations—and if you're excluded from the second market, those numbers are large enough that they can affect your ability to compete in the first.

These comments suggest that philanthropic investments of debt or equity or donations to for-profits have far fewer adverse consequences to market-based competition than do pure donations to nonprofits. Jonathan Schorr of NewSchools Venture Fund (NSVF) explained that making philanthropic investments in for-profit companies—which NSVF does—can help "nudge them in the right direction," for example, by encouraging them to serve lower-income customers. On the other hand, Jonathan Harber of Schoolnet and Pearson asserted that donations to nonprofits "sponsor solutions that are not market-driven." For donors who agree with Harber, that markets are a powerful mechanism for solving longer-term problems sustainably, the analysis here suggests that those donors think more about supporting the for-profit sector through investments, direct donations, or other means. Except in the specific, limited circumstances when nonprofit is a fundamentally superior option, the interview findings suggest that philanthropies and government donors interested in systemic long-term changes should move beyond any notion that nonprofits are inherently better suited to serve the greater good.

For the Charter School Movement

If interviewees are to be believed that for-profits are not fundamentally less socially valuable or more corruptible than their nonprofit peers, it suggests that anti-for-profit legislation and commentary are misguided. Therefore, charter school advocates, if they agree with the interviewees' arguments, should support and encourage nondiscriminatory legislation for for-profit and nonprofit charter school operators.

Every single one of the interviewees who discussed the matter agreed that both for-profit and nonprofit charter schools should be allowed to thrive. Nina Rees, a former executive at for-profit Knowledge Universe and former official in the U.S. Department of Education, captured this perspective. She said, "I don't think it's worthwhile to set up artificial boundaries between nonprofits and for-profits. . . . Nowadays, with the focus on outcomes, it's much more about getting the results than your tax status."

The government officials agreed (though to be certain, both have previous executive experience at for-profit charter school networks). Asked whether there should be any education policies that discriminate by tax status, Chris Cerf, the New Jersey acting commissioner of education, replied, "My general answer is no. Those sort of differences are based on a very primitive, anti-free-enterprise attitude that permeates American culture and really always has." And Jim Shelton of the U.S. Department of Education said, "I don't think that for the sake of accountability, it makes sense to set up separate rules for nonprofits and for-profits." When asked about topics beyond accountability, such as eligibility for government programs or watchdog initiatives, he maintained that the focus should be on "weeding out bad actors," rather than making policy distinctions based on tax status.

Jimmy Wales, the Wikipedia cofounder, suggested a shift, referring to the example of Apple Computer:

> I think actually the idea that if somebody's trying to make money that this is offensive doesn't fit with our natural moral instincts in other spheres. Why is it different here? Can we move our minds into a situation to say "Yeah, my kid goes to an Apple school, that Apple guy who started the school made a fortune, and I don't have a problem with that at all"?

However, with the exceptions of Ebbie Parsons, a former executive at for-profit Mosaica Schools, and Casey Carter, a former president at for-profit National Heritage Academies, nearly everyone with whom I spoke expressed pessimism about the prospects of for-profit charter schools in American education, given the harsh political climate. Richard Barth, CEO of the nonprofit KIPP Foundation and a former executive at the for-profit Edison Schools project, said that for the issue of for-profit charter schools, the "what is" is a different matter from the "what should be." He said, "You have to focus on what you want your battles to be, and this issue isn't my top priority." Many others made similar comments. Even the NewSchools Venture Fund, which openly invests in for-profit companies and in charter schools, has "never seen a proposal for a for-profit school operator that we feel fits with what we do," said Jonathan Schorr.

So there was a clear disconnect: Those I interviewed believed that for-profits should be given equal opportunities to thrive, but generally expressed that the political challenges to do so would be too great. Below are two brief suggestions for how the case could be made.

First, charter advocates should explain that there is a chicken-and-egg problem: Policy that generally makes life harder for for-profits means that those networks may necessarily only exist on the fringes, which leads precisely to critiques that for-profit charter schools are fringe operators. Instead, if policy changes make it reasonable for an ambitious entrepreneur to believe that he or she might be able to form a national network of schools within a reasonable time frame and have an equity stake in the success of the company, the cycle would break. Given the potentially enormous social and financial opportunities, the enterprise of charter schooling would become instantly attractive to the very best educator-leaders in the country. But until that point, plenty of talented and ambitious educators and entrepreneurs will turn their talents elsewhere.

Second, charter advocates should respond forcefully to the argument that specific examples of poor behavior and disappointing results are sufficient evidence to believe that for-profit charter schools are fundamentally inferior—the Edison Schools project perhaps being chiefly cited on the latter account. After all, disappointments and failures are natural consequences of market forces at work. When a dot-com company fails, for example, nobody suggests that for-profits should be banned from the Internet. Charter school advocates should explain the reality more clearly: Even though some for-profit charter school networks will underperform, those failures will be required to close, and create space for the successes to grow. Moreover, as we have seen, given equal opportunities, for-profit successes are better suited to grow more rapidly than their nonprofit peers.

CONCLUSION

For-profit status is the default choice for entrepreneurs seeking to form a new business in just about every industry. But there certainly are reasons to believe that K–12 education should be different. After all, in K–12 education, the government is the largest customer, and the product is seemingly more social good than business.

But the extensive interviews with education leaders and executives undertaken for this chapter suggest that for-profit should be the default option for education entrepreneurs, too. It offers several universally powerful advantages with no comparable universal disadvantages. That said, as interviews demonstrated, nonprofit status can still be preferable in some specific circumstances—though even then, can come with some significant compromises.

For philanthropies, policymakers, and others interested in systemic change, the interviews suggest that for-profits and nonprofits should be encouraged and supported with equal vigor and enthusiasm. As interviewees explained, for-profits tend to operate in a more efficient and powerful marketplace than their nonprofit peers—and are no more or less virtuous than nonprofits simply for the fact of their IRS classification. Nonprofits, on the other hand, will always fill vital niches, but under more limited conditions, as we have seen. Of course, we need only look to the extraordinary success of Wikipedia to understand that these nonprofit niches are in no way less vital to the cause of educational advancement in America.

For the general public, the comments and insights suggest that we take a closer look at our assumptions about the role of for-profits in K–12 education. Mawi Asgedom, founder of the for-profit character education company Mental Karate, offered a story that captured the pragmatism of the entrepreneurs with whom I spoke:

> I was talking to a friend one time and he said, "You help kids for money." And he made it sound like it was some horrible thing. And my friend happens to be a pediatrician. And I said to him, "You know what? You save kids' lives for money. You don't do it for free. You're a doctor, and you'd stop being a doctor if you weren't being paid. So don't give me this whole holier-than-thou attitude."

CHAPTER 3

Crossing to the Dark Side?

An Interview-Based Comparison of Traditional and For-Profit Higher Education

Ben Wildavsky

The past few years have certainly not been lacking in controversy for the for-profit higher education industry. The fast-growing sector, which now accounts for some 10% of all students enrolled in U.S. postsecondary institutions, up from about 6.5% as recently as 2007 (and less than 1% 4 decades earlier), has come under unprecedented scrutiny from policymakers, regulators, and the media.[1] Critics have zeroed in on a range of concerns about for-profits, from sometimes dubious recruiting tactics and overblown promises to students about their future employability to excessive student debt and problematic default rates.

In a representative commentary, the *New York Times* editorialized in support of tougher federal regulation of higher education for-profits by declaring that new rules must be "strong enough to protect students from unscrupulous schools that strip them of aid, saddle them with crippling debt, and give them nothing in return."[2] For their part, for-profit colleges and universities have deployed a formidable lobbying apparatus to argue that their efforts are being unfairly maligned with apples-to-oranges comparisons that do not properly take into account the important education access they provide to previously underserved students.

Largely missing from the debate, however, has been a more fine-grained look at the ways traditional and for-profit institutions differ from one another. How does the experience of instructors and administrators compare and contrast? What about questions of mission and governance? Why do students enroll in for-profit degree programs? In what ways is the culture of for-profit education distinctive? This chapter is an effort to examine these questions from the point of view of individuals who have had firsthand experience moving from the traditional to the for-profit sector—or have kept a foot in both.

Those interviewed for this chapter—a nonrandom sample of administrators, board members, instructors, and a recent graduate—have all spent time in public or private not-for-profit higher education. All but one are now affiliated either full- or part-time with some of the best-known for-profit institutions: Kaplan University, the University of Phoenix, Capella University, DeVry University, Walden University, and Rasmussen College. Perhaps because of this, they are highly supportive of the mission of for-profits and almost entirely positive about their performance. At the same time, their occasional critical comments suggest that for-profits may be in the kind of shakeout phase common to all disruptive innovations, to use the term coined by Harvard Business School professor Clayton Christensen.[3] According to Christensen, disruptive innovations often experience significant growing pains and quality problems at their outset but improve quickly, create new markets, challenge the status quo, and ultimately have a transformative effect on their sectors. Thus, we can understand the interviewees' "from the trenches" observations and arguments about what for-profits add to the higher education world not simply as advocacy but as a sign of things to come for a much broader range of postsecondary institutions.

These insiders' comments, drawn from telephone interviews and follow-up email exchanges in the fall of 2010, highlight the characteristics that the respondents say distinguish the for-profits where they work from the nonprofit institutions with which they are also familiar. The interviews suggest that beyond an effort to make profits, these relatively new institutions distinguish themselves by their targeted efforts to serve nontraditional students; their creation of market-driven, career-oriented degree programs; their consistent focus on data collection and measuring learning outcomes; and their willingness to standardize curriculum and faculty roles to a degree that is rare in conventional colleges and universities. Taken individually, none of these approaches is unique to for-profits, of course. Advocates may well be guilty of overselling for-profits' educational innovations while downplaying their well-publicized shortcomings. Nevertheless, at a time of soul-searching about the ability of most colleges and universities to serve increasing numbers of students more effectively, there is good reason to believe that practices like these, when implemented together on a consistent basis, have value well beyond the for-profit context.

ECLECTIC LEADERS AND UNLIKELY CONVERTS

What would motivate a professor, administrator, or board member at a traditional university to join a for-profit institution? The individuals interviewed for this chapter say they were drawn to the for-profit sector for a variety of reasons, notably the chance to work within organizations that serve nontraditional students and the opportunity to be part of institutions not tied to conventional practices.

Other motivations are more practical; for example, one instructor found that a part-time teaching position fit well into a broader professional life by allowing him to keep a hand in the world of education while running his own consulting business. Outsiders often assume money is a big draw for participants in the for-profit sector, and at least one interviewee observed that compensation played a role in his decision to join a for-profit board. But another, a dean who was recruited to Kaplan, noted that his new salary is lower than his counterpart's at the large state university he recently left.

Several of the well-known academic administrators interviewed for this chapter previously worked on nontraditional ventures within conventional institutions, so their transition to the for-profit sector was not made out of the blue. Peter Smith, senior vice president for academic strategies and development for Kaplan Higher Education, was the founding president of Vermont's statewide community college system. "I have been very interested in community-based, life-based education," he says, referring to institutions in which outcomes-oriented, experiential student learning, rather than research, has a central place. Later in his career he became the founding president of another unconventional institution, California State University, Monterey Bay, which focuses heavily on enrolling first-generation college students, significant use of technology, service learning, and measuring learning outcomes. When he was recruited to the Kaplan post, he did not hesitate to move to a money-making venture. "I thought, 'You've been doing this—taking risks—all your life. Why should you not take a risk now?'" Despite his background in nontraditional public higher education institutions, he had been disappointed in some respects with the sustainability of reform. "Too often, even successful change in higher education is like a sand castle before the tide comes in," he says. "When the champion leaves, when budgets get cut, much of the value is lost." He is more optimistic about the prospects for successful new ideas to become embedded at Kaplan.

Smith's colleague Geri Malandra, who became provost of Kaplan University in 2010, had previously overseen the development of the 15-campus University of Texas system's well-known performance-based assessment model as vice chancellor for strategic management. In an earlier job, she spearheaded another accountability system at the University of Minnesota and also established an off-campus technology education center that was initially envisioned (though without ultimate success) as a for-profit division of the huge state university. "This particular private-sector university sorts for leaders that have very eclectic experience," she says.

Indeed, another well-known for-profit figure, Jorge Klor de Alva, president of the Nexus Research and Policy Center and former president of the University of Phoenix, was also involved with nontraditional ventures from the beginning of his otherwise conventional and successful academic trajectory. As a young professor at San Jose State University, he met a fellow instructor, John Sperling, who was already working outside the university on practical training programs for nontraditional students such as police officers and firefighters. Drawn to the chance to work with a student population that he felt San Jose State "had zero interest in," Klor de Alva became involved with the fledgling University of Phoenix even as he pursued an academic career that took him to a tenured professorship at the University of California, Berkeley. His decision to leave that job to head the fast-growing and controversial for-profit institution was not as big a surprise as some of his Berkeley colleagues may have thought, he says: "I had one foot in the for-profit world from the beginning."

By contrast, if some for-profit leaders had always played somewhat unconventional roles within traditional academe, other stalwarts of the higher education establishment never expected to find themselves in cutting-edge (and controversial) institutions. "If you had asked me 15 years ago would I ever be participating in any way in the for-profit sector, I would have dismissed it out of hand," says Harold Shapiro, former president of Princeton University and the University of Michigan. "One, I didn't know very much about it, and two, what I did know wasn't very flattering." But Shapiro got to know DeVry Inc. cofounder Dennis Keller when Keller served as a Princeton trustee. When Shapiro retired from the Princeton presidency in 2001, he was asked to join the board of DeVry, which owns DeVry University, Chamberlain College of Nursing, Keller Graduate School of Management, and other for-profits. "By that time I'd begun to think that some of the firms in the sector were really addressing a problem that was overlooked by the traditional higher education sector," says Shapiro, who continues to carry a full teaching load as an emeritus professor of economics at Princeton. "There was a portion of the population that for various reasons was not being served by the traditional sector. I began to realize that there was potential for a great social product there." In 2008, he became DeVry's board chairman.

Another perhaps unlikely champion of the proprietary higher education sector, Henry Bienen, former president of Northwestern University, was recruited to the for-profit world by a Northwestern University alumnus and donor, Robert King, chairman of Rasmussen College, Inc. Bienen joined the Rasmussen board while he was still president of Northwestern. When he stepped down from the presidency, he became vice chairman and later chairman of the board; he also spends about 30 days per year working for the company. Rasmussen offers bachelor's degrees in subjects such as nursing, business, information technology, criminal justice, and early childhood education. Many of its courses are offered online, and 17 Rasmussen College campuses offer both in-person teaching and blended instruction that includes an online component. A Rasmussen subsidiary, Deltak, offers master's degrees in partnership with institutions such as St. Joseph's University and Loyola University, New Orleans.

Like Shapiro, Bienen saw for-profits filling a role that conventional institutions have not always performed well: "I thought, 'There's a lack of institutions in the United States putting together jobs and skills, which is striking. . . . It's a lacuna in the higher education system.'" Community colleges were meant to serve this function, he notes, but have delivered mixed performance and, in any case, are "crammed to the gills right now" as workers pour into cash-strapped public institutions to upgrade their skills in a faltering economy.

Bienen says that his wife, a law professor at Northwestern, was somewhat skeptical about whether he should join a for-profit. But she agreed with him that colleges like those Rasmussen runs have the potential to provide much-needed educational opportunities. "These are important institutions for the country if you can get them right, if you can maintain good standards and fulfill your mission: Train people to do jobs and get them into the employment market," he says. He is also candid about the financial appeal of the for-profit sector, as well as the value to Rasmussen of his understanding of the postsecondary world and his access to policymakers in Washington, D.C. "I thought I could bring something to the table of some use, knowing higher education reasonably well. Obviously, I wanted to do well for myself financially, while doing something that interested me, while at the same time doing something that was good for the world. Some of these places can do some good—the good ones."

Still, the potential virtues of for-profit universities are by no means immediately apparent to many academics on traditional campuses. Professional colleagues sometimes make this clear to Jim Goes, a former professor of health care and management at the University of Minnesota and the University of Alaska, who began teaching doctoral students online at the University of Phoenix and Walden University after he left conventional academe to launch his own management consulting firm. "The toughest thing for me to manage personally has been the question of legitimacy," he says. He has published in top journals in his field and has long been a member of the Academy of Management, a professional association of business academics. Yet, he says, "When I go to conferences and they say 'University of Phoenix?', they kind of look at you as if [to say], 'What happened to you?' There's enormous snobbishness in education."

Klor de Alva suggests that, in at least some cases, the reaction of traditional academics when their colleagues move to vastly different for-profit colleges and universities does not just reflect their perception—a common one—that those institutions provide a substandard education. He maintains that a move like his, which was particularly unusual because of his status as a tenured professor with an endowed chair at an elite university, may also be a little threatening to members of the university establishment.

"When I left Berkeley, I felt a little bit the way you do when you have a group of couples who are friends, and one of them gets divorced. It always sends a kind of ripple of consternation and reflection among your whole little group," Klor de Alva says. "So when I left I could easily understand how upset they were with me. Because I was basically saying, 'Look, I found something else, other than what we are doing together, of great value.' These are all people who identify what they're doing as a job to die for—how could you leave it? And yet I was putting that into question." Michael Offerman, who holds a Ph.D. in educational policy from Northern Illinois University, was dean of continuing education at the University of Wisconsin–Extension and later became president of Capella University. He echoes this view: "I gave up tenure at Wisconsin, and that's something that people don't do."

Whatever their backgrounds, many interviewees were willing to acknowledge in general terms that all is not rosy in the for-profit world. After all, to take just one example, recent data showed that for-profits nationally had average 3-year student loan default rates of nearly 23%, much higher than those of publics (11%) and nonprofits (7.5%). Insiders concede that concerns about poor academic quality and inadequate consumer protection have some factual basis. They simultaneously make the case that their own institutions are effective, that many of the problems facing for-profits are common to all postsecondary institutions serving nontraditional students (which also have above-average default rates), and that regulatory overkill risks closing off access to students who could benefit from higher education. "I have said publicly, and to Secretary [Arne] Duncan, that there are quality issues for many for-profit schools," Bienen says. "Some do not provide a decent career-oriented education. I think we do at Rasmussen." He recognizes that the for-profits' rapid expansion has had some downsides but cites potential upsides, too. At a time when President Obama and many others are pushing to expand college-going rates, he notes that heightened scrutiny from Washington has made for-profits less willing to take risks on marginal students, some of whom could benefit from what these institutions have to offer.

TRIAL, ERROR, AND MEASUREMENT

Perhaps the biggest appeal for-profits hold for Klor de Alva, Offerman, and others who have joined the sector is that that they are relatively new postsecondary institutions—educational works in progress in which experimentation is encouraged and inevitable. In his previous job, "I was getting bored," Offerman says. He initially worried that when he got to Capella, which offers online-only degrees to students 24 years old and up, "everything was going to be about the bottom line and was going to be ruthless." What he found instead was "a very thoughtful mode," in which the company took a long-term view of building its reputation without being tied to traditional assumptions and models.

He cites Capella's focus on learning outcomes not just for core skills like writing and analytical reasoning, but also at the program or major level. Capella's learning-outcomes work gained the company an award from the Council for Higher Education Accreditation—the kind of recognition that would not have come had the institution been focusing solely on short-term financial returns, Offerman says. "The issue isn't that for-profits are so much better at this," says

Offerman. But their newness and distinctive mission "allows us to innovate and experiment in ways that I didn't see happening as much when I was in public institutions." Capella and other for-profits create "curriculum maps" leading to defined outcomes tailored to skills valued by employers. Offerman contrasts this practice with the ethos of many traditional institutions where, he argues, "the interests and research experiences of the available faculty determine what is emphasized and what is taught."

To illustrate Kaplan's ability to experiment, Thomas Boyd, dean of Kaplan University's School of Business Management, cites the firm's practice of comparing and contrasting different pedagogical approaches in, for example, a marketing class with a highly standardized curriculum. With large numbers of essentially identical courses, he says, Kaplan is able to test out new ideas systematically and on a large scale. New tutorial software has been piloted in some sections and not others, for example. Kaplan also gives students the chance to try seminar-style classes as an alternative to conventional instruction. Administrators can then look at student learning outcomes to compare success rates in classes using existing and alternative approaches. "We've created a laboratory for improving education," says Boyd, who joined Kaplan in 2010 from California State University, Fullerton, where he was a professor of marketing and associate dean for academic programs at the College of Business and Economics. "We don't get it right every time. Some of the stuff bombs, and we drop it. We say, 'Whoops, that didn't work.' But we're there trying new things all the time."

Along with the capacity to tolerate more trial and error than traditional institutions, entrepreneurial for-profits are able to move much faster to create new programs, adjust staffing levels, and make curriculum changes, according to Malandra, who says this became apparent to her soon after she joined Kaplan. "I was amazed at how quickly program suggestions can be developed and brought online," she says. That ability to make rapid program changes contrasts with many traditional universities, in part because of for-profits' ability to staff new or expanding programs on short notice. "In a regular university it's very hard to add faculty positions; it can be done, but it's hard," she says. "Here it can be done relatively easily if there are strong market reasons." Kaplan's online classes are offered at multiple starting points each year to let students enroll at their convenience. So the firm's recruiting, hiring, and orientation procedures are set up to quickly accommodate fluctuations in demand for course sections; part-time, adjunct faculty can be hired on short notice when needed. It is true, of course, that traditional universities also have a large and expanding core of adjuncts, but those positions tend to be filled on a less flexible schedule because of the traditional semester system, she adds. "This is not a judgment of better or worse—just different business models."

Kaplan can also react speedily when course content needs to be updated, Malandra says. "One of the biggest contrasts is that we can adjust and improve our curriculum much more quickly than I was able to see at public universities. Not because the faculty wouldn't want to do that, but you have [factors including] limitations because of resources, the timeline it takes to add new people, different levels of internal and external review," and so forth. In the public systems where Malandra worked, she says, "it could take a year or more for programs to go from idea, through department, college, board, and state coordinating board approval." She recalls one online doctoral program that took many years to get a green light. "Because it is so rare to eliminate programs, it makes sense that the public systems would be careful," Malandra says. "As an administrator, the checks and balances along the way were valuable, but it was frustrating to the academics." At Kaplan, there is also what she calls a "rigorous, multistep process" to evaluate new programs, but, averaging 3 to 6 months from beginning to board approval, the process is much faster. Kaplan also employs a large staff of curriculum developers focused on keeping course material up-to-date and ensuring that it can be delivered effectively online. According to Boyd, more than half of Kaplan's business courses went through major revision last year, while many others received minor tweaks.

The ability to standardize curriculum is particularly important to the success of for-profits, interviewees stressed repeatedly. Klor de Alva says this represents a huge philosophical shift from faculty-controlled curriculum decisions in the traditional sector. "Berkeley was a place where everybody was truly their own boss—as the Brazilians say, '*todos são os donos da verdade*' (everybody is the owner of the truth)." Peter Smith agrees. "The culture of faculty governance is hostile to anything that in a consistent way will impinge on the autonomy of the individual faculty member, period," he says. "They're the kings and queens of their own courses. You can teach ten accounting courses with ten teachers and have ten entirely different sets of curriculum."

As the University of Phoenix grew, in contrast, its leaders applied the principles of standardization and mass production across the board. The company felt no need to reinvent its design template each time it opened a new facility in its chain of campuses, Klor de Alva says. It tried to maintain the same look and feel in each building, even using the same furniture. It followed the same model with its courses. "The idea was that when you were in the second week of Organizational Behavior in Tampa, or Dallas, or Oklahoma City, or San Diego, the student was learning the exact same things, and the faculty member had been trained to teach," he explains. "So your success in class did not depend on which side of the bed the faculty member got up on, or how good or bad the faculty member was."

Part and parcel of for-profits' inclination to standardize the material in each course is the ability such a system gives them to systematically measure whether students learn what they are being taught. A repeated theme of the interviews was that for-profits have developed a culture in which student learning outcomes are carefully designed, then regularly assessed. Malandra, who pushed hard for better assessment of student learning in the University of Texas system, boasts that nearly every one of Kaplan's 900-plus courses in some 125 certificate, bachelor's, and master's programs has a rubric spelling out the goals of the course and the specific outcomes students are expected to master. Courses are effectively reverse engineered: Once the desired outcomes have been established, administrators and instructors can create content for each week and semester. Data are collected from each class, allowing administrators to map outcomes by program, course, instructor, and more.

To determine where changes are needed in a particular course section, Kaplan creates detailed scatter charts analyzing how student outcomes compare with overall grades for the course as a whole. Sections for which the upper left-hand quadrant shows both low average overall course grades and low median scores on unit tests within the course are immediately flagged for improvement. Kaplan also uses testing data to overhaul course design. Boyd says that Kaplan recently revised aspects of a marketing class by adding new multimedia exercises when a detailed breakdown of tests showed that about 10% of students were not improving their grasp of certain subtopics.

Not all assessment is the same, of course. Although agreement on the need for more outcomes measurement in a range of postsecondary institutions is growing, the shape it takes in for-profits needs to be highly individualized, Malandra argues. Instruments like the Collegiate Learning Assessment (CLA), which is now mandatory for all University of Texas campuses, rely on relatively small student samples to produce results intended to represent student achievement at the entire institution. Traditional public universities and private not-for-profits are often wary of assessment regimes like the CLA on the grounds that one-size-fits-all tests cannot capture their complexity as institutions.

Malandra's views on the need for individualized assessments are based on a different argument—that overall measures of an institution's teaching effectiveness based on testing a small group of students are not what students at for-profits need or want. Sampling makes sense, she says, for large institutions that have been around a long time, have relatively well-prepared students, and are supported by policymakers who generally value the importance of higher education. But for-profit students are self-supporting—with a hefty assist from federal student loans, of course—"so for them there's no way that sampling of student outcomes makes sense," she says. "We don't want to know 'on average' anything. We want to know about actual live students and how they're doing and how we can improve their experience one by one."

For-profit administrators say they conceive of learning outcomes very practically. At Capella, "We have identified program-related learning outcomes development by talking to the people who hired our graduates. It's not just a bunch of people sitting around a room," Offerman says. Other for-profit leaders echo the theme. What students should learn, they say, and the knowledge and skills on which they are evaluated, is a function not simply of students' desires or of the preferences of the institutions where they study, but of institutions' efforts to respond to market needs.

At Rasmussen, Bienen says, "If employment demands are shifting in some way, we could start up new programs in ways that a lot of traditional places can't [easily do]. You know what academic institutions are like; they're often quite slow to do this." At Rasmussen, without the need for faculty committee approvals for every new program, an accounting program could be established within about a year. At Northwestern, Bienen says, even when an undergraduate business program was put in place fairly quickly by traditional standards, the process took 2 years. Rasmussen gauges the need for particular course offerings by talking to firms that hire its graduates. In an area like Minneapolis–St. Paul, for example, which has a high concentration of health-care firms, Rasmussen officials meet regularly with human resources staff at large companies to discuss what programs and courses would be particularly useful in meeting their needs. This approach to assessing market demands is not just a practical necessity: It is a philosophical dividing line between the traditional sector, particularly at the elite level, and money-making institutions, says former Princeton president Shapiro:

> In elite higher education, you think you know what people need, so you produce that. You're not out there asking firms or consumers, "What do you want?" [At traditional universities,] we know what we want. Whereas at a place like DeVry, which is much more focused on career education, management is out there all the time talking to businesses, asking, "What do you want?" [They are] talking to students, asking, "What do you want in a professional sense?" Obviously, the for-profit sector has to be much more attuned to customer needs—students and employers. And the not-for-profit sector has more general guidelines in that respect and maybe longer-term guidelines.

In this environment, it goes without saying that returns to shareholders matter. "After all, this is a profit-making business," Shapiro says. But he maintains that attention to the bottom line is fully compatible with serving the practical needs of student-consumers. "The thought is you do well by doing good. You produce a product that people want, and then you'll make a profit."

RETHINKING THE FACULTY'S ROLE

For-profit institutions that value trial and error, a heavily standardized curriculum, careful assessment of learning outcomes, and responsiveness to consumer demand depend heavily on instructional staff to make all this work. The result is that their faculty tends to look quite different from their counterparts at many traditional public and private not-for-profit institutions. First and foremost, for-profits' faculty are instructors rather than researchers. "At DeVry we're hiring people who want to teach," Shapiro says. "If you want to do research, DeVry is not the place for you." The proportion of full- to part-time faculty at DeVry varies by institution. Professors at institutions such as Ross Medical School in the West Indies are almost all full-time, but many instructors in other DeVry divisions are part-time adjuncts. The company says that its goal is to have 60% of the credit hours it offers taught by full-time faculty.

The understanding that teaching is the central responsibility of faculty is not hugely different from the expectations of faculty at community colleges; large, nonselective regional public universities; and some small, private colleges. But Peter Smith of Kaplan maintains that there are, nevertheless, some contrasts. Kaplan's faculty (which is 70% female) includes not just instructors with terminal degrees in their fields, but many practitioners as well. Also, Smith maintains that instructors at Kaplan, while having some latitude in how they deliver materials, must focus particularly carefully on student learning outcomes because of the company's emphasis on assessment of those outcomes both during and at the end of each course.

More broadly, for-profits' emphasis on faculty as classroom instructors is quite different from the conception of a professor's core job at many research universities. Klor de Alva says he saw this firsthand at Berkeley, where, by his account, the reward structure for professors was based almost entirely on their professional advancement as scholars, both on campus and beyond. "The percentage of folks who focused on research to the near total disregard of students was pretty high," he contends. Though many would dispute this view, Klor de Alva asserts that the general attitude among Berkeley faculty was that students "were a bother, and they took up time" that could otherwise have been devoted to research. (He recalls that teaching was considered a higher priority at Princeton, where he taught before moving to Berkeley.)

To be sure, as University of Southern California professor Guilbert Hentschke notes, it may be more appropriate to compare for-profit faculty to instructors at community colleges than to tenured professors at major research institutions, who are tasked with creating or adapting new knowledge. Others liken for-profit instructors to the adjuncts who increasingly staff many large undergraduate classes at traditional universities. But Capella's Offerman says that his entry into the for-profit sector dispelled some stereotypes he held about the kinds of instructors he would find. "I had drunk the Kool-Aid at the publics and the nonprofits," he says, referring to the assumption that for-profit faculty were almost all low-level adjuncts with no benefits and few other prospects. Instead, he says he discovered "a whole new world" of instructors: independent contractors who had little interest in the publish-or-perish world of traditional research universities. Many have degrees from respected institutions, he notes—typically terminal degrees for those teaching in Capella's graduate programs. Offerman says these instructors self-select based on their desire to focus on teaching, much like those at the University of Wisconsin–Stevens Point, the regional campus where he once worked in continuing education. Capella's faculty are employees; Offerman says their compensation levels are set using pay rates at similar institutions as defined by the Carnegie classifications.

To create effective teachers, for-profits also do something that is unusual in many traditional colleges and universities: They evaluate prospective hires on their teaching skills and give new instructors explicit pedagogical training. "DeVry actually trains people how to be better teachers. I'm not aware of any traditional universities who do that," Shapiro says. That is an expansive claim that would no doubt elicit disagreement from the many institutions trying to upgrade teaching quality on their campuses. But the 3-week intensive teaching seminar that DeVry offers faculty before they begin teaching, plus ongoing training, certainly is not common practice at most colleges and universities.

When Goes, who already had considerable teaching experience, first began working with Walden in 1999, the company flew him to Minneapolis for an orientation session in which he was shown how to evaluate a large research and writing project, known as a Knowledge Area Module, then in widespread use for doctoral students at Walden. At Phoenix, he went through an online training program devoted largely to learning the mechanics of the course platform. Next, he taught a class under the online supervision of a current faculty member, receiving regular feedback on his success at engaging students. When the class was finished, he received a formal evaluation before Phoenix decided to hire him. "They check you out," he says.

Once on the payroll, for-profit instructors are also evaluated much more systematically than many of their peers in the traditional academic world. Since becoming an instructor at Phoenix, Goes has been through several evaluations by faculty members or administrators, who assessed his performance on a variety of criteria, including whether he met "minimum set" or "best practices set" criteria. Goes says that Phoenix officials are aware of the criticism that professors in online classes are not actively engaged—that students are, in effect, teaching themselves. So his online activity is monitored weekly to ensure that he is interacting regularly with students and providing them substantive feedback on their papers and contributions to class discussion.

He finds the exercise useful, he says, and something that "rarely, if ever" took place at the traditional institutions where he has taught. Although student evaluations are routine in the not-for-profit world, they often "go off into a black hole," according to Goes. "You can access them, but I never had any direct feedback from anybody in the institution about them." To be sure, he says he has not received feedback at Walden and Phoenix based explicitly on student course evaluations. Still, Goes says that the culture of faculty evaluation at those two institutions is pervasive—and valuable. At four traditional universities where he has taught, he explains, including two Carnegie I research institutions, teaching abilities "received relatively little attention." He got one "attaboy" from an administrator and a favorable acknowledgment of strong student evaluations when he was granted tenure at the teaching-oriented University of Alaska Southeast campus. The exception to the general lack of interest in teaching evaluations he has experienced at traditional institutions, Goes says, is in an Executive MBA (EMBA) program sponsored by a consortium of several Oregon universities in which he has taught for the past decade. "In this case, evaluations matter a lot, because EMBA is a very competitive market," he says.

Shapiro agrees that oversight of teaching quality is weak in the traditional sector. He maintains a full teaching and research load at Princeton and says that traditional institutions rarely criticize or reward faculty based on student evaluations. "I get feedback telling me that students liked or disliked this or that aspect of a course. It would be much more unusual, however, for the dean to call a faculty member and say, 'Hey, I've looked at your evaluations, and I'm concerned about them,' or 'I congratulate you on them.' Whereas at DeVry, that feedback is organized, and it happens all the time." Course evaluations at DeVry are conducted from all directions, Shapiro notes: Every course is evaluated by students, faculty, and a dean.

Does the for-profits' focus on instructors' classroom success mean that poor performers are dismissed? Goes says that faculty turnover at both Walden and Phoenix is fairly high: "There seems to be a lot of churn." That is probably in part because some instructors simply do not care for the online mode. Goes is personally aware of at least a few cases in which Walden faculty members have been fired. "Let's be clear: This is at-will employment, and there is nothing resembling tenure," he says. "However, I think if you meet the standards for a faculty hire and continue to meet the standards in your work, you're reasonably safe at either institution." Flexible employment arrangements mean that the drama of terminating an instructor simply is not needed in most cases. "The work is all contractual, so if they decide they don't like you anymore the most likely event is that they will no longer offer you courses or other work," Goes says.

Why is it so much harder, by these interviewees' accounts, to use evaluations to boost teaching quality in traditional institutions? Boyd, the Kaplan business school dean, explains that administrators at many universities have very limited ability to oversee professors. When he was associate dean of the CSU Fullerton business school, he was frustrated by a culture in which his authority was severely constrained. "It was sort of a protocol that you had to walk on eggshells when you talked about what they were doing in their classroom," he says. "Of course you couldn't go into the classroom and observe a professor. You could ask their permission, but you couldn't drop in on classes. That was considered very inappropriate, to watch how they were teaching." Similarly, administrators could obtain a professor's syllabus for a particular course, "but you had no way to make sure they were following their syllabus. You would frequently encounter professors who would say, 'I ran out of time, so I skipped the last two chapters,' or 'I never knew much about marketing channels, so I didn't cover that.' There was very little you could do about that."

Perhaps unsurprisingly, Boyd identifies tenure as a significant barrier to improving teaching, consistency of the curriculum, and student learning. He recalls a tenured faculty member who taught a large section of a Principles of Marketing class using 20-year-old handwritten notes and refused to use the same textbook as other instructors. "He wasn't a bad teacher. He wasn't bad with students," Boyd says. But the professor's stubbornness "made it much harder to make sure students were exposed to the material. Current marketing practice has evolved dramatically in the last 10 to 15 years." The upshot: Quality control was hard to exercise, which in turn meant that "despite people's best efforts, it was also very hard to measure student learning."

Like other tenure critics, he worries that the system has devolved from giving freedom to faculty engaged in potentially controversial research to protecting professors who do not pull their weight. Many faculty members at CSU Fullerton, he says, go well beyond the minimum—publishing, teaching, mentoring junior faculty, and otherwise serving their departments. But the minority who do not serve as a barrier to a culture of excellence. He cites another run-in with a tenured professor, whom he asked to attend a Thursday morning meeting. "He said, 'I'm not going to come. I only come to campus on Wednesdays, and you can't make me come.'" This exchange "is illustrative," Boyd says. "It is not an extremely widely held attitude, but it is held, and it holds back institutions."

PRACTICAL INSTRUCTION AND STUDENT SUPPORT

One reason among others that tenure is unheard of in for-profit colleges is that many of them hire working professionals or retired college instructors to teach courses whose emphasis is relentlessly practical. When Phoenix was created, says Klor de Alva, "we wanted practitioners. We used to say that you were teaching in the evening what the students would be able to apply to their workplace in the morning." That focus is attractive for some professors. Goes, for example, says helping students think through the kinds of real-world problems they encounter in their workplaces makes his teaching at Phoenix and Walden distinct from the classes he has taught at other institutions. "These are people who have life experience; they're not 20-somethings reading about business in a book," he says. "They're 40-somethings who have a lot of practical experience, who are trying to improve their lives. . . . It's wonderful to work with people who are dealing with real-world problems, and real-world business problems, and they need help working them through."

This hands-on orientation, where academic theory often takes a distant back-seat to practice, was attractive to students like Laura Parker, the director of the Children's Discovery Center, a preschool in Riverside, California, owned by the Seventh Day Adventist Church. Parker recently earned a degree in human services from the University of Phoenix. Before her 17-year career in early childhood education, she had worked as a respiratory therapist. That is certainly not a theoretical subject, but she complains that the "perfect scenarios" that were used to teach the respiratory therapy class she took many years ago did not prepare her for the reality she encountered in the emergency rooms where she worked later. In her Phoenix classes, which she took at a bricks-and-mortar facility near her home in Orange County, California, "the teachers had real experience in the field," she says. "So you're not getting someone who's just book smart—you're getting people who are actually out there working. And I think you get a clearer picture of what you're going to be up against in the field you've chosen."

Career advancement, of course, is the payoff promised by for-profit institutions—and their failure at times to deliver on that promise is at the center of today's controversy. For Parker, whose boss explicitly promised her a $7,000-per-year raise if she earned her bachelor's degree, a clear financial incentive combined with her slight embarrassment at having no formal postsecondary credential was enough impetus to take on a significant new commitment. Along with giving her a higher salary in the near term, her degree would qualify her to pursue a master's program at nearby Loma Linda University. A master's would in turn prepare her for her eventual career goal—working as a medical social worker in a children's hospital. Although she is known and respected within her community, Parker says, "I couldn't market myself [in the wider world] without my degree." Jim Goes says that his doctoral students have also seen career doors open because of their Phoenix and Walden degrees, even though such qualifications do not carry much academic cachet. "I've seen some real success stories for people who are dead-ended in their jobs, even at mid-to-upper levels in the corporate world, for whom this doctoral level was a revelation. [It] has changed the trajectory of their professional lives. It has opened up new opportunities for them."

Student convenience is a frequently cited selling point of for-profits, which market themselves not just on the basis of the practical, career-oriented courses they offer, but also for the way they accommodate the real-world demands of older students juggling work and family obligations. Once recruited, students can begin classes quickly, thanks to year-round enrollment cycles that do not abide by the traditional fall-to-spring academic calendar. A much-noted distinguishing characteristic of Phoenix is that its branches are conveniently located near freeway exits. Classes typically run 4 hours or so 1 night per week, with assignments and group projects scheduled on an accelerated basis, permitting a semester of course credit to be earned in about 5 weeks for courses held in bricks-and-mortar "on-ground" campuses. For Parker, the opportunity to earn a degree within a few years while still working was crucial. She took just under 3 years to earn her Phoenix bachelor's degree and says that despite her high student debt—around $50,000—she does not regret the choice. Previously, she had attended community college 2 or 3 nights a week, taking one or two classes per semester, and sometimes had trouble finding courses that met in the evenings. "It was wearing me down at that rate," she says. "I felt like I was never going to be done with school. . . . I felt like I needed to do something, regardless of cost."

To keep nontraditional students on track, for-profits say that they make student engagement a high priority. Despite what educational traditionalists might expect, for-profits often keep classes small, both in person and online. That can contrast favorably to most students' public-sector alternatives. Before enrolling at Phoenix, Parker took classes at Riverside Community College, which often had 30 or 40 students per class. She had minimal contact with her instructors and was frustrated when she wanted to contribute to a class conversation and was lucky to get in a brief comment. By contrast, her Phoenix classes had no more than 20 students, and she felt that her contributions were encouraged.

As a beginning Phoenix student, Parker says, "I was scared to death when I walked in." With the exception of a few community college classes, she had been out of school for years and was worried about a heavy workload. But she received weekly phone calls from a university staffer, which she found reassuring. "They really mentor you when you start the program," Parker says. "You feel like that's their goal, to help you succeed. . . . I always felt like I had a sense of security with them; I didn't feel like I was lost." When she attended nearby Riverside Community College, by contrast, although counselors were available, getting attention was not as easy, and she felt the personal touch was lacking: "To me it felt more like a cattle call."

Malandra of Kaplan underscores how much support is needed for students with one or more of the risk factors often associated with failure to complete a degree: Many are first-generation college students; ethnic or racial minorities; or older, working adults with children. Many would simply never be enrolled at traditional colleges and universities, where students often enter with stronger preparation. Many students at for-profits "would crash and burn before the end of the semester in a regular university, and they know that," Malandra says. Big state university systems "are not set up for these students—and I'm not sure they should be." Kaplan provides a large network of advisors who give its students guidance on topics from financial aid to core academic skills. "If they're struggling in any way, we'll help right away," she says.

The flip side of enrolling many nontraditional students who are often poorly prepared for college is that the potential to improve what they know and can do is significant. Malandra draws an analogy between what for-profits can do for their students and the kind of educational gains seen by nontraditional students at unselective regional public universities. When the University of Texas began administering the Collegiate Learning Assessment at relatively open-access, mostly Hispanic-serving campuses such as UT Permian Basin and UT El Paso, value-added measures of student learning were much higher than at the state flagship in Austin. Although students may have come in with poorer abilities on average, their gains while on campus outstripped those of their peers. Students at Kaplan have a similar set of risk factors, Malandra says, and are similarly likely to gain disproportionately from postsecondary education.

Those who have worked in both traditional and for-profit institutions almost invariably bring up web-based learning when comparing the sectors. Although online education is spreading throughout higher education, Offerman contends that for-profits have had unique success in leveraging the efficiencies of web-based instruction. "Most traditional institutions have actually found that online [education] adds costs rather than reducing costs or achieving efficiencies," he says. "My theory is that they're laying a new delivery mode over the old structure, over an old set of assumptions."

Indeed, when asked what the traditional sector can learn from for-profits, Shapiro says the key is learning to respond quickly to new developments in the surrounding society. "So the question for a place like Princeton, for example, is 'Are we really deploying all the newest technological devices . . . as effectively as we could, or are we married to the old pedagogy?'" Although institutions such as the University of Illinois and Carnegie Mellon University have earned a reputation as early adopters of new learning technology, he adds, "Those of us at the Princeton and the Michigans of the world ought to be saying, 'Are we being agile enough, or are we just sitting on the monopolistic position we hold?'"

Online education has helped drive the fast growth of for-profits, which account for more than 40% of all fully online enrollments in postsecondary education. But it is not for everybody. Kaplan's Boyd says that probably the most important of the "very strong positives" he continues to see in the traditional sectors is "the face-to-face opportunities for students to go and sit in professors' offices and talk to them." That said, the two are not mutually exclusive: For-profits have pioneered blended learning, a hybrid of online and classroom instruction that is becoming increasingly popular in both for-profit and not-for-profit institutions.

QUALITY CONCERNS AND GOVERNANCE

For-profits are controversial, of course, because some of their practices seem to exploit nontraditional students rather than help them. Those who have moved from one system to the other are generally quick to acknowledge some serious problems while underscoring that such nontraditional students often face comparable difficulties and frequently experience poor outcomes in conventional institutions. "I hold no favor for some of the abuses that have been discovered across the board—they're wrong; they're disgusting; they shouldn't happen," says Peter Smith of Kaplan, referring to allegations, for instance, that for-profit recruiters have misled prospective students about the labor-market value of certain degrees. At the same time, he adds, alluding to a controversial Government Accountability Office "secret shopper" report on alleged unethical practices by for-profits, investigators applying similar scrutiny to traditional institutions would "see and record some things that are every bit as bad," such as rock-bottom graduation rates at community colleges or dubious athletic recruiting practices at 4-year schools.[4] Like others at Kaplan, he highlights the company's new "Kaplan Commitment" program, which gives every potential student a 5-week window to test out course offerings without financial commitment. James Goes also says critics are only partly right: "There certainly seem to be some abuses going on," he says, "but these institutions have been reaching an audience and a market that traditional education could not. And that piece gets lost in the discussion." (He stresses that he is "not an apologist" for either Walden or Phoenix, which he does not significantly rely on to earn a living.)

Shapiro, too, does not hesitate to concede that quality is "very variable" at for-profits. But in the same breath he notes that "there are good schools and terrible schools within the traditional sector. DeVry is not perfect—nor is Princeton, for that matter." Asked whether for-profits are more likely than other institutions to be of poor quality, as their battered image (and numerous critics) would suggest, Shapiro demurs: "I cannot say if for-profits are more likely than others to be of poor quality, since I have not reviewed them as a whole." Like other interviewees, he stressed that the goals and accomplishments of for-profits must be seen in context. "I try to pay attention to the issue of 'Can we or can't we serve an important sector of the population in a way that helps them?' If we can, we'll be okay. If we can't, we ought to get out of the business," he says. He believes that for-profits have every reason to applaud a policy environment in which increasing attention is paid to how well all kinds of institutions serve students. "This idea that, going forward, we're all going to be held to account, is on the whole a very positive thing," Shapiro says.

The reputation of for-profits is based on many things beyond student debt and future employment prospects, of course. One is the quality of faculty. In institutions focused very heavily on teaching practical subjects, measures of what constitutes a good instructor may differ somewhat from those in traditional colleges. But among traditional academics, suspicions run high that faculty who teach in for-profits that offer advanced degrees have subpar academic credentials and abilities. Goes says there is some truth to such concerns. "There's a great deal of variability in my experience." Some of his faculty colleagues are "very competent and academically credible," he says. Nevertheless, he adds, "I've had to deal with people at both institutions [Phoenix and Walden] who, in my mind, are not entirely credible scholars or academics." Some of these faculty received their degrees from the same institution where they now teach or from other online institutions. Some of those hired in the early days of Phoenix and Walden, Goes says, "have established a bureaucratic position in the institution . . . and they're embedded. They're not what I think of as credible colleagues on par with how I think of myself."

He acknowledges that these weaknesses are significant, but he does not see them as insurmountable. He believes for-profits are making progress in setting higher expectations for faculty. And his acknowledgment of significantly uneven quality in for-profits fits right in with his broader analysis of these relatively new institutions as exemplifying Clayton Christensen's notion of disruptive innovation. In the case of for-profit postsecondary institutions, he argues, "The real question is, 'how fast are they improving, and how fast can they move up market?'"

Goes says he has seen some former doctoral students go on to establish mainstream academic reputations. But others have had no luck getting a foot in the door at traditional institutions because their for-profit credentials were viewed as suspect. Yet he believes this ethos will gradually change as for-profit graduates with advanced degrees who can write well get published and begin to prove themselves. "I think meritocracy will win out in the end," he says.

On the governance front, notwithstanding the built-in differences between for-profits and not-for-profits on such core matters as faculty control of the curriculum, more structural similarities exist than outsiders might imagine. "If you looked at our administrative manual, it would be similar to what you'd see in other colleges and universities," Malandra says of Kaplan University. Kaplan has curriculum committees, policy review committees, an administrative council, a new programs steering committee, and a faculty senate. This is not a coincidence, she explains, because such structure and internal processes are needed to comply with accreditation requirements. (Kaplan is accredited by the Higher Learning Commission.)

Malandra, who weathered political controversies as an administrator in the Minnesota and Texas state university systems, sees commonalities between the close oversight those institutions received and the current firestorm surrounding for-profits. "I know what it was like when we were being attacked by the legislature in Texas," at a time when the university was under pressure to explain how and why it provided value to taxpayers, she says. "I know what it's like being in a room with people discussing communications and legislative strategy. . . . That part feels the same to me." Similarly, she recalls being horrified the first couple of times she was chastised by Minnesota legislators during debates over issues such as legislative scrutiny of the university budget and proposal to close county-level offices of the university extension services in favor of a regional model. "But eventually you learn that it's a political process. It's not the end of what will happen," she says. Malandra says her past experience has helped her stay relatively unperturbed by the current period of heightened for-profit scrutiny by Washington legislators. "There's a part of me that says, 'This, too, will end.'"

What about board leadership at for-profits versus traditional universities? Here again, commonalities exist among the inevitable differences. Strategic thinking matters wherever you are. Shapiro recalls that one of his riskiest decisions as president of the University of Michigan was rebuilding the university's medical center during the oil crisis of the 1970s. With $1 billion needed for the project and just $140 million in funds, selling the university board on the project was not easy. "We were actually putting the foundation in before we even designed the upper floor," Shapiro says. In retrospect, the move was enormously beneficial to the university.

He compares that judgment call to his role in DeVry's decision to expand its online presence significantly in 2003. The company had previously offered its business, technology, and management technology degree mostly on physical campuses. Shapiro reasoned that the company had flourished over the years by finding a market niche that others had not yet exploited. Yet such opportunities "are only worth a decade or so of profits, so you've got to figure out where your next niche is." DeVry was not the first online institution, but it was well positioned to expand more quickly than others. It now offers nearly all of its undergraduate and graduate classes online, with about a quarter of all students taking only online courses, another quarter taking only onsite classes, and 50% mixing the two. "We wouldn't be anywhere near where we are now if we hadn't done that," Shapiro says. "Times come when you have to take unusual steps, and to me that's when leadership counts the most."

CONCLUSION

It would be overreaching to suggest that a series of interviews with a relatively small group of individuals could yield an authoritative taxonomy of lessons the organization and culture of for-profits might hold for the much larger world of public and private not-for-profit colleges and universities. Nevertheless, those interviewed for this analysis bring valuable firsthand knowledge to an ongoing and increasingly urgent debate about the best paths to higher education reform.

The interviewees emphatically make the case that the controversy surrounding for-profits risks stigmatizing a sector of postsecondary education that has systematically used innovative practices to give educational opportunities (albeit, at times, of uneven quality) to previously underserved student populations. This effort to reach new groups of students comes as traditional institutions are under growing pressure to improve their own mixed record of enrolling and graduating nontraditional students. The accounts of the insiders quoted here suggest that even educators and policymakers who are sharply critical of for-profits or simply agnostic about their performance can learn something from the approach they take to such fundamental matters as who is taught, what they are taught, who teaches, how they teach, and how teaching effectiveness is measured.

To sum up, the lessons that for-profits can teach the rest of the postsecondary world begin with flexibility and speed. Institutions closely attuned to the practical needs of consumers, defined to include both students and prospective employers, can change course quickly when market demand for a particular vocational specialty changes. In principle, there is no reason that traditional institutions should not be able to innovate quickly, but in practice they often lag in this area. The same is true of experimentation—a core principle for institutions like Kaplan, which by the accounts of business school dean Thomas Boyd and others do not hesitate to test out different pedagogical approaches for identical classes to see which yield the best learning outcomes.

This kind of results-oriented trial and error depends, in turn, on several other defining characteristics of for-profits. They have a high comfort level with a standardized curriculum and very limited autonomy for instructors, who must follow course rubrics in which specific learning outcomes are outlined in prescriptive terms. Progress reaching those outcomes is measured frequently—both for students and, crucially, for their professors—in a culture that values data as much as any other business venture. Again, none of these practices are unheard of in conventional institutions. But for a variety of reasons, both philosophical and practical, they are not often implemented on a widespread basis, despite their potential benefits for students.

For-profits can take the approach they do in the classroom—whether bricks-and-mortar or online—only because of an understanding of the faculty's role that deviates sharply from the norms of many traditional colleges and universities. As Michael Offerman of Capella notes, for-profits often recruit from outside traditional academe, seeking instructors with practical experience and, typically, little interest in research. Once trained, instructors at for-profits must be comfortable in environments in which (1) they are not viewed as the ultimate authorities on curriculum and pedagogy; (2) they are evaluated regularly on their teaching abilities; and (3) without the job security afforded by tenure, they must hew closely to the wishes of the administrators who hire and supervise them. This model would, in at least some respects, not be appropriate for faculty in major research universities or in some liberal arts institutions. But colleges and universities that are, or should be, almost entirely teaching institutions could learn much from a conception of the faculty's role that is more flexible (in hiring of part-timers, for example), gives instructors little room to act autonomously, and is more focused on measurable results.

Many other questions for the traditional sector are raised by for-profits' success in appealing to undergraduates who might not otherwise have enrolled in postsecondary education. How have these upstart institutions adopted online delivery mechanisms so quickly? How have 2-year for-profits succeeded in graduating their students at nearly triple the rate of community colleges (despite the dismal graduation rates of 4-year for-profits)? How are the most successful for-profits able to support high-risk students, many of them Black or Latino, from recruitment to graduation more systematically than some open-access publics? What might institutions like community colleges and vocationally oriented 4-year institutions learn from for-profits' close connections to employers? How could conventional colleges and universities make better use of assessment to prove to students, policymakers, and taxpayers that they are teaching effectively?

No doubt the for-profit nature of institutions like the University of Phoenix has contributed to some of their problems: heavy pressure for fast growth and profits, an emphasis on enrolling students quickly, and incentives to capture a growing pool of federal aid without accompanying incentives to ensure that students' future employment prospects are as strong as promised. As Shapiro acknowledges, "One has to be aware that the market does not generate the most socially responsible incentives, and one has to continually monitor operations to guard against perverse incentives taking hold." But he also makes an eminently fair point when he adds, "The same is true, of course, for both the for-profit and the nonprofit sector, although the source of the incentives might differ." In other words, different institutions operate in different kinds of markets, whether profits are involved or not. For instance, public universities whose state funding depends in part on filling seats but not graduating students are, perhaps understandably, better at doing the former than the latter.

It is worth remembering that the same money-generating incentives that sometimes get for-profits in trouble also give them high motivation to respond quickly to the needs of students and employers in what seem to be useful ways. Their newness and independence from existing arrangements permit them to innovate. This doesn't mean that all students need a dramatically different model, of course. Hentschke of the University of Southern California observes that for-profit innovations ought to be viewed not as a one-size-fits-all alternative to traditional institutions, some of which are fulfilling their core missions well. Instead, for-profits should be seen as part of a growing menu of options that have particular promise for the marginal students who make up a subpopulation of traditional universities and a large fraction of the community college population.

Critics notwithstanding, for-profits' long-term business incentives would seem to lie in improving their existing operations, not in exploiting students. Where regulation and oversight are concerned, it is hard to argue with the insistence of for-profit officials that all postsecondary institutions should be assessed on a level playing field, particularly when it comes to serving nontraditional students with multiple risk factors. Low graduation rates, for example, are a problem everywhere. As Peter Smith of Kaplan says, "While we need to improve, others do as well." Better measures of learning outcomes throughout postsecondary education are badly needed, and it seems reasonable for all institutions to be asked to demonstrate success in student learning, completion, employment after graduation, and debt repayment.

For-profit colleges and universities will certainly need to work hard to prove their own worth as they remain in the regulatory and media spotlight for the foreseeable future. But for all their flaws, for all the dismaying practices and bad actors that continue to be associated with the sector, their innovative characteristics are well worth studying. The observations and experiences of those interviewed for this chapter suggest that traditional colleges and universities will be badly mistaken if they assume that the travails of for-profits today mean that profitable lessons cannot be drawn from their successes to date—and those likely to occur in the future.

CHAPTER 4

Unequal Access

Hidden Barriers to Achieving Both
Quality and Profit in Early Care and Education

Todd Grindal

Children's early experiences can have a profound impact on their subsequent academic achievement, physical and mental health, and success in the workforce.[1] High-quality early care and education programs can help children and families take advantage of this developmentally sensitive period and can yield short- and long-term benefits for children and society. However, the potential positive benefits of early childhood education are contingent upon children's attending high-quality programs, and many child-care programs in the United States, regardless of their tax status, fail to meet that bar.[2]

As previous chapters in this volume note, U.S. public policies generally limit for-profit companies' participation in the provision of public K–12, vocational, and higher education.[3] Although this skepticism of for-profit providers can also be seen in some publicly funded early care and education programs, private enterprises are key partners of many of these programs. For example, state and federal policies permit parents to use public funds to attend for-profit early childhood education (ECE) programs through Childcare and Development Fund (CCDF) programs or the Child and Dependent Care Tax Credit (CDCTC). Furthermore, nearly all of the public prekindergarten programs now operating in the 40 U.S. states that have them allow for at least some participation by for-profit child-care providers.

From a policy perspective, early care and education programs for children from birth to age 5 serve two broad purposes. First, they help children develop in ways that support the skills and habits of mind essential to later school achievement and economic success. Second, they facilitate parents' participation in the workforce by providing care for children during business hours. Public-sector entities such as public schools and state prekindergarten programs are often able to meet the first of these purposes. A growing body of evidence from quality public prekindergarten programs in places like Tulsa, Oklahoma, and Boston, Massachusetts, indicate that public entities such as traditional public and charter schools are well positioned to support the developmental needs of 4-year-old children. Yet, public-sector programs are often less able to meet parents' employment-related child-care needs, and these programs often do not have the capacity to serve the millions of families of children 3 years old and younger.

Private enterprise is critical to filling these gaps. For-profit ECE programs rapidly adapt to the employment-related needs of families by offering extended hours or convenient worksite locations, and provide much-needed access to care for parents who work outside the home—particularly for parents with children under age 3 and those who work nonstandard hours. Private enterprises are flexible and convenient and are well positioned to support parents' employment-related child-care needs. Yet, the for-profit model may fall short in preparing children for school success. Research conducted in the 1980s and 1990s suggested that, although quality varied substantially from one for-profit early care and education program to another, on average, for-profit programs ranked below public and nonprofit programs on many indicators of program effectiveness.[4]

Despite the fact that this research is nearly 2 decades old, these findings nevertheless continue to fuel concerns about the role of private enterprise in early care and education. There are a number of plausible explanations for why researchers have found differences in the quality of for-profit ECE programs and their public and private not-for-profit counterparts. Caring for young children is an expensive endeavor. In most areas of the United States, basic health and safety regulations limit the number of children who can be cared for in a given space and by a given number of adults. Although unable to control these regulations, child-care programs interested in maximizing profits can either generate more revenue through higher tuition or reduce costs by paying lower salaries to their workers. With tuition costs already higher than many families can bear, profit-oriented programs might choose to pay staff as little as possible, thus attracting low-skilled, poorly prepared adults to teach.[5]

Another potential explanation for these differences in quality is that many child-care programs concentrate on aspects of program quality that can be easily observed by potential customers. In general, parents must make decisions about whether to enroll their child in a particular child-care program based on limited information. Parents can readily see if the facility is clean, safe, and staffed by caring teachers. Those parents who choose to look more closely might also observe important structural quality indicators such as the child-to-teacher ratio or the number of books in the classroom.

But even the most thorough and conscientious of parents would likely unknowingly overlook the more important indicators of quality such as the day-to-day interactions among children, teachers, and instructional content. Economists refer to this dilemma as "information asymmetry."[6] Program operators may be able to gauge the quality of all aspects of the care they provide, but parents cannot. If parents are unable to make purchasing decisions based on a complete picture of quality, it makes little financial sense for child-care providers to invest in the types of costly, ongoing professional development necessary to improve performance on these hidden quality indicators. Although this information asymmetry exists throughout the child-care sector, there is some evidence that the problem may be more acute in for-profit programs.[7]

Must the convenience and flexibility of for-profit ECE necessarily come at the expense of quality? No. To maximize the potential of private enterprises to support the needs of young children and their families, parents must be given the tools to better observe the most important elements of program quality. Moreover, public policies must provide all programs—public, for-profit, and private not-for-profit alike—with equitable levels of oversight and support.

In this chapter, I discuss the role of private enterprise in the early care and education of children in the United States. I begin by presenting research detailing the importance of quality early care and education for children, families, and society. I subsequently outline how changes in employment patterns and public policies have shaped the child-care marketplace in the United States over the last 75 years. I then discuss how for-profit companies have responded to these changes and provide examples of how private enterprises currently participate in publicly funded systems of early care and education. I likewise present research from the 1980s and 1990s on the strengths and weaknesses of for-profit programs before suggesting how parents, policymakers, and providers can improve access to high-quality child care by maximizing the strengths and minimizing the weaknesses of for-profit child care.

WHY SHOULD WE CARE ABOUT CHILD CARE?

The science is indisputable: The years from birth to age 5 represent a uniquely sensitive period for the development of children's long-term cognitive, physical, and emotional capacities. The character of children's experiences during this period profoundly influences their subsequent development. Four decades of research provide strong evidence of a relationship between early experiences and later academic achievement, as well as physical and mental health.[8] Many children in the United States spend a substantial proportion of their critical early years in early care and education programs. Today, more than 12 million U.S. children (or 62% of all children) under 5 years old are regularly cared for by someone other than a parent. Of the young children who are enrolled in nonrelative child-care programs, most spend approximately 32 hours each week in these settings.[9]

Child-care programs have, in some cases, shown a remarkable capacity to improve short- and long-term results for children across a variety of outcomes related to school success. In the 1960s and 1970s, experimental studies of the Perry Preschool and Abecedarian programs demonstrated that intensive, high-quality preschool programs could dramatically improve the later academic achievement and long-term economic productivity of low-income children. More recently, quasi-experimental studies of larger-scale school-based pre-school programs for 4-year-old children in Tulsa and Boston have demonstrated that preschool can have an impact on the school readiness of low-income and non–low-income children alike.[10]

A key finding of early education research is that only high-quality programs yield positive results for children and society. Quality in early care and education programs is typically measured using two types of input-based indicators—those that measure classroom processes (such as the quality of the interactions between children and teachers) and those that measure elements of the program's structure (such as teachers' levels of education, teachers' salaries, and teacher-to-child ratios). Though neither of these indicators singularly guarantees positive outcomes for children, each has been shown to have some association with children's cognitive and social development. There are no comprehensive studies of the quality of early care and education in the United States, but scholars, advocates, and policymakers generally agree that many young children are cared for in programs where quality is unacceptably low.[11]

Based on this research, Nobel Prize–winning economist James Heckman argues that public investment in quality early childhood programs provides a higher long-term economic benefit than do infrastructure projects or other educational programs such as K–12 schooling or higher education.[12] Former chairman of the Minneapolis Federal Reserve Arthur Rolnick agrees: Most of the numerous projects and initiatives that state and local governments fund in the name of creating new private businesses and new jobs result in few public benefits. In contrast, studies find that well-focused investments in early childhood development yield high public as well as private returns.[13]

THE MIXED CHILD-CARE MARKETPLACE

Preschool and child care have become common components of children's early experiences in the United States. This care is provided in a wide range of settings. Some young children attend organized care programs such as day care, nursery schools, or prekindergarten programs, while others are in less formal settings such as home-based child-care centers, nannies, or babysitters. Some ECE programs serve hundreds of children each day, while others serve as few as one child.

Auspices for these programs vary both within and across settings. Though home-based programs are typically for-profit, both private nonprofit and private for-profit entities operate center-based programs. In many parts of the country, nonprofit and for-profit entities also provide child care in partnerships with state and local governments through CCDF programs or state prekindergarten programs.

For-profit entities represent a larger proportion of the early care and education sector than they do in the K–12 and higher education sectors. Precise numbers are not available, but my best estimates suggest that approximately one-half of children under the age of 5 who regularly attend child care are cared for in nonpublic programs. Of these nonpublic programs, for-profit entities outnumber nonprofit providers at a rate of approximately two to one.[14]

Public-sector early care and education programs (for example, Head Start, Early Head Start, state prekindergarten, prekindergarten provided through public elementary schools, and publicly funded early intervention programs for children with disabilities) can be distinguished from three types of non–public-sector programs:

1. Private independently operated not-for-profit child care programs (tax-exempt organizations such as community organizations or faith-based institutions);
2. Informal for-profit early care and education (babysitters, nannies, or home-based, owner-operated programs with no employees); and
3. Formal for-profit early care and education (center- and home-based, taxable entities with at least one employee).[15]

Although this taxonomy provides a useful tool for understanding the complex child-care marketplace, the reader should be cautious when making inferences across an entire category. Programs with similar tax statuses, for example, may differ in terms of their size, structure, and instructional quality. Furthermore, distinctions between these different types of programs are often blurred. Formal for-profit programs in some cases provide state-funded prekindergarten programs, and private not-for-profit programs often serve as Head Start grantees. That said, as I will discuss, research suggests some potentially important differences across these categories.

A BRIEF HISTORY OF CHILD CARE IN THE UNITED STATES

The U.S. child-care marketplace has developed over the last 75 years in response to changes in parental employment patterns and a hodgepodge of public policies. When labor shortages encouraged large numbers of women to work outside the home during World War II, the federal government provided funding for workers' young children to attend child-care programs during work hours.[16] In the 1960s, educators and policymakers began to view child care not only as a means to facilitate maternal employment but also as a potential tool for improving child health and development. The creation of the Head Start program in 1965—a key component of President Lyndon Johnson's Great Society programs—sought to provide low-income families with both child care and family support services through grants to community-based agencies.[17]

The Head Start program facilitated access to child care for many low-income families, but it was not designed to address the growing need for child care among middle- or upper-income families. By the early 1970s, approximately 30% of mothers with children under the age of 5 were employed outside of the home. Although some parents could rely on friends or family to care for their children, demand outpaced supply. Federal policymakers attempted to address the growing need for child care with the 1971 Childcare and Development Act (CCDA). Designed to structure a universal system of early care and education, this bill passed both houses of U.S. Congress with bipartisan support, but was vetoed by President Richard Nixon out of concerns that it would promote communal child-rearing approaches that would weaken the American family.[18]

Although nothing like CCDA ever again passed both houses of Congress, the federal government did provide some support for the child-care needs of middle-income families through the expansion of the CDCTC in 1976. This credit allowed families to deduct as much as $3,000 for the care of one child or adult dependent and $6,000 for the care of more than one. Approximately 4 million U.S. taxpayers currently take advantage of this credit every year.[19]

The 1996 Personal Responsibility and Work Opportunity Reconciliation Act (PRWORA) expanded public involvement in the child-care marketplace. PRWORA provided a large increase in the amount of public child-care subsidy dollars available to low-income families. Designed to encourage families receiving public assistance to transition from welfare to work, PRWORA limited the amount of time families could receive cash benefits and required recipients to participate in job training or other work-based programs. This led to a large-scale movement of mothers of young children into the workforce that, in turn, increased demand for child care. Through Childcare and Development Fund programs (for example, Temporary Assistance to Needy Families [TANF] and the Childcare Development Block Grant [CCDBG]), state and federal policymakers provided families transitioning from welfare to work—as well as other low-income families—with vouchers with which they could purchase child care from a provider of their choosing.

As shifts in employment patterns and public policy have reshaped the early care and education marketplace over the last half-century, private enterprises have consistently stepped in to meet families' needs. As Roger Neugebauer notes in his 2010 review, the formal for-profit early care and education sector has enjoyed strong and steady growth over the last 4 decades. Although the majority of for-profit programs in the early 1970s were small "mom-and-pop" operations, many in the business community expressed excitement about the potential for growth and profit in the child-care market. Neugebauer cites a 1971 article in *Barron's Financial Weekly*, which listed more than 100 companies with aspirations of creating nationwide chains of child-care programs. *Barron's* likened the enthusiasm for the growth potential of early care and education in the 1970s to the expansion of the electronics industry a decade earlier.[20]

The for-profit early care and education model may not have met *Barron's* lofty projections, but it has proven to be a dynamic and profitable industry.[21] Annual revenues of for-profit child-care programs increased nearly tenfold over the last 2 decades, jumping from a total of $2.8 billion in 1986 to more than $20 billion in 2008.[22] A few large companies have indeed emerged over this period; however, formal for-profit child care today remains, by and large, a mom-and-pop industry. Estimates suggest that the 50 largest formal for-profit child-care organizations represent less than 10% of the overall center-based for-profit child-care sector. Put another way, approximately nine out of ten formal for-profit child-care programs operate between one and five centers and serve fewer than 1,000 children.[23]

The publicly funded portion of the early care and education sector has also experienced substantial growth in recent decades. Annual funding for state preschool programs more than doubled to a total of $4.6 billion from 2001 to 2008 because of growing evidence about the importance of children's early years.[24] Today, 40 states and the District of Columbia provide publicly funded care and education for all 3- and 4-year-old children. In 2010, in addition to the approximately 1 million children from birth to age 5 supported by CCDF and the 1.4 million children enrolled in federally funded special education, Head Start, and Early Head Start programs combined, another nearly 1.2 million children were enrolled in state-funded preschool programs.[25]

BRIDGES AND BARRIERS: PRIVATE ENTERPRISE AND THE EXPANSION OF PUBLIC EARLY CARE AND EDUCATION

The growth in publicly funded preschool presents both opportunities and challenges for for-profit child-care providers. In many states, private not-for-profit as well as informal and formal for-profit entities have partnered with state governments to help fund child care with public dollars. This has given some child-care providers access to a new market of families who otherwise might not have been able to afford this care. The expansion of publicly funded child care also creates unique challenges for nonpublic child-care providers. To better understand this dynamic, we should look more closely at child-care regulations and the basic business model of a for-profit early care and education program.

Staff and space represent the majority of operating expenses in a typical child-care program. On average, labor and occupancy costs account for 62% and 20%, respectively, of a formal for-profit child-care program's operating expenses.[26] These costs are to some extent fixed, as state and local regulations generally mandate that programs maintain a minimum number of square feet and adults per child. These regulations vary based on the age of the children served. This makes sense from a developmental perspective—infants demand more attention and care from adults than do toddlers, and toddlers demand more attention than 3- and 4-year-old children. Child-care regulations in most states therefore allow programs to combine 3- and 4-year-old children into comparatively larger groups with fewer adults. Thus, caring for children under 3 is often substantially more costly for providers than caring for children 3 years old and above. Many for-profit and private not-for-profit programs construct their business models based on these differences in returns by child age. Although a program may break even or lose money by serving infants and toddlers, it can often make up for these losses by providing less cost-intensive services for 3- and 4-year-olds.

Publicly funded child care, by and large, supports children at the upper end of the preschool age range. In 2010, more than 40% of 4-year-olds and 14% of 3-year-olds were enrolled in state-funded prekindergarten or Head Start programs across the country. Rates of enrollment in public early care and education vary widely from state to state. While more than 75% of 4-year-old children in Florida, Oklahoma, and West Virginia were enrolled in publicly funded early care and education programs in 2010, in Nevada, New Hampshire, and Utah, this figure was less than 13%.

In addition to competition from publicly funded programs, formal for-profit providers also face competition from unregulated informal providers. These home-based child-care programs (sometimes called family child care) are particularly popular with families of infants and toddlers. In most states, formal center-based programs (both for-profit and not-for-profit) face much stricter scrutiny from state and local officials than the small programs based in private homes, even though home-based programs are in some cases eligible to receive public funds. Half of the states do not require annual inspections of small child-care programs operated in private homes. In nine states, home-based programs serving six or fewer children are permitted to operate without any licensing or substantial oversight from the state. An additional eight states do not require inspections or visits of home-based child-care providers prior to licensing. Center-based programs, by contrast, are required to undergo annual inspections in 44 states, 8 of which require programs to be visited at least every 3 months. Center-based programs are also subject to regulations regarding teacher education, ongoing professional development, and instructional content from which many small home-based providers are exempt.[27] Despite this limited state oversight, many unlicensed child-care programs are permitted to receive public money to care for children through TANF and CCDBG funds.[28]

The low level of regulations for the informal care combined with the increasing number of public schools and state prekindergarten programs offering free and reduced-cost options for 3- and 4-year-old children has the potential to squeeze for-profit providers out of the market.[29] On the one hand, it is difficult for formal for-profit centers to compete with free or reduced-cost public options for 4-year-olds. On the other hand, it is difficult for formal for-profit centers to compete with low-cost, unregulated, informal home-based providers for younger children. Unlike nonprofit programs, for-profits cannot supplement revenues through fundraising campaigns. In the current child-care marketplace, for-profit programs therefore seem to have two basic choices: (1) they can forgo public funding and compete directly with the public-sector programs by providing an alternative product or (2) they can partner with the public sector to provide publicly funded care to young children. The following are some examples of for-profit enterprises that have adopted these two strategies.

Bright Horizons Family Solutions, one of the largest providers of formal for-profit child care in the United States, has distinguished itself by creating good alternatives to public programs. The company states that it aims to foster quality through highly qualified staff, providing an innovative curriculum, and maintaining low child-to-teacher ratios. Bright Horizons has engaged in some partnerships with state governments and, in some cases, has received public funds to provide child care. However, the core of its business is based on partnering with employers to provide parents with flexible, quality child care at or near their workplace. This type of workplace child care is popular with parents and employers. For parents, onsite child care provides convenience, affordability, and the opportunity to visit their child or, in some cases, breastfeed without leaving the office.

For employers, some evidence exists that onsite child care improves employee productivity and reduces worker absences. Currently, Bright Horizons operates more than 700 centers across the United States and provides onsite child care to more than 90 Fortune 500 companies, including Bank of America, Eli Lilly, Citigroup, and Time Warner. This focus on onsite child care, in part, helped Bright Horizons grow its business by an estimated 69% between 2002 and 2009, despite competition from the public sector.[30]

Smaller mom-and-pop formal for-profit child-care companies such as Metro Montessori in Rockville, Maryland, have also responded to the increase in publicly funded ECE for 4-year-olds by creating alternatives to public programs. One of Metro's preschools, the Franklin Montessori School in Washington, D.C., has grown nearly tenfold in the last decade despite being located less than a mile and a half from two public elementary schools that offer prekindergarten programs free of charge.[31] Metro co-owner Josh Oboler attributes this success to providing a combination of consistency and flexibility that is absent in school-based programs. He states that while public school policies and programs shift with changes in leadership, parents can be sure that Franklin's core educational program remains the same. At the same time, for-profit entities such as Franklin can quickly respond to parents' evolving child-care needs. Oboler cites Franklin's recent adoption of afterschool sports programs and year-round schooling options as examples of how private enterprises can rapidly respond to the changing needs of their community.

Knowledge Universe (KU)—the largest formal for-profit provider of care for young children in the United States—has embraced the increase in public support for early care and education. In a 2008 interview, now former CEO Felicia Thornton stated that the increase in public prekindergarten enrollment represented a potential challenge for the formal for-profit child-care industry. She was nevertheless optimistic, noting that KU was collaborating with more than 20 state systems to provide child care. She also stated that she hoped to leverage KU's longstanding relationships with many school districts to serve an increasing number of 3- and 4-year-old students through the publicly financed system. Thornton said that these public–private partnerships were good for the industry, children, and families:

> Private providers have the capacity, the history of serving younger children, the early childhood expertise; and we can play a significant role in the success of schools if we are afforded the opportunity to lay a foundation of learning with these children before they enter the public school system.[32]

Many publicly funded early care and education systems permit the kinds of partnerships envisioned by Thornton. In contrast to other areas of education policy, for-profit enterprises are deeply involved in the provision of publicly funded early care and education in many states. Here, it is important to make a distinction between policies and programs for different age groups—namely, those for children from birth to 3 years old, and those for 3- and 4-year-old children. Infants and toddlers primarily receive publicly funded care and education through voucher programs such as TANF and CCDBG. Three- and 4-year-old children are also served through these programs, but are increasingly served through Head Start and state prekindergarten programs. Following are some examples of how private enterprises participate in these different types of publicly funded early care and education.

Child-Care Programs for Children from Birth to Age 3

TANF and CCDBG help support the early care and education of nearly half a million children age birth to 3 years old across the country. These programs support families currently receiving or transitioning out of welfare, as well as other low-income families, primarily through the use of vouchers. Parents can use these vouchers to purchase care from any legally operating child-care provider, including family members, faith-based providers, and for-profit providers. The federal government recommends that states set subsidy rates equal to or higher than 75% of the local market rate for child care, but few states meet this mark. According to research conducted by National Women's Law Center, subsidy rates in many states are very low. In fact, 24 states set the subsidy rates for infants at 55% or less of the local market rate.[33] Though it is possible to track the types of child-care settings these families use, no data currently exist on the degree to which families use these subsidies to attend for-profit or private nonprofit programs.

Child-Care Programs for 3- and 4-Year-Old Children

Publicly funded programs for 3- and 4-year-old children are also generally amenable to private sector involvement. Although nonschool Head Start grantees are private, nonprofit corporations, many state programs rely on the private sector to help meet families' needs for early care and education. Yet the extent of for-profit participation varies substantially from state to state. The following are descriptions of two large state ECE programs—Florida and Oklahoma—that offer contrasting approaches to partnering with the private sector. In Florida, for-profit providers are a critical component of the delivery of publicly funded preschool, while they are nearly nonexistent in Oklahoma's publicly funded system.

Florida: Access and Accountability. In 2002, Florida voters amended the state's constitution to mandate universal access to preschool. As a result, all Florida 4-year-old children are now eligible to receive 540 hours of preschool instruction free of charge. Parents may choose to enroll their children in a range of ECE settings, including programs based in public schools, private not-for-profit programs, informal for-profit programs, and formal for-profit early care and education programs. To qualify as a provider of Florida Voluntary Prekindergarten (VPK), nonpublic programs must be accredited and adhere to standards regarding teacher training, class size, and teacher-to-child ratios.

VPK programs are also accountable for their students' performance once they reach kindergarten. Within the first month of school, all Florida kindergartners are tested using the Florida Kindergarten Readiness Screener (FLKRS). The FLKRS evaluates children's skills and knowledge of language and literacy, mathematics, social and personal skills, science, social studies, physical development, and creative arts. The Florida Department of Education uses these results to determine the percentage of a program's children who are prepared for kindergarten. Programs that consistently perform below the state's established minimum readiness rate are designated as low-performing and are subject to sanctions. After 4 years of poor performance, programs are no longer allowed to provide VPK-funded services.[34]

Florida had provided publicly funded prekindergarten to a small number of low-income children since the late 1970s, but when the Florida Universal Pre-Kindergarten (PreK) Amendment 8 passed in 2002, the state system did not have the capacity to serve all of its 4-year-old children. Florida policymakers therefore relied heavily on nonpublic ECE programs of all types to meet the voter mandate. In 2010, approximately 155,000, or 68%, of Florida 4-year-olds attended more than 6,000 different preschool programs using VPK funds; 84% of these were nonpublic programs.

This high level of participation by for-profit and private not-for-profit early care and education providers was intentional. After failing to pass expanded prekindergarten legislation through Florida's legislature in 2000 and 2001, the supporters of the 2002 PreK mandate were eager to build a broad base of support for the ballot initiative. PreK amendment supporters therefore worked closely with members of the for-profit and faith-based preschool communities to craft amendment language and ensure that VPK neither threatened the autonomy of for-profit providers nor put them out of business.[35]

While this big-tent approach helped ensure easy passage for the PreK amendment, some have suggested that it made it difficult to guarantee that VPK programs would provide high-quality services for children and families. The standards for programs interested in participating in the VPK system are low. Of the ten quality benchmarks established by the National Institute for Early Education Research (NIEER), VPK programs need meet only three.[36] VPK programs are responsible for children's results on later measures of school success, but there are concerns that this outcome-based accountability system may lead preschool programs to narrow their curricula or seek to exclude children who might receive low scores on the kindergarten readiness measures. There is some evidence that this may be the case. In 2009, public programs served higher percentages of low-income students, English language learners, and students with disabilities. Interestingly, despite serving a population of students that was, on average, more disadvantaged, children who attended VPK programs based in public schools demonstrated higher average kindergarten readiness rates than those who attended nonpublic VPK programs.[37]

Oklahoma: High-Quality Early Care and Education Based in the Public Schools. Oklahoma offers the most expansive access to public early care and education in the United States. In 2010, 71% of Oklahoma 4-year-olds participated in the state prekindergarten program. When combined with the 14% of 4-year-old children who attend publicly funded Head Start programs, Oklahoma provides prekindergarten instruction to a higher proportion of its 4-year-olds than any other state in the nation.

In contrast to Florida, Oklahoma's publicly funded 4-year-old prekindergarten program is operated almost entirely through its public schools; 98% of Oklahoma school districts participate in the state prekindergarten program.

The state encourages districts to collaborate with outside organizations to provide prekindergarten, but these represent a relatively small proportion of the public prekindergarten in Oklahoma. In 2010, approximately 5,550 (15%) of 4-year-olds in the state prekindergarten program were served outside of public schools. Approximately 80% of these nonpublic programs were private, nonprofit organizations affiliated with Head Start rather than private enterprise providers.

Georgetown University researchers Walter Gormley and Deborah Phillips argue that situating prekindergarten in the public schools has some important implications for the quality of Oklahoma programs. First, closely connecting early care and education programs with the public schools ensures that prekindergarten teachers earn wages on par with other public school teachers. This means substantially higher wages than ECE staff would otherwise earn.

Gormley and Phillips estimate that teachers working in state prekindergarten programs earned approximately double the average annual salary of an Oklahoma teacher working in a nonpublic, center-based prekindergarten program. These higher wages permit Oklahoma public early care and education programs to attract more highly educated candidates. In contrast to Florida, where prekindergarten teachers participating in the VPK school year program need only have an associate's degree, teachers in Oklahoma programs are required to hold at least a bachelor's degree. Oklahoma's school-based early care and education programs feature other indicators of program quality. Staff-to-child ratios cannot exceed 1 to 10, and groups of children can be no larger than 20. Programs are regularly monitored by the state, and teachers receive an average of 15 hours per year of training and support.

Evidence suggests that Oklahoma's focus on quality has translated into positive results for children. A 2005 study published in the journal *Science* indicated that 4-year-old children who attended a state-funded, school-based prekindergarten in Tulsa demonstrated an additional 5 to 9 months of development on measures of their reading, writing, and mathematics skills when compared with children who had not attended preschool. While Latino and English language learners demonstrated the largest gains, children from a wide range of income, ethnic, and language backgrounds all demonstrated significant positive impacts of attending a Tulsa prekindergarten program.

Although the cases of Florida and Oklahoma are instructive, it is important to note that they represent two extremes regarding the inclusion of private enterprise in publicly funded early care and education. In most states, the picture is much more mixed, with a range of public and nonpublic entities providing early care and education in a variety of settings. Nevertheless, the contrasting picture of quality in the Florida and Oklahoma systems raises some important questions about the quality of for-profit early care and education providers.

THE QUALITY OF FORMAL FOR-PROFIT CHILD CARE:
A CAUSE FOR CONCERN?

Some prekindergarten advocates have celebrated the growth of programs such as those in Oklahoma and Florida as a critical first step in improving the skills and achievement of U.S. students. Yet, research clearly indicates that simply attending an early care and education program does not yield long-term benefits for children or society. It is only through attending high-quality programs that children realize the results that have so excited parents, scholars, and policymakers.

Presently, no contemporary studies comparing the quality of early care and education in U.S. public school-based, nonprofit, and for-profit child care programs exist. However, evidence from older studies suggests that for-profit programs—on average—lagged behind public and nonprofit programs on multiple input-based indicators of child care quality. Now more than 20 years old, this research does not reflect the expansion of state child-care licensing regulations or recent cross-sector initiatives to improve the quality of child care. Nevertheless, numerous studies from the 1970s and 1980s found that for-profit programs had consistently higher child-to-teacher ratios, fewer services for parents, and less sensitive caregivers when compared with nonprofit centers.[38] Interestingly, these findings were not replicated in the 1990s Cost, Quality, and Child Outcomes study. Here, researchers compared the quality of for-profit and nonprofit programs and did not find any clear differences between the two.[39]

The most recent comparison of quality in U.S. public, nonprofit, and for-profit programs comes from the National Institute of Child Health and Development (NICHD) Study of Early Care and Youth Development. Using data collected in the early 1990s, researchers found statistically significant differences between the average quality of for-profit and nonprofit programs. On average, nonprofit programs paid higher wages to teachers, had fewer children per classroom, and experienced less staff turnover than for-profit centers. Caregivers in nonprofit programs were also more likely to engage in positive caregiving behaviors with their students (for example, giving prompt and appropriate responses to the children's needs and stimulating children's cognitive development) when compared with teachers in for-profit programs.

Although nonprofit early care and education generally outperformed their for-profit counterparts, there were some important within-sector differences. The NICHD study indicated that for-profit chain programs generally provided lower-quality care than independent (mom-and-pop type) for-profit providers. They also found differences between specific types of nonprofit programs. For example, nonprofit community-based programs generally earned moderate to high marks for quality, while the ratings for nonprofit faith-based providers were low and on par with those of for-profit chains.

Research comparing for-profit and nonprofit or public child care in other parts of the world also points to lower quality in the for-profit sector. A 2007 study of child-care programs in the United Kingdom found the quality of public programs to be, on average, superior to that of for-profit programs.[40] Gordon Cleveland and colleagues reviewed multiple studies of the quality of child-care programs in Canada and found that for-profits consistently lagged behind nonprofit programs on nearly every input-based quality indicator. The city of Toronto was so concerned about the findings regarding the quality of for-profit child care that it no longer permits parents to use government child-care money to attend for-profit programs.[41]

INFORMATION ASYMMETRY:
CAN PARENTS ACCURATELY ASSESS A PROGRAM'S QUALITY?

In many areas of the United States, parents may choose from a range of government for-profit and private not-for-profit providers. To survive in this competitive marketplace, one would assume that programs would constantly endeavor to improve their quality and efficiency. It is possible that the research from the 1980s and 1990s on the relative quality of for-profit child-care programs no longer represents the current child-care landscape. But if, as this research suggests, the quality of for-profit programs is generally lower than that of government-provided and private nonprofit programs, why is it that for-profit programs continue to represent a large and growing share of the early care and education market?

One explanation for this disconnect is that parents struggle to distinguish between high- and low-quality programs.[42] Economists refer to situations such as this—when consumers do not have access to the same information as producers—as information asymmetry. Parents consider a variety of factors such as safety, cost, convenience, child-to-staff ratio, or perceived caregiver warmth when choosing an early care and education program for their child. Although the relative weights of these factors vary widely by parent background and child age, multiple studies suggest that parents are poorly informed about what constitutes quality in early care and education. Jennifer Sumsion and Joy Goodfellow argue that even those parents who are knowledgeable about the components of program quality may find them difficult to observe.

Before enrolling their child, a parent can inspect a facility to determine whether it is safe and clean. A particularly thorough parent might track down information on the program's child-to-teacher ratio or the number of books in the classroom. Yet the important day-to-day interactions between children, teachers, and content remain largely hidden from view. A parent might draw on "word-of-mouth" information from friends and social networks to learn about the quality of a given program, but this too can be unreliable. The high levels of staff turnover in some ECE programs can make the quality of those programs unstable. Once a child is enrolled, parents generally spend little time observing classroom practice. Moreover, the young children who are the direct consumers of these early care and education services are often unable to determine the quality of these services or to communicate these ideas to their parents.

Parents tend to overestimate the positive quality of their children's early care and education programs. For example, when parents and trained assessors rate the quality of an early care and education program, parents consistently provide higher ratings. Unsurprisingly, the gap between parent and assessor ratings is larger for those aspects of quality that are less visible.[43] This has led some to suggest that for-profit companies intentionally skimp on these hard-to-observe elements of quality. John Morris and Suzanne Helbrun examined this question by comparing for-profit, private not-for-profit, and public schools' early care and education programs on aspects of quality that were easy for parents to observe (for example, furnishings, play materials, meeting areas for parents) and those that were harder for parents to observe (for example, teacher–child interactions and professional growth opportunities for staff). The results were mixed. Public schools, parent cooperatives, and nonprofit private schools provided the highest level of quality on hard-to-observe indicators of quality. For-profit, chain ECE programs did appear to skimp on aspects of quality that were hidden from parents, but so too did nonprofit, community-based providers and some faith-based child-care providers.[44]

The early care and education marketplace provides a unique look at the benefits and challenges of permitting private enterprise to participate in the delivery of public education. Private enterprises have long been an integral component of the U.S. early care and education system. Through innovative strategies—such as partnering with employers to create onsite programs, experimenting with unique pedagogical approaches, and providing flexible programming to meet the changing needs of families—for-profit entities have provided parents with the choice and flexibility to manage their professional and family lives. Yet, because parents are often unable to effectively discern program quality, some providers may not invest in the unseen elements of program quality. I provide two suggestions for how to correct these failures in the ECE market and to marshal the strengths of for-profits to help provide quality, affordable care to U.S. children and families.

MOVING FORWARD:
RECOMMENDATIONS FOR POLICY AND PRACTICE

1. Provide Parents with a Clearer Picture of Program Quality

Markets do not function efficiently when consumers are unable to accurately rate the quality of goods and services. Because of the unique nature of early care and education, the individuals making child-care purchasing decisions are often blind to the key components of quality. In Florida, policymakers have attempted to offer parents this sort of information by providing data on students' performance once they reach kindergarten. This represents a step in the right direction, but it is ultimately insufficient. The Florida system measures children's skills and ability upon entry to kindergarten, but provides little insight into the effectiveness of that child's early care and education program. A kindergarten child's skills and abilities represent the culmination of 5 years of educational inputs and experiences, not solely the effectiveness of his or her ECE program. Even if these measures were effective in measuring the actual impact of a child's 4-year-old program, kindergarten readiness scores do not indicate the quality of that child's early care and education settings prior to age 4.

Quality rating systems (QRS) have the potential to offer parents this information. More than 25 states and local areas across the country are currently operating or developing quality rating systems. The details of these programs vary, but, in general, they provide independent assessments of early care and education on structural quality indicators such as licensing compliance, staff qualifications, teacher-to-child ratios, and group size. Some QRS take a closer look at process quality and gauge the fitness of a program's curriculum or child-assessment tools. Based on these and other indicators, programs are awarded either a numerical score or a substantive rating of their overall quality.[45]

QRS scores or ratings serve a number of purposes. Kathryn Tout and colleagues conducted an extensive survey of QRS across the country and found that nearly all provided participating programs with training linked to QRS indicators. These trainings covered a range of topics including assessment of the classroom environment and business practices as well as analyses of children's cognitive, social, and emotional development. QRS scores can also be connected to financial incentives. Two-thirds of QRS are connected to systems of tiered reimbursement by which programs that receive public funds (by serving children with state child-care subsidies) are paid at higher rates for demonstrating higher scores on QRS indicators.

Quality rating systems can provide parents with the information they need to make rational decisions regarding early care and education programs. Yet the impact of QRS on correcting information asymmetry in the child-care marketplace will be limited if parents cannot find consistent information on all types of early care and education providers. Nearly half of the systems that Tout and colleagues examined provided ratings on 30% or fewer of the programs in their area. In some states, Head Start programs are rated using a different set of criteria than are used on other programs. It is also unclear how well this information is being distributed to parents. For example, Tout and colleagues found that 12 QRS programs did not have a budget to support the marketing of QRS information.[46] Furthermore, the effectiveness of QRS depends on providing real incentives for programs to reach and maintain higher levels of quality. In most states that offer tiered rates of reimbursement, the amounts paid to the highest-quality providers still fall well below the local market rate.[47]

Private enterprises have worked and should continue to work closely with states on the development of QRS to craft systems that provide parents with an accurate picture of program quality and that give programs incentives to reach and maintain high levels of performance. By providing child-care programs with clear financial incentives to improve quality and by giving parents the tools to become more informed consumers, QRS will encourage providers of all types to focus on the aspects of program quality most important for children's health and development.

2. Provide Equitable Oversight and Support for All Caregivers of Infants and Toddlers

Emerging research suggests that school-based programs provide effective and developmentally appropriate instruction for 4-year-old children. Evaluations of school-based prekindergarten programs in Tulsa, Boston, Miami, and Los Angeles indicate that school-based programs can help 4-year-old children develop the skills and habits of mind critical to later school success.[48] Though the trend toward integrating preschool and elementary school has slowed slightly during the recent recession, the extension of formal schooling into the preschool years is likely to continue. In the coming decades, 4-year-old prekindergarten programs may become as common a component of elementary school as kindergarten and 1st grade.

The critical question then becomes how best to support the early care and education of children 3 years old and younger. As more and more 4-year-old children are educated through the elementary school system, we must reassess the real cost of caring for young children. As noted above, the higher staff-to-child ratios required in infant–toddler classes makes them substantially more expensive than programs for 4-year-olds. Some early care and education programs mask the true cost of these services by subsidizing more expensive care for infants and toddlers with funds from less cost-intensive 3- and 4-year-old children. The real costs of care for infants and toddlers are further obscured by the availability of low-cost, unregulated child-care providers.

Private enterprise should be a key component in shaping this new child-care landscape. When large numbers of women began entering the workforce in the late 1960s, for-profit providers stepped in to help deliver access to safe and reliable care for working families' young children. Now, as the child-care landscape is again reshaped by the adoption of school-based prekindergarten programs, the creativity and flexibility of the private sector will be essential in meeting the needs of young children and their families.

If private enterprises are to be effective partners in meeting the needs of this evolving marketplace, state and federal governments must make changes to the way they regulate and support early care and education. First, states must provide clear, consistent, and fair regulation of all early care and education programs. State oversight of formal and informal early care and education programs is often uneven. This regulation imbalance between large and small providers allows some home-based providers to operate at lower costs than formal providers and jeopardizes the healthy development of children in these lower-cost, lower-quality programs. This bias toward small providers makes it difficult for successful, innovative for-profit providers to grow their programs to serve a larger number of children and to maintain quality of care. Child-care regulations provide important safeguards for young children and have far reaching implications for children's development. States should therefore work to apply uniform standards to all those who care for children, regardless of program auspice or size.

Second, the capacity of for-profit providers to participate in state child-care systems could be further facilitated by better integration of the various state subsidy programs. As Hannah Matthews and Danielle Ewen note in their 2011 paper, state TANF and CCDBG programs often differ in important ways such as the amount and duration of subsidies they provide to families.[49] This creates unnecessary bureaucracy and confusion for both families and providers. States should find ways to combine these and other subsidy programs to provide a more seamless integrated system.

Third, state subsidies must better reflect the actual cost of child care for young children. Less than 15% of states currently meet the federal government's recommendations for determining the appropriate dollar amount of child-care subsidies. If for-profit programs are to participate in the provision of publicly funded early care and education, they, as well as nonprofit providers, need to be compensated at a fair market rate. High-quality child care requires high-quality teachers. In 2011, the median-salaried child-care worker earned less than $9.50 an hour. This means that caregivers of young children are on average paid at a slightly lower rate than parking lot attendants and animal caretakers.[50] To attract high-quality staff, providers of all types need to offer higher wages and benefits to caregivers and program leaders. This must in part come from higher rates for subsidy-supported children.

Finally, the federal government should increase the amount of the CDCTC of parents of children under 3. Currently, the CDCTC allows families to deduct a maximum of $3,000 for one dependent or $6,000 for more than one, regardless of the dependent's age. This credit should be reformulated to provide additional relief to families who need care for children from birth to age three. This extra cash would provide parents with the additional money necessary to pay for quality care for their children.

CONCLUSION

In a 1970 *McCall's* magazine article, writer Alice Lake outlined emerging concerns about the participation of private enterprise in early care and education: "Everybody wants day care centers, and businessmen are rushing to supply them. But can you serve children the same way you serve Kentucky Fried Chicken?"[51] Over the last 40 years, parents, scholars and policymakers have moved beyond these simple caricatures of for-profit child-care programs and have come to recognize that private enterprise is an integral part of the child-care system in this country. For-profit institutions have played an important role in meeting the changing needs of children and parents throughout this period—a role that they often cannot play in other education sectors.

Today—as evidence about the long-term importance of children's early experiences and the growth of school-based preschool again reshape the child-care landscape—for-profit enterprises will once more be important in meeting the dual purposes of child care. Promoting quality care in this evolving child-care marketplace will require difficult decisions at all levels. Increasing the amount of state child-care subsidies may mean decreasing the number of eligible families. Increasing the amount parents can deduct for the care of their children from birth to age 3 may require a corresponding decrease in the amount deducted by parents of older children. Employers interested in keeping their employees productive and happy may need to employ the services of site-based child-care programs such as Bright Horizons. For some families, the high cost of care for children in their early years may necessitate a reevaluation of the efficacy of both parents working long hours outside of the home. Regardless, fulfilling both the parental employment and child development purposes of child care will require the energies of all of the players in the child-care marketplace, public, nonprofit, and for-profit alike.

CHAPTER 5

Beyond Good and Evil

Understanding the Role of For-Profits in Education Through the Theories of Disruptive Innovation

Michael B. Horn

The role of for-profit companies in public education—education financed by the government—has attracted increased scrutiny over the past few years. On one hand, for-profit entities such as textbook companies have had contractual agreements with public schools for decades yet have received scant attention. On the other hand, several for-profit universities have attracted significant negative attention of late for questionable marketing practices around recruiting students and for what some government officials and others perceive as low graduation rates. As this controversy heated up, it has prompted a wider debate about the role of for-profit companies in education, which has been fueled by the emergence of new for-profit K–12 education companies along with increased interest in education from private capital sources, including angel investors, venture capitalists, private equity firms, and companies such as News Corporation.

Many in public education assume the worst when it comes to for-profit corporations. One oft-repeated assumption is that for-profit companies are money-grabbing entities that will shortchange the public good. Some critics see profiting from public funds designed to serve children as an evil to be rooted out of the system.

Others—seemingly fewer in number in public education circles—view for-profit corporations as a force for good that can harness the profit motive to attract top talent and scale quality in public education. Many in this group see nonprofit and government organizations as inherently bloated—and consequently slow to scale and quick to waste public funds—and view for-profits as a needed counterbalance that can drive efficiencies.

These depictions have taken on lives of their own in public education circles. The government often perpetuates these divides by drawing lines in the sand of what activities companies can and cannot do based on their corporate structures. Recently, for example, regulations prohibited for-profit companies from applying directly to the Department of Education's Investing in Innovation (i3) program. Despite the two extreme views on for-profits, however, the reality is different.

This chapter seeks to explore the reality of for-profits in education and move beyond the caricatures—both good and bad—of for-profit companies both generally and in public education specifically—pre-K through higher education. The chapter does not defend for-profit companies per se, nor does it dive into a deep analysis of the recent events that have transpired in higher education, for example. Instead, it examines the basic incentives and structures of for-profit and non-profit companies by using the theories of disruptive innovation to deduce what drives them and what opportunities and dangers their corporate structures create. Broadly speaking, the theories of disruptive innovation are a set of theories that help make innovation (both the disruptive and nondisruptive, or sustaining, kind) far more predictable and successful. They have been built inductively and tested deductively across categories—from the for-profit to the nonprofit and government worlds and from highly regulated industries to deregulated ones—and through anomalies.

The use of these theories in examining for-profits and nonprofits deductively is not intended to imply that certain for-profit or nonprofit entities in education are disruptive, but instead is used to understand the dynamics that drive all organizations, as the theories help explain the interplay within and between organizations. Previous chapters have already explored *why* there exists suspicion around the for-profits. By approaching the issues surrounding for-profits in a new way, this chapter presents an opportunity for fresh thinking on the role of for-profits in public education. Ultimately, this chapter finds that there are a striking number of similarities between for-profit and nonprofits, but that each appears to have some unique advantages as well. The findings suggest some implications for public policy.

First, for-profit companies are not inherently good or evil. Some corrupt for-profits flagrantly violate the law, but many others accomplish remarkable things. Likewise, some for-profit companies are wildly successful and others are wildly unsuccessful. Successful for-profits solve the problem or do "the job" that customers—the entity or person paying for the product or service—hire them to do.[1] Over time, the most successful companies (according to what have become the widely accepted ways of measuring success in the United States) improve, grow, and serve more demanding customers with better products—and consequently return increasing value to their shareholders. When there is a viable, publicly financed market opportunity in front of them, successful for-profit corporations respond by chasing the customer's—in this case, the government's—dollars by doing what it asks them to do, much of which is codified in policies and regulations. As a result, as they build their business, *successful* for-profit companies will do what regulations offer incentives for them to do—not much more and not much less. If there are "smart" regulations and policies in place that cause the government customer to make "smart" purchasing decisions, successful for-profit companies will do "good" things. If there are "stupid" ones in place, then they will do "bad" things. For-profits that receive plenty of investment up front but do not ultimately satisfy the customer and therefore do not gain traction in the marketplace will be unsuccessful. Trying to deliver products or services that the company perceives to be of moral value will not have an impact if customers do not value them as well.

Second, there are far fewer inherent and predetermined differences between for-profit companies and their nonprofit counterparts than many assume. Much of the debate over whether for-profits or nonprofits are more or less virtuous is a red herring to what the real questions should be. For the government paying, the question should be, "Is this given company, regardless of corporate structure, delivering on what society is paying it to do, as specified in the law?" And more important, the government should ask, "Is the law asking this entity to do the right thing?" As mentioned above, there are corrupt for-profits, but there are also corrupt nonprofits (recall the United Way scandal several decades ago). Furthermore, both for-profit and nonprofit corporations must bring in revenue to sustain their operations. Contrary to the name, the most successful nonprofits (called nongovernmental organizations, or NGOs, abroad), like their for-profit counterparts, make a "profit," as they bring in more revenue than they spend. They then reinvest in their business to serve more people and improve their offerings. When the government is the customer, both for-profits and nonprofits may or may not be aligned with the needs of their targeted end user, as the end user is often not the one paying. That all depends on how well the government's policies—which dictate what products or services will receive payment—align to the end users' actual needs, as opposed to their perceived ones. The notion that for-profits are inherently motivated to cut costs at the expense of doing their job—or that nonprofits inherently have less discipline in controlling costs and therefore are far less streamlined and efficient—has proved largely to be a smokescreen in public education to this point.

Third, the biggest inherent differences between for-profits and nonprofits stem from their fundamental corporate structures, which determine what they are able to do with their profits—and thus affect their ability to attract capital and scale—as well as what opportunities look attractive. Of course, for-profits and nonprofits are regulated in different ways. For-profits pay corporate taxes, for example, and nonprofits do not. But this is not their most salient difference and, in theory, could change at any point. They do have fundamentally different corporate structures, however. For-profit corporations have owners or shareholders; nonprofit corporations do not. Having owners means, first, that for-profits may not always reinvest all their profits into their core business, as successful nonprofits will, but instead have the option to return some of those profits to their owners. This is not necessarily a bad thing, however, as many assume. The reason is that because for-profits provide returns to their owners, for-profits naturally attract even more capital to grow and scale operations and attract more top talent when there is a viable market. Nonprofits do not share this natural tendency, although they can overcome this. As a result, if they are performing a valuable service that society considers "good," then for-profits have a more natural ability to scale a solution. This means that successful for-profits tend to be crystal clear about their end objective: Make increasing profits by doing the job their best customers pay them to do. Nonprofits lack this easy metric, which makes it relatively harder for many of them to stay focused on a particular job. This focus and ability to scale can be critical tools in a policymaker's arsenal. Bad policies that reward the wrong things can also be a significant risk. Nonprofits play a vital role because without shareholders, they can remain invested in a sector even in the absence of a viable market—a circumstance from which successful for-profits retreat, as they will not be able to provide meaningful returns for their owners.

These conclusions raise important considerations for policymakers and society. First, the government should employ both for-profits and nonprofits to serve the public good. Legislation that creates artificial roadblocks by favoring one over the other—although sometimes useful for political sloganeering—does not advance the public good and may even shortchange it. Given the ability of for-profits to scale a solution by attracting increased capital in addition to government funding, there is significant pressure on the government to craft policy and regulatory conditions that will capitalize on for-profits' incentives for growth and profit when there is a viable, publicly financed market opportunity. Critically, for-profits and nonprofits alike will only move the needle if the government customer demands continual improvement. Laws and regulations should therefore focus on and define the desired outcomes where possible without specifying the processes or inputs used to achieve them. They should also reward organizations that achieve the best outcomes for the best price relative to the competition and, in cases like education where the purpose is to serve an end user—such as a student—in addition to society, align those outcomes with what the end user actually needs.

WHAT IS A "SUCCESSFUL" FOR-PROFIT COMPANY MOTIVATED TO DO?

To move beyond the overly simplistic question of whether for-profits are inherently good or evil, it helps first to understand how a "successful" company functions—what incentives it responds to, as well as what it does and does not do. The theory of disruptive innovation sheds light on this, as it answers the fundamental question: "Why do successful organizations ultimately fail?"

Before diving into this analysis, it is important to note that not all for-profits define success in the same way. All successful for-profits share a certain baseline in that they have to nail "the job" that their customer is paying them to do. After that, there are a variety of ways for-profits can judge and measure success, which in turn determine their actions. Some so-called "mom-and-pop" for-profits do not aspire to grow beyond a certain limited market and do not seek to deliver results for investors measured in the same way that most venture-backed or publicly traded companies do. Of course, smaller for-profits that lack ambition to grow do not seem to drive the controversies or questions in public education circles as much as the more ambitious for-profits do. In contrast, the majority of companies driven in part by investor concerns use the same measures—no matter how flawed—to guide and illustrate their performance.[2] This chapter uses the behavior of successful for-profit companies—defined as those that dominate markets or are growing and seek to dominate markets—for its analysis concerned with the ability of for-profits to improve, grow, and scale. To a certain extent, the theories of disruptive innovation are predicated on this behavior. This acknowledges that this behavior is something that is "on average" to for-profits and not necessarily causal of being a for-profit—that is, just because a company is a for-profit does not mean it will follow this behavior. That said, the corporate status serves as a good proxy and does create a causal mechanism—the ability to attract capital to scale—that for-profits can choose to use.

The diagram in Figure 5.1 represents any given market. In the figure, the vertical axis measures the quality of the product or service, and the horizontal axis charts this performance over time. In every market, there are two trajectories of performance. The first, represented by the dotted line, reflects what the average customer is able to use. As the figure suggests, customers' needs tend to be relatively stable over time. The second trajectory, represented by the solid line, is the pace of technological progress. This shows that technological progress almost always outstrips customers' ability to use the improvements. This means that a technology that is not good enough to meet customers' needs at a certain time (the left side of the figure) is likely to improve and eventually overshoot what customers can use.

Some of the innovations that improve product performance are incremental ones; others are dramatic breakthroughs. But both are called sustaining innovations so long as their purpose is the same—to help companies sustain their movement upward along the trajectory of performance improvement to make better products that can be sold for better profits to their best customers. Research shows that companies that lead their industries on the left side of this figure, before the battles of sustaining innovation begin, are almost invariably still the leaders in their industries when these battles are over.[3] It does not matter how technologically difficult the innovations are. The leading companies in the industry invariably find a way to get it done because their motivation to do so is high.

Figure 5.1. Trajectory of Sustaining Innovation

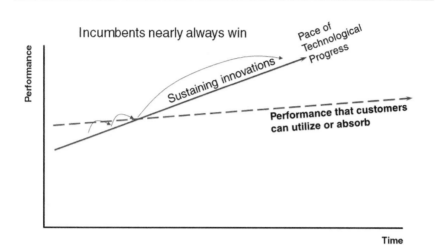

For example, recall the early personal computers from the 1980s. Powered by Intel's 286 microprocessor, the machines could barely run a basic word-processing program. But true to form, Intel improved the microprocessor year after year and retained its market dominance, as the company was consistently motivated to implement features that would allow it to sell better products for better profits to its best customers. The same phenomenon has held true in many other industries, from steelmaking to airlines.

Equally important for this discussion, if implementing a new feature, improvement, or innovation would *not* help a company sell better products for better profits to its best customers, that firm is *not* motivated to do it. We see this most clearly when looking at another kind of innovation, which has historically proved almost impossible for the industry leaders to catch. We call this a disruptive innovation.

A disruptive innovation is not a radical, breakthrough improvement along the existing trajectory in Figure 5.1. Instead of sustaining the leading companies' place in the original market, it disrupts that trajectory by offering a product or service that is *not as good* as what companies are already selling, as judged by the traditional measures of quality and performance. Because the innovation is not as good as the existing product or service, the customers in the original market cannot use it. Instead, the disruptive innovation extends its benefits to people who, because of a lack of skills, money, or access, are unable to consume the original product—so-called nonconsumers (shown in the new plane in Figure 5.2).

Figure 5.2. The Theory of Disruptive Innovation

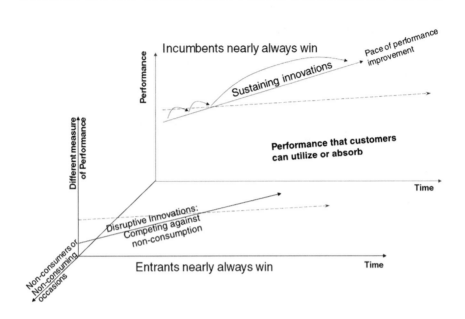

Disruptive innovations tend to be simpler, more affordable, and more decentral-ized or more convenient than existing products. This allows them to take root in simple, undemanding applications in a new market. Here, what constitutes qual-ity, and therefore an improvement, is different from the quality and improvement in the original market.

Little by little, the disruptive innovation improves. At some point, it becomes good enough to handle more complicated problems, and customers from the back plane rapidly adopt it, as they are delighted with this simpler, more affordable, and more convenient product. Over time, therefore, a disruptive innovation re-places the original product or service—which is relatively complicated, expensive, inconvenient, and centralized—with a product that is more affordable, simple, convenient, and accessible. This process has transformed countless sectors—from computing, where personal computers disrupted mainframe and minicomputers, to accounting, where many now use TurboTax instead of accountants for their taxes. It is also currently happening in postsecondary education, where some insti-tutions powered by online learning are in the early stages of disrupting traditional colleges and universities by making education far more convenient and, in some cases, affordable.

Because the definition of performance is so different in the front plane compared to the back plane, and the industry leaders' customers cannot use the disruptive product initially, the leading companies have difficulty implementing disruptive innovations. When the leading companies on the sustaining-innovations trajectory are faced with the choice of making better products that yield better profit margins for their existing customers versus making lower-priced, simpler products that yield slimmer margins for people who are not their best customers, they invariably find it more attractive to build and offer more and better. In other words, they respond to incentives by doing what their best customers pay them to do so they can make more money and be more successful (as success is commonly defined in this arena). As a result, new companies almost invariably enter and grow to dominate the industry by introducing or competing with disruptive innovations. This is why Digital Equipment Corporation, a leader in the manufacturing of minicomputers, was disrupted by the personal computer industry, and why the Detroit automakers were unable to fend off the upstart Japanese automakers.

This insight is important to understand when evaluating the track record of for-profit universities, for example—and for-profits more generally. Companies do what their customers offer incentives to do—not much more or less. The United States' dominant higher education policies have focused on expanding access for more than half a century—allowing more students to afford higher education regardless of true cost—through mechanisms such as Pell grants and other financial aid programs, subsidies, and access to low-interest student loans. As a result, the government has, in essence, been the true customer for a significant portion of higher education.[4] Although regulations such as those around preparing students for gainful employment set a minimum bar for not burdening students with too much debt, for example, they have been just that—a low bar. Because the federal government historically has had all-or-nothing access to its funds as opposed to a sliding scale where an institution's performance determines how much of its operations it can finance through government funds, it cannot set the bar too high lest it roll back its chief priority of access. Its policies have not focused on lowering higher education costs or on graduating more people per se. Instead, the government pays money for enrolling students. True to form, for-profit universities have followed suit and done what the customer—the government—has given them incentives to do: expand access.

Some for-profit universities have seized hold of online learning to capitalize on these incentives even more successfully—only now many in society are questioning whether the incentives focus on the wrong thing by ignoring graduation rates and the debt levels students face when they graduate. To say that for-profits— or any organization fulfilling this set of policies—are evil or of poor quality misses the point. Quality is defined by what a customer is paying someone to do, and in this case, for-profits were doing a spectacular job of expanding access. The stories of low graduation rates and students facing high debt with limited prospects to repay it are predictable, as government policies do not go beyond expanded access in defining the job to be done and how the government will pay for it. This is not inherently the fault of the for-profit institutions. The government and society have offered incentives for this behavior and have gotten what they have paid for, so to speak. Blaming for-profits for doing what we have asked and paid them to do from the outset misses this bigger picture.

HOW EASY IS IT TO CHANGE THE POLICIES?

A natural question arises from this analysis. Once society (or a segment of it) recognizes the problem—that it is not paying for the job it actually wants done—is the fix as simple as changing the regulations so the companies will change their actions to meet demand? Unfortunately, it is not always as easy as that. It is important for policymakers to get the regulations right early or else there will be a struggle. The presence of different players built to take advantage of the desired changes can help avoid some of this struggle, but these new entities are not always emerging at the time that policymakers seek to make changes.

To explain this, we first need to understand what a business model is and how it locks a system into place. Business models are comprised of four interdependent elements, as depicted in Figure 5.3. They start with a value proposition: a product or service that helps users do a job they have been trying to do more effectively, conveniently, and affordably. To deliver that value proposition, the organization must assemble the required set of resources—such as people, products, technologies, equipment, and facilities.

As the organization repeatedly uses its resources to deliver its value proposition, processes—habitual ways of getting recurrent things done—coalesce that are both explicit and, even more often, implicit. This is where an organization's culture resides. As Edgar Schein, one of the world's foremost scholars of organizational culture, wrote, culture is "a pattern of basic assumptions—invented, discovered, or developed by a given group as it learns to cope with its problems of external adaptation and internal integration—that has worked well enough to be considered valid and, therefore, to be taught to new members as the correct way to perceive, think, and feel in relation to those problems."[5]

When an organization's capabilities reside primarily in its people, change is relatively simple to manage because those who are not willing to change can be fired as needed. But when the capabilities reside in its processes—or its culture—change is extraordinarily difficult because processes designed for certain tasks usually perform efficiently, but the same process employed for a different task often seems bureaucratic. In other words, a process that is a *capability* in executing a certain task can be a *disability* in executing other tasks. Think of trying to follow

Figure 5.3. The Elements of a Business Model

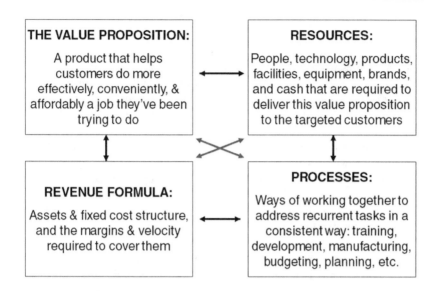

THE VALUE PROPOSITION:

A product that helps customers do more effectively, conveniently, & affordably a job they've been trying to do

RESOURCES:

People, technology, products, facilities, equipment, brands, and cash that are required to deliver this value proposition to the targeted customers

REVENUE FORMULA:

Assets & fixed cost structure, and the margins & velocity required to cover them

PROCESSES:

Ways of working together to address recurrent tasks in a consistent way: training, development, manufacturing, budgeting, planning, etc.

the same precise steps for building two different LEGO designs. Processes by their very nature are meant not to change. They are established to help employees perform recurrent tasks in a consistent way, time after time, without needing intense managerial monitoring.[6]

As the organization follows its processes to deliver the value proposition, a profit—or revenue—formula emerges. The profit formula defines how large the organization must be to break even and what kind of profit it must bring in to cover the cost of its resources. The profit formula in turn determines the kinds of value propositions the business model can and cannot offer.[7] These four elements of the business model quickly become interdependently locked.[8] In education, for example, textbook companies make money from selling large volumes per title. Even though many within those companies would love to offer more targeted products for specific groups of learners, books that promise only short print runs or modular pieces of content intended for small niches do not make sense within their business model, as this would hurt their profitability.

An organization's resources, processes, and priorities embedded in its business model show what it is capable of doing, but they equally show what it is *not* capable of doing.[9] Thus, once a company—and indeed an industry—is developed, it is difficult to alter completely what the company will and will not produce by changing some regulations and thus incentives. Innovations that conform to the business model are readily funded. When an innovation emerges to address a new need in the market but does not fit the four elements of the business model, the organization sometimes rejects the innovation. More frequently, however, the organization co-opts such innovations by forcing them to conform to the business model to get funded.

One way to understand these forces is to visualize how the legislative process works. A congresswoman sees a pressing societal problem and envisions an innovative solution. She drafts the enabling legislation and introduces the bill. Within a few weeks, the labor unions inform her that unless she modifies the legislation to address their concerns, they will block it. She changes her bill to win their support. A short time later, the Chamber of Commerce announces its opposition to the bill unless it is modified in certain ways, so she again amends her proposal. Then she learns that a powerful senator will not support it unless she adds special considerations favorable to his state, and so on. To win the support needed for Congress to enact the proposed legislation into law, the congresswoman shapes the bill to fit the interests of those with powerful votes; as a result, what comes out at the end of the legislative process looks *very* different from what went into it.

The same forces are at work in every organization. Organizations shape each innovative idea to fit the interests of the groups that must support the proposal for it to receive funding. Innovative ideas never pop out of the innovators' heads as full-fledged plans. Rather, they are fragments of a plan. As the innovator tries to sell the idea to the powerful entities in the organization, he runs into hurdles that are frightfully comparable to those the congresswoman encountered. To win the support of those whose endorsement is critical to getting the innovation funded, the innovative idea morphs into a concept that fits the business model of the organization, rather than the market for which the innovator originally envisioned it. In other words, organizations cannot prioritize those things that do not naturally sustain and fit their processes, priorities, and economic models. This is a core reason why incumbent firms are at a disadvantage relative to entrant companies when disruptive innovations emerge.

As a result, when policymakers try to change existing regulations that alter the fundamental job around which the leading organizations have built a large, successful business model, the members of the existing order will predictably fight it because meeting a new job is not something their core business can do naturally. In other words, the change in regulations will cause them to lose profitability. This is precisely what has happened with for-profit universities, as they fought hard against any dramatic regulatory changes.[10]

It is not just companies in one part of the industry that will fight against change, either. Companies are embedded in value networks, within which they establish their cost structures and operating processes and work with suppliers and channel partners to respond profitably to customers' common needs. Each of the players at different parts of the value network has its own business model, economic incentives, and rhythms of innovation and technological paradigms that are consistent and mutually reinforcing.[11] As a result, as companies grow and gather power, they build strong partnerships and constituencies embedded within the value network, all of which stand ready to support and defend the way they have always made money—which, in the case of education, is within a certain regulatory framework. Although small changes or tweaks to that regulatory framework are not ideal from the lens of their profitability, they are not an insurmountable problem. Regulatory changes, however, that redefine the fundamental job or value proposition they are delivering are often an existential threat. This causes the coalition of groups to use its considerable resources to lobby against such changes. In the saga of for-profit universities, it has not just been the universities that have pushed back against a proposed overhaul in the regulations. Their partners, industry trade groups, and lobbyists, who have much to lose from fundamental changes, also put up a formidable fight.

All this means that saying the customer always has the power is not quite accurate. In this case, the customer—the government—actually has less power than it would like, as the causality of why products are made has to some extent been reversed. The reason is that the companies' business models are now driving what products they are making, not necessarily the needs of the customers. This has several implications. First, it is hard to fight against a group that has benefited mightily and built up substantial resources from the old regulatory order and has much to lose from a fundamental shift. It is harder still if there is no strong constituency with plenty of resources that will benefit from and stand up for the new order. Second, even changing regulations to create different incentives will not create the new results politicians desire because the companies they want to change are, through no intentional malice on the part of their managers, nearly incapable of doing so.

In the case of for-profit universities, this analysis explains what happened. The Department of Education was able to make some regulatory changes to include a stronger metric around quality, not just access. Many for-profit universities subsequently have had to change their practices accordingly such that student enrollments—and their profits—have shrunk. For example, many of these universities no longer offer incentives to recruiters for enrollment starts. Enacting these changes, however, required a grueling struggle, and the new regulations fall far short of a sweeping overhaul that would have created a fundamentally new value proposition. Indeed, the Department of Education was somewhat hamstrung, as it could not create a new value proposition without at least temporarily rolling back the gains that it has made around extending access—a job that it still has as a priority—and on which it has said it will need the for-profits universities' help.[12]

This analysis suggests that there is a dynamic that could change the equation. If there were a different group of companies with lots of resources or an emerging set of disruptive innovators amassing considerable resources that stood to benefit even more from a change in regulation that would reward the value proposition they delivered, then this group could throw support behind the proposed changes *and* could deliver on the dramatic changes.[13] This would increase a policymaker's chances of success. Consider again the textbook companies and their business models that demand large volumes per title. Politicians in Florida and elsewhere have sought to use digital resources that begin to move the system toward a more modular, less expensive one. But in the absence of disruptive companies—and, perhaps even more important, a new channel of partners outside the standard textbook-adoption process ready to step up—these efforts have produced few real results and much frustration as new regulations have produced outcomes similar to those they sought to change. Of course, government officials can always move ahead with the regulatory changes despite the massive fight. If new regulations fundamentally alter the job to be done, then existing for-profit companies may simply go out of business, but that doesn't mean the officials will have solved their actual problem, nor does it mean that the absence of those companies will necessarily be the lesser of the two evils.

This analysis suggests that for-profits are not inherently good or evil, but are beholden to their customers and, after some time, their own business models. Companies are honed to deliver on a particular value proposition, which, in the case of public education, is shaped by the job that the policy and regulatory environment pays them to do. For any company to be successful, delivering on this job is vital, regardless of whether the policies and regulations are asking them to do something smart or stupid. As companies craft a business model that delivers on this value proposition, they are motivated to implement improvements that will allow them to grow and make more money. They lack the motivation to make changes that their customers do not signal as important. As their business models solidify, the same companies also lack the capabilities to deliver on a fundamentally new value proposition, which can, in certain cases, hamstring the ease with which the government can make certain sweeping changes.

ARE NONPROFITS THAT DIFFERENT FROM FOR-PROFITS?

Does leaving for-profits out avoid the pitfall whereby the customer (the government) loses some power as the for-profits mature and grow? It's not clear because nonprofits and for-profits are far less different than many assume. Importantly, both for-profits and nonprofits have business models that define over time what they can and cannot do, and what they prioritize.

Consider higher education. Some nonprofit career institutions in higher education as well as nonprofit industry groups, in addition to the for-profit universities garnering most of the attention, were affected by Department of Education's gainful-employment regulatory changes.[14] They were just as motivated as their for-profit counterparts to fight fundamental changes. Even more visibly, in 2005 the Commission on the Future of Higher Education—also known as the Spellings

Commission—announced its recommendations for reforming postsecondary education more broadly through tough accountability measures that would have dramatically changed the rules of the game for the majority of nonprofit and public universities. Just as for-profit universities have fought against changes to gainful employment, nonprofit and public universities were highly motivated to fight against the Spellings Commission's proposals and ultimately stymied any real changes, arguably more successfully than their for-profit counterparts. In other words, the incumbent universities had established business models that were not compatible with a new value proposition and were just as desperate to fight any changes that would undermine them.

Nonprofits, like their for-profit counterparts, have business models that allow them to deliver on their value proposition. Instead of a profit formula, they have what could be called a revenue formula, which serves a similar purpose. It dictates the levels of funding nonprofits need to support their existing organizations in accomplishing their missions. Like for-profit companies in the disruptive diagrams, nonprofits and governmental organizations respond to similar incentives—only, in their case, rather than pursuing profit and growth, they pursue prestige.[15] The ambition to do more and have a bigger footprint—an ambition driven both by administrators and alumni in higher education, for example— precipitates a behavior similar to profit maximization in the for-profit world. In addition, as processes and priorities coalesce in nonprofit organizations, just as in for-profit organizations, various groups often become entrenched in the organization's value network, and they naturally strive to expand, grow, and preserve themselves. Consider how difficult it is to introduce fundamental changes in the structure of a university. Faculty departments and members have a right to weigh in, and will do so, if they think the changes will affect their work in a negative way. As a result, fundamental changes to a university's business model are nearly impossible to make.

In higher education, this has led nonprofits to respond to incentives just as for-profits have. The California Master Plan for Higher Education adopted in 1960—which established by law whom the University of California, California State University, and community college systems could serve—cemented the definition of quality and thus what their upward trajectory would look like. It established that the colleges allowed first crack at the brightest students, as measured by standardized tests, would "also get the most money, enroll the most graduate students, run the biggest research projects, and have the most prestige."[16] Other states adopted similar plans over the next decade, which triggered a race to move up the ranks to "be eligible for more cash from federal and state governments, not to mention alumni. . . . Whenever and wherever they could, normal colleges became state teachers' colleges, became state colleges, became state universities. The best proxies for prestige are spending per student and selectivity, both of which drive up costs. The perception, and sometimes the reality, has been that colleges for the poor must be poor colleges."[17]

The popular perception that for-profit universities have lower graduation rates than nonprofits is true in the aggregate. A key reason for this may be that the majority of nonprofit and public universities have strong incentives to serve the brightest students with the most potential and strong disincentives to serve high-risk students because the government does not tie more money and incentives to graduating them. It is less clear, however, that nonprofits maintain this advantage in terms of quality student outcomes when controlling for the percentage of high-risk students that an institution serves.[18] Conflicting research exists. According to one study, for-profit universities not only serve more high-risk students on average—by roughly 20 percentage points—but they also deliver graduation rates that are significantly higher than their nonprofit and public counterparts for this population.[19] Another study, however, while not adjusting directly for the types of students that the institutions serve per se, suggests that among students entering associate degree programs, there are "large, statistically significant benefits from obtaining certificates/degrees from public and not-for-profit but not from for-profit institutions."[20] The point of this analysis is not to conclude definitively whether for-profits, nonprofits, or public institutions are better or worse. That there is evidence on both sides of the debate suggests that categorizing the world by for-profit versus nonprofit is the wrong categorization scheme and not a sound way to build good theory. In other words, what we see is that the nonprofit and public universities, like their for-profit counterparts, seem to be following their incentives and doing the job the customer has historically asked them to do. Again, if there are "smart" regulations and policies in place that cause the government customer to make "smart" purchasing decisions, universities will do "good" things. If there are "stupid" ones in place, they will do "bad" things.

Another perceived difference between for-profits and nonprofits manifests itself in two ways—either that for-profits are inherently motivated to cut costs at the expense of serving the customer or the reverse, that nonprofits inherently have less discipline in controlling costs and therefore for-profits can be far more streamlined and efficient to the benefit of the taxpayer and end user. It is certainly true that there are strong incentives in place for for-profit companies to cut costs to increase profitability. These incentives are explored further in the next section. For-profits are not motivated to do this, however, at the expense of customer satisfaction *that would be detrimental to their bottom line.* Recall the earlier analysis. For-profits are highly motivated to make better products that they can sell for better profits to their best customers, but they are not motivated to do things that will not allow them to make better products for their best customers for better profits. If something in a product or service is critical to a customer, for-profits are not motivated to shortchange it because their customers will punish them—by choosing another vendor—for doing so. But if customers do not signal that something is important—by showing no change in their willingness to pay—for-profit companies are willing, and sometimes quick, to cut the offering if it is not valued. As a result, if successful for-profit companies are shortchanging the government, it is generally because the government has not put in place the correct incentives and regulations that pay for the value proposition it wants.

The emerging segment of K–12 online learning companies provides evidence that for-profit companies have a strong disincentive to cut corners if it would compromise the quality their customers demand, but also that they appear to have little incentive to do much more than the regulations require. Negative media stories appearing about full-time online schools—most of which are operated by for-profit educational management organizations—are in many ways remarkable less for what they reveal about full-time online schools and more for what they reveal about the shortcomings in the American education system more generally. Colorado, for example, has historically paid a school all of its funds on a "count day" on October 1 based on the number of students enrolled on that day. If students leave afterward, then the original school still keeps the funds. If students enroll elsewhere, then the new school receives no funds. In essence, the policy environment incentivizes schools to enroll students but little else beyond that. Of course, schools still try to educate students and comply with various other regulations. They also seek to please the students that they serve, as they are fundamentally schools of choice that can build good or bad reputations in the market. But according to reports, some full-time virtual schools have taken the count-day regulation quite literally and focused very little on student outcomes, which isn't all that surprising. This mirrors some of the struggles in the existing education system more generally, which, as many have noted, is focused far more on compliance and meeting the input requirements than student outcomes. What's also interesting now is to see how negative stories in the press are potentially preventing full-time virtual school providers from opening schools in new states, which will limit their growth. As a result, the schools have a strong incentive to do what is necessary to meet their customers' needs to gain access to these new states or else suffer the consequences from limited growth prospects, or even worse, see existing states where they have schools revoke their charters and roll back their business.

A key question arises from this: When for-profits improve profitability and streamline operations, does the government spend less and get similar outcomes—thereby allowing taxpayers to keep more of their dollars—when contracting with for-profit providers? In education, the answer historically has been no. This is not to say that there are not mechanisms that could make this happen, but to this point, because funding tends to be determined through formulae based on inputs, the cost of services in previous years, and other such factors, the true cost has been tough to identify. Although for-profit universities operate at lower costs than their nonprofit and public counterparts on average, their tuition prices are often the same or higher, which means that the public often has to pay more money through

Title IV financing. The same has largely been true in K–12 education. Although a district may find a vendor that offers services for less, this frees up resources to be spent elsewhere, not to return funds to the government or taxpayers.

As a result, to this point, though there are those who claim that the for-profit sector would save taxpayers more money than nonprofits or public universities, the evidence for this is not clear. Ultimately, all entities that serve the public—whether for-profit, nonprofit, or governmental—are public entities in some sense because they are publicly funded. Advances in education policy may change this, but for now, the refrain that the for-profit sector saves the public money has not proved true.[22] In sum, those who want to castigate for-profits or nonprofits as inherently good or bad often are categorizing the world in the wrong way. There are far fewer distinctions between the two, as nonprofits, like for-profits, have business models, and both will follow the incentives that their customers—be they donors for nonprofits or otherwise—lay out for them. Although for-profits have clear motives to cut costs to improve profits, they won't do it if doing so will make their customers dissatisfied *and* hurt their bottom line. Equally so, to this point, having for-profits involved in public education has not realized real savings for taxpayers because policies have not created a way to capture any savings. All this points to the idea that governments should not discriminate between for-profits and nonprofits as a matter of blanket policy. Instead, a government entity should ask if the company with which it is contracting, for-profit or nonprofit, is delivering on what society is paying it to do, as determined by both the spirit and letter of the law. And policymakers more broadly should be asking if the law is asking these organizations to do the right thing.

SCALE, FOCUS, AND ATTRACTIVENESS: THE DIFFERENCES BETWEEN FOR-PROFITS AND NONPROFITS

Although there are many similarities between for-profits and nonprofits that run counter to conventional wisdom, they do have some inherent and important distinctions that stem from their fundamentally different corporate structures.

Scale

For-profit corporations have owners or shareholders; nonprofit corporations do not. This means that for-profits do not have to reinvest all their profit into their core business, as successful nonprofits in theory do, but instead have the option to return some of that profit to their owners. Although many in education believe this is a bad thing, it actually has huge benefits for a sector trying to attract more, not less, capital and create sustainable success.

Given that for-profits will not take shortcuts if their customers will punish them for doing so, this ability to scale has fewer risks than many believe. By the same token, however, for-profits are always weighing tradeoffs to boost their profitability. Simply put, they can either make investments to improve their product for which their customers will reward them or they can cut costs. As a result, companies may sometimes shortchange certain elements in a product that in an ideal world customers would love to have but will not necessarily punish companies for not having. This is a real scenario. That said, because for-profits offer returns for their owners, they can naturally attract even more capital to grow and scale operations and attract more top talent when there is a viable market—which means that they have an easier time scaling a solution that meets customer demands than do nonprofits when having increased capital is a critical input in scaling. Thus, in some ways for-profits can combat the risk that although the solution they produce might not always be optimal, the alternative might in fact be no solution at all.

The reason they have this ability to attract more capital is that shareholders invest to make returns, so capital flows naturally to places where those returns will be most attractive. To maintain attractive returns for investors, for-profit companies have to deliver results that offer an upside surprise because investors discount a company's stock price by whatever rate of growth they foresee a company achieving. In other words, expected growth—no matter how fast—is already factored into the share price. To satiate investors' needs, companies have to grow faster than shareholders expect. This drives them to find ways to scale an effective business model as quickly as possible. Capital, in turn, is always searching for companies that can offer that surprise—and pushes for-profit enterprises to scale faster.[23]

By not having shareholders, nonprofits lack this natural pathway. Although many have tried to bring investment principles to the nonprofit sector in choosing which organizations they support and how they fund them, in many cases, these actors (often foundations and philanthropists) instead operate like customers—as they provide the revenue that sustains the business, not growth capital in addition to revenue. As a result of these dynamics, for-profit companies spend between $2 and $4 raising capital for every $100 they bring in, whereas nonprofits spend $10 to $24 for every $100 they raise.[24]

In education, this is a principal reason why several for-profit universities have been able to seize the advent of online learning, a technology that enables disruption, and scale much faster than their nonprofit and public counterparts. Seeing the market opportunity to create new models that serve adult learners and others—particularly minorities and low-income students—who have historically been overlooked by traditional universities, for-profit universities have tapped vast sums from private capital markets to create offers that do the job the government has paid them to do: expand access to postsecondary education.

Focus

Because of this clear pressure and drive to deliver for their shareholders, success-ful for-profits tend to have a crystal-clear idea of what their metrics and "bottom line" are. If they do their job well, they make more money, which equates to suc-cess (even if it ultimately leads them into the innovator's dilemma, in which by consistently choosing to make products with higher margins over those with lower margins, companies ultimately open the door to their disruption; thus, there is a legitimate question if their metrics of success are in fact the right measures).

Nonprofits lack an easy metric, such as shareholders demanding monetary returns, which makes it relatively harder for them to focus and judge if they are successfully delivering on their mission. There have been suggestions of how to overcome this—such as measuring success by whether the cost of customer ac-quisition falls over time, as well as countless articles that have documented how certain nonprofits have escaped this trap—but to date, none of these suggestions has become commonly accepted wisdom and practice across the whole sector.[25]

This focus problem is one of the reasons why nonprofits, on average, are slower to streamline operations and redirect dollars to more useful pursuits. Such shifts are often slowed at for-profits and nonprofits because of personalities or attachments—managers may have personal relationships with people they need to let go, veteran employees may like certain perks, and groups will fight to pre-serve themselves. But without investors to reap the benefits of new efficiencies and push aggressively for cost savings, nonprofits tend to make the switch much more slowly in the absence of clear metrics or a certain kind of leadership. Self-interest tends, on average, to encourage a more aggressive pace at for-profits.

What Opportunities Appear Attractive

Nonprofits play an important role because not having shareholders allows them to remain invested in a sector even in the absence of a viable market. The K–12 online learning world presents a classic case. Two of the more successful companies, K12 Inc. and Connections Education, are highly motivated to do the jobs that their customers pay them to do and deliver a sound education. What is also intriguing, however, is what these companies are not motivated to do. Although both offer a high-quality curriculum, it is in essence a fixed and linear one. Their learning soft-ware is *not* built on an adaptive-learning platform, one that is automated to offer curriculum in a nonlinear fashion by improving the quality of what it offers each individual student in real time—much as Netflix, Pandora, and Amazon do for movies, music, and books. Neither one has made the sizable investment in a next-generation curriculum—which would likely be, for them, a sustaining innovation. The reason is that their best customers will not reward them for doing so. There is no viable market with the needed critical mass among states and districts. Indeed, current policies encourage school districts to make their purchase decisions based on price, not efficacy. Districts are motivated to increase offerings, save money, and offer something that aligns to standards—but there are not many incentives to do more than that.

A case study of an educational startup company called Time to Know presents more evidence for this. The company spent at least $60 million on developing a beautifully engineered and polished curriculum that pushes the envelope, yet it has struggled to gain rapid adoption by school districts. The company was naturally mystified because, from their perspective, they are offering a "great" product. Why aren't more districts realizing this and buying it? One reason is that many districts do not define quality in the same way—and quality can only be defined in relation to the job customers will pay for. To make a reasonable return on the big upfront investment, Time to Know must either enroll lots of customers quickly or charge high amounts. But by targeting price-sensitive districts with long buying cycles, the company risks running into a significant headwind.

In contrast, the Florida Virtual School (FLVS), a public online school, has already experienced success as an early leader in the K–12 online learning movement; FLVS is now pioneering new approaches to learning such as video game–based courses and constructive curricula. At this point, there is less concrete evidence about the efficacy of these approaches and, more significantly, unclear willingness on the part of customers to pay. One of the reasons FLVS might be able to pursue approaches that are not yet highly valued in the marketplace is because it is not a for-profit. It therefore does not have shareholders who would discourage it from going in this risky direction. Hence, nonprofits (and, in this case, governmental organizations) can still operate in an arena where there may be a pressing public need but few customers with the willingness or ability to pay for a product or service—in which case it is nearly impossible to make attractive profits or returns for investors. Unlike their for-profit counterparts, with the generous gift of just one individual (or foundation)—who is not expecting returns and therefore is not a shareholder, but instead is essentially the paying customer—nonprofits can support an operation to serve these types of missions. This circumstance will most often occur in niche areas with little demand (where it is hard to galvanize a market). In this way, nonprofits can inspire action even in the absence of a traditional, well-functioning market.

CONCLUSION

As AEI's Frederick M. Hess wrote, "So long as we recognize that it is no wiser to romanticize them than to demonize them, we absolutely ought to welcome for-profits into the education sector."[26] For-profits are not inherently good or evil, and they have far fewer differences from nonprofits than most assume. Indeed, successful for-profits and successful nonprofits share many characteristics, as previous chapters in this volume have articulated.

But there are some important differences between for-profits and nonprofits in their fundamental corporate structure that allow for-profits to more readily address the struggles faced in education—from finding sources of capital to sustainability and scale. If people want investment and capital to flow into and support the education sector, the most natural way is to enable self-interest to take hold by allowing for-profits to operate in a functioning marketplace. For that reason, the U.S. government's decision to favor nonprofits and public operators and to marginalize for-profits in areas such as i3 and higher education appears shortsighted. Whenever the government creates a market as the customer for services, by allowing for-profits to compete it creates a multiplier effect, whereby private capital comes in on top of the government's funds. As a result, if they are performing a valuable service that society considers "good" and there is a robust market opportunity, then for-profits have a more natural ability to scale a solution. This, along with their laser focus, can therefore be a critical tool in a policymaker's arsenal—one reason why Secretary of Education Arne Duncan has said that for-profit universities are vital for realizing President Barack Obama's goal of dramatically expanding the percentage of Americans with postsecondary credentials.

Of course, for-profits do present some risks. With bad policies in place that reward the wrong things, scaling up a solution rapidly can create a significant problem, as it will create an industry intent on maintaining the status quo. This is not unique to education. The government faces this problem in all sectors when it acts as the customer. In the absence of perfect foresight, the best the government can do in creating a market to solve a problem is to be clear about the goals and spirit of its policy and proceed with a measured approach to creating new programs by recognizing that they may not be successful.[27] In addition, creating policies that first and foremost reward and pay for outcomes, as well as efficiency or productivity—and do not regulate the inputs or processes to achieve those outcomes—is vital, as it will align the interests of for-profit companies around the correct end goals. To date, federal, state, and local governments in the United States have done little work in creating policy in this vein.

Crafting smart policy is a vital job of elected officials. Ceasing to use the benefits that for-profits bring is not smart policy. It does not address the root causes of misaligned incentives, and it potentially shortchanges the public good by making it harder to scale solutions. It also perpetuates many of the stereotypes in education that have held back these potential forces for far too long. Although for-profits are not a panacea for what ails society, using what they do well in conjunction with policy that rewards the right outcomes—and is open to an honest debate about what those should be—can start to move us closer to solutions that have a far better chance of working at scale.

CHAPTER 6

Odd Man Out

How Government Supports
Private-Sector Innovation, Except in Education

John Bailey

Federal policy has traditionally supported efforts to engage the private sector in solving some of the most challenging and intractable social challenges. Policymakers use a number of policy tools, including grants, loans, loan guarantees, and tax credits, not only to incentivize private-sector engagement but also to stimulate consumer demand for new solutions and innovations. The underlying drive behind these policies is that public good results from attracting private-sector entrepreneurs to tackle pressing social challenges.

For example, the military and intelligence communities engage commercial partners to help improve their mission and operational capabilities. The American Recovery and Reinvestment Act of 2009 (ARRA) invested billions to foster private-sector innovation in clean technology (cleantech) and health care. One such investment was more than $20 billion in financial incentive payments to help medical practices and hospitals—public as well as private—purchase electronic health records (EHR) from dozens of for-profit technology providers. In March 2010, President Barack Obama announced more than $150 billion to support cleantech, telling CEOs, "Your country needs you to mount a historic effort to end, once and for all, our dependence on foreign oil. . . . And in this difficult endeavor, in this pursuit on which I believe our future depends, our country will support you."[1] President Obama has also proposed canceling several NASA space-flight programs and instead calling on commercial vendors to develop spacecrafts to send astronauts into orbit.

In all of these areas, the federal government has actively sought ways to engage the private sector by stripping away regulatory barriers that impede new entrepreneurs from launching new ventures or by providing a mix of funding and financing programs to support innovators in areas policymakers have deemed important to the country's future. Policymakers understand that government alone cannot address these challenges. As a result, various federal initiatives support public–private partnerships to explore possible solutions.

The federal government's posture, however, has been entirely different with respect to engaging the private sector in addressing one of the country's most serious challenges—improving education. Instead of involving the private sector, education policymakers have actually created policy and funding barriers that skew support to nonprofits and prevent for-profit entities from participating in programs aimed at improving teaching or learning. These barriers exist at nearly every level of government—local, state, and federal—further isolating education from potential innovations and discouraging entrepreneurship.

President Obama has set the ambitious goal of leading the world in college completion by 2020. To achieve this goal, Secretary of Education Arne Duncan has also challenged the country to turn around 5,000 of the country's lowest-performing schools and help every child graduate high school ready for college and work. The only way to achieve these goals is through marshaling the forces of every segment of America—the private sector, nonprofits, philanthropy, and government. The urgency of the need requires public policy to be open to solutions that work and deliver high-quality results, regardless of who provides them. Just as tax incentives are helping to stimulate demand for alternative energy, education policymakers should use similar incentives to stimulate demand for alternatives and options for students. Just as government uses programs to lower financial risk for investors in low-income neighborhoods or in sectors with entrenched incumbents like energy, so too should they look for ways to lower risk for investors in solution providers tackling intractable challenges in our most troubled schools. Just as the government is open to embracing private-sector solutions that were once core government missions, so too should education be open to engaging the private sector for delivery of core services.

However, the federal government has tied one hand behind its back by engaging only public and nonprofit entities. Instead of attracting private-sector innovators, many programs explicitly exclude them based not on the quality of their solution, but simply on their for-profit tax status. Congress, for example, wrote the authorizing legislation for the Investing in Innovation (i3) fund in such a way as to specifically shut out private entities from the competition. Nonprofits could receive up to $50 million in direct federal support to scale their solutions, but for-profit entities had to go through a lengthy procurement process with a school district or nonprofit entity or operate as a subcontractor for, typically, modest sums only after the grant was awarded. Instead of inviting the private-sector entrepreneurs to solve education problems, our public policy encourages them to stay away and employ their creativity and innovation in other sectors such as health care, energy, and economic development.

This chapter builds on Horn's use of disruptive innovation in Chapter 5 to understand the potential role of for-profits in education. Namely, to reach the president's college completion goal, we need to engage all solution providers—for-profit and nonprofit—to help create new interventions, technologies, school models, and systems. Unfortunately, to date, the tax status of for-profit education providers has been used to keep them off the playing field. This raises an important question for our country's policymakers: If the federal government can support the private sector in addressing climate change, improving health care, and sending astronauts into orbit, then why can it not support the private sector in addressing education challenges?

FEDERAL EXAMPLES

Most federal agencies in some way seek to engage the private sector in addressing their policy priorities. These agencies are charged by legislation not only to identify and support innovative companies, but also to use policy levers such as tax credits to stimulate consumer demand and accelerate new-technology adoption. Here are several examples from federal agencies.

NASA

In 2008, the White House Office of Science and Technology Policy established the Review of U.S. Human Spaceflight Plans Committee and tasked it with exploring spaceflight options after the planned space shuttle program retirement in 2011.[2] The committee included a recommendation for NASA to investigate broader use of commercial spacecraft. Under this scenario, a private company would design and build the spacecraft instead of NASA, which would oversee quality assurance and safety. The review argued that this would free NASA to focus its attention and investment on developing more advanced capabilities, particularly in deep-space exploration. And in an attempt to address concerns of privatizing the space fleet, the review noted that all of NASA's spacecraft, including the space shuttle, have been built by private contractors.

In January 2010, President Obama announced his intention to adopt the review's recommendation. His 2011 budget proposed a $6 billion, multiyear initiative that would allow private firms to compete to build and operate spacecrafts to carry astronauts into space and resupply the International Space Station. The budget also requested more than $300 million in additional incentives to encourage private providers to compete for contracts to deliver commercial space cargo. The new system would limit taxpayers' financial exposure by promoting competition and inviting companies to share in the financial risk, which gives them a bigger stake in the outcomes.

Peter Diamandis, chairman and CEO of the X PRIZE Foundation, praised the initiative, saying, "The U.S. Government doesn't build your computers, nor do you fly aboard a U.S. Government owned and operated airline. Private industry routinely takes technologies pioneered by the government and turns them into cheap, reliable, and robust industries. This has happened in aviation, air mail, computers, and the Internet. It's about time that it happens in space."[3] Phil McAlister, acting director of NASA's Commercial Space Flight Development group, reflected, "It's a historical truth that government goes into those areas in which there is no private-sector profit motive, and the private sector follows behind. We think the time is right to transition that part to the private sector."[4]

Both traditional aerospace companies such as Lockheed Martin and Boeing and a number of new aerospace startups are expected to compete. Space Exploration Technologies Corporation (SpaceX) is developing a family of launch vehicles for commercial cargo and human spaceflight. The company made history on December 8, 2010, when its Dragon capsule was sent into orbit by its Falcon 9 booster and returned to Earth for a successful recovery.

"The December 8th flight of the Falcon 9/Dragon, for us, demonstrated that the United States commercial sector is prepared to meet the needs of NASA to carry crew to orbit," said Tim Hughes, vice president and chief counsel of SpaceX, at the Annual FAA Commercial Space Transportation Conference.[5] Such a system could carry astronauts at less than half the cost of what Russia charges to send astronauts into orbit using the Soyuz spacecraft. In fact, the total cost of the Falcon 9/Dragon, including the launch, was only $800 million, mostly paid by NASA as part of a program to encourage commercial space capabilities. By contrast, NASA has spent nearly $10 billion over the last 6 years on the Aries I rocket and the Orion capsule and is still years and billions of dollars away from even a workable prototype.[6]

The remarkable part of the SpaceX story is not its vehicles, but rather the entrepreneur behind the effort. In 1999, Elon Musk founded a company that facilitated e-commerce payments, which would eventually become PayPal. Musk then went on to found SpaceX in 2002 with the financial backing not of the typical aerospace industry backers, but instead of the cofounders of Google, Larry Page and Sergey Brin. And as with many serial entrepreneurs, Musk is involved with other startups, including Tesla Motors, a pioneering company that creates electric automobiles, of which he is the founder and CEO.

Musk brought a Silicon Valley mindset to tackling the challenges of spaceflight and energy independence. But more important, the federal government backed his approach. Federal funding helped launch both of Musk's two most recent ventures with NASA, including a $1.6 billion contract in 2008 for 12 flights of the Falcon 9 rocket and Dragon spacecraft. Tesla also received a $465 million loan from the U.S. Department of Energy to build a nonunion electric auto assembly plant on a former NASA base. The federal government also supported the location of the plant by providing regulatory flexibility under the Brownfields Program, which allowed Tesla to redevelop a plot of land that had formerly been contaminated. In other words, Musk's pioneering ideas were supported by government through direct subsidies, loan financing, and deregulation.

Electronic Medical Records

Health care is, perhaps, more analogous to education than any other sector. Both are fragmented systems: The country's health-care system is populated with more than 5,795 hospitals, 650,000 physicians (often in small practices), and nearly 2.5 million nurses.[7] This is not too dissimilar from the nearly 15,000 school districts and more than 3.4 million teachers in education.[8] The government spends well over $1 trillion in both sectors. Both have federal laws protecting individual privacy of sensitive information (HIPAA and FERPA). And each of these sectors is struggling to develop data systems that drive informed decision making, provide early warning alerts for troubling trends, and increase efficiencies while improving outcomes.

In health care, EHRs are seen as a way to not only improve coordination of care but also prevent the as many as 195,000 deaths each year that result from medical errors.[9] EHRs provide doctors with instant access to a patient's medical history, lab test results, MRI/CAT scans, prescribed medications, and allergies. Many systems also have the capability of transmitting orders electronically so that they arrive not only faster, but with fewer errors. EHRs can also strip personally identifiable information and share data with regional and national health information networks to help researchers sift through volumes of patient data in the hope of accelerating new treatments and spotting potential problematic trends and outbreaks.

Policymakers have taken an interest in EHRs after studies have shown how these systems can increase efficiencies and reduce duplicative procedures, helping reduce health-care costs by as much as 20%.[10] And unlike many other areas of health-care reform, strong bipartisan support exists for EHRs. In a 2004 speech, President George W. Bush said, "Medicine ought to be using modern technologies in order to better share information, in order to reduce medical errors, in order to reduce cost to our health care system by billions of dollars. To protect patients and improve care and reduce cost, we need a system where everyone has their own personal electronic medical record that they control and they can give a doctor when they need to."[11] In January 2009, President-elect Obama delivered a speech with a similar call to action. "To improve the quality of our health care while lowering its cost, we will make the immediate investments necessary to ensure that, within five years, all of America's medical records are computerized," Obama said. "This will cut waste, eliminate red tape and reduce the need to repeat expensive medical tests."[12]

ARRA contains a section entitled the Health Information Technology for Economic and Clinical Health Act, which charges the U.S. Department of Health and Human Services (HHS) with providing $20 billion of incentive payments through Medicare and Medicaid to physicians and hospitals when they not only adopt, but also "meaningfully use" EHRs to achieve improvements in care delivery.

In consultation with hospitals, physicians, EHR providers, and other experts, HHS developed a program with an escalating set of measures that phase in over the next 5 years based on desired health outcomes. For example, doctors will initially need to use EHRs to record patients' demographic data; height, weight, and blood pressure; medications; allergies; and smoking behavior. Other performance measures require physicians to transmit a certain percentage of their prescriptions electronically.

Attached to these measures are incentive payments. Beginning in 2011, a doctor can receive EHR incentive payments of up to $44,000 under Medicare and $63,750 under Medicaid, while hospitals can receive as much as $6 million. Early adopters will be rewarded with higher incentive payments, while late adopters will receive lower payments. These financial "carrots" end in 2015, at which point a "stick" of financial penalties kicks in for physicians who do not meaningfully use EHRs.

This is another instance in which the federal government is providing direct subsidies to private entities to accomplish a public good, in this case ensuring that every person in the United States has an EHR by 2014 to improve care and reduce costs. The eligibility for the incentive payments was not limited to just nonprofit hospitals and clinics, nor were the certification standards written so as to apply only to nonprofit EHR providers or force physicians to adopt only nonprofit or open-source solutions. The result has been a vibrant, competitive marketplace with well over 100 EHR providers of all sizes and types. Established technology titans such as Microsoft, HP, GE, and Dell have developed solutions, and entrepreneurs are also experimenting with other platforms and models, including nearly a dozen open-source options. Others are trying different business models such as Practice Fusion, which offers a free web-based EHR that is supported by advertising. Physicians wanting to opt out of the advertising can pay $100 per month. Kalorama Information forecasts the EHR market to nearly double in size over the next 4 years, reaching $31.9 billion in 2015.[13]

Early survey results indicate broad support for the program. In 2012, 66% of physicians reported intending to participate in the incentive program. Adoption rates of EHRs are increasing as well. A CDC study found that 72% of physicians used an EHR system representing a 26% increase from 2011 (57%). The percentage of physicians who reported having a system that met the meaningful use criteria also increased from 34% to 40%.[14] The public also supports this approach, particularly its engagement of the private sector. A Greenberg Quinlan Rosner/

Public Opinion Strategies poll found that 81% of Americans support developing public–private partnerships between government, industry, and universities to maximize U.S. resources and expertise in medical innovation and research.[15]

Energy

The U.S. government's philosophy toward energy policy is nearly the opposite of its approach in education. The Obama administration's summary of our country's energy challenge is that "our addiction to foreign oil and fossil fuels puts our economy, our national security, and our environment at risk."[16] In response, the president has sought to engage a broad spectrum of solution providers, as well as consumers, through the use of grants, loans, and tax credits. In rallying the involvement of cleantech innovators, the president said, "As we recover from this recession, the transition to clean energy has the potential to grow our economy and create millions of jobs—but only if we accelerate that transition. Only if we seize the moment. And only if we rally together and act as one nation—workers and entrepreneurs; scientists and citizens; the public and private sectors."[17] The president's narrative around solving our country's energy crisis does not exclude for-profit enterprises; he knows that to realize his goals, he needs their involvement.

Tied to this policy are dozens of incentive programs that help support demand by consumers as well as supply from providers, including:

- *The Advanced Technology Vehicles Manufacturing Loan Program (ATVM):* The Energy Independence and Security Act of 2007 established this program, which provides both grants and direct loans for up to 30% of the cost of retooling, equipping, or establishing manufacturing facilities used to produce energy-efficient vehicles or component parts. The loan program has $25 billion in loan authority, supported by a $7.5 billion appropriation to fund the credit subsidy. To qualify, automakers and eligible component manufacturers must promise to increase the fuel economy of their products by 25% over the average fuel economy of similar 2005 models. The Obama administration announced the first four awards, ranging from $465 million to $5.9 billion, to Ford Motor Company, Nissan North America, Tesla Motors, and Fisker Automotive. The size of these loans makes the U.S. Department of Energy the largest investor in certain energy segments.
- *Advanced Energy Research Grants:* The Advanced Research Projects Agency—Energy (ARPA-E) was created in 2007 though the America COMPETES Act to apply the Defense Advanced Research Projects Agency research model for military innovations to energy technology development. It funds high-risk, high-reward research that might

not otherwise be pursued because of the costs involved with projects with a high risk of failure. Rather than limiting ARPA-E to traditional government research partners, Congress tasked the office to engage all sectors. ARPA-E received $400 million in funding from ARRA for grants that ranged between $500,000 and $20 million. Yet again, those eligible included corporate researchers, not just nonprofits and universities, so as to cast the widest net possible to identify and support the best ideas and solutions. For example, Pellion Technologies received $3.2 million to develop a rechargeable magnesium-ion battery for electric and hybrid vehicles.[18]

- *Improved Energy Technology Loans*: This loan guarantee program was created by the Energy Policy Act of 2005 to accelerate and scale commercial deployment of innovative clean-energy technologies in support of job creation, reducing dependency on foreign oil, improving the environment, and enhancing American competitiveness. A loan guarantee is a contractual obligation between the government (in this case, the U.S. Department of Energy), private creditors, and a borrower that promises the federal government will cover the borrower's debt obligation if the borrower defaults. This allows the government to share some of the financial risks of projects. The program has committed nearly $25 billion to support almost two dozen projects, most of which are run by commercial entities. Solyndra received a $535 million loan guarantee—nearly as much as the entire U.S. Department of Education's i3 fund—to finance construction of the first phase of a new solar manufacturing facility. The prudence of this investment is rightfully being debated in light of Solyndra's recent troubles and questions around their selection. It is important to scrutinize any government awarding of funds, be it to a nonprofit, private enterprise, school district, or university. However, the purpose of this chapter is highlight the willingness of the federal government to engage private-sector companies.

- *Hydrogen Fuel Excise Tax Credit*: A major challenge in the commercialization and adoption of new alternative energy–based vehicles is the cost of building out the infrastructure for fuels such as hydrogen. To provide incentives for both the adoption of these cars and the building out of the infrastructure, the federal government offers a tax credit of 50 cents per gallon for hydrogen that is sold for use or used as a fuel to operate a motor vehicle.

- *Clean School Bus USA:* This public–private partnership focuses on reducing children's exposure to harmful diesel exhaust by limiting school bus idling, implementing emission-reduction technologies, improving route logistics, and switching to clean-fuel buses. Grants are available to nonprofits, for-profits, and school districts for projects that advance these goals.

USING INTERMEDIARIES TO FORGE
PUBLIC–PRIVATE PARTNERSHIPS

In addition to this slew of direct support from agencies to for-profit entities to advance their goals, several federal agencies have seen the need to unleash the full power of this sector through even more creative arrangements. To do so, they have begun using intermediaries to engage the private sector without the bureaucratic red tape and limitations that restrict the agencies' ability to engage in even more flexible funding approaches. Often, these intermediaries attract individuals with necessary expertise who might not otherwise join a government agency. They are also often free from many of the constraints imposed on public agencies, allowing them to be more flexible in their investment approaches.

In-Q-Tel

In-Q-Tel is a not-for-profit venture capital firm that invests in high-tech companies for the sole purpose of keeping the Central Intelligence Agency (CIA) equipped with the latest technology for delivering enhanced intelligence capability. In the 1990s, the pace of commercial information technology innovation was outpacing the ability of the intelligence community to access and adopt the latest innova-tions ahead of the private sector. In 1998, the director of the CIA engaged former Lockheed Martin CEO Norman Augustine (who would later head the commission that produced the National Academies report *Rising above the Gathering Storm*, which highlighted the need for science, technology, engineering, and mathematics reform) to create and launch In-Q-Tel.

In-Q-Tel's mission is "to exploit and develop new and emerging information technologies and pursue R&D [research and development] that produce innova-tive solutions to the most difficult problems facing the CIA and Intelligence Com-munity."[19] The company works with the intelligence community to identify critical technology needs and engages with entrepreneurs, companies, and researchers to deliver solutions and capabilities.

From this needs analysis, In-Q-Tel develops an investment blueprint using $37 million of federal funding appropriated by Congress each year through the CIA. A typical investment can range from $500,000 to $2 million over a 6-month to 2-year period. The rationale is that any investment of less than 6 months will es-sentially produce a solution that could just be purchased. Any investment of more than 2 years is essentially just basic research. All proceeds from investments are reinvested back into In-Q-Tel operations, technologies, and programs to further benefit the CIA.

In-Q-Tel is similar in some respects to traditional government R&D organiza-tions such as the Institute of Education Sciences or the National Institute of Stan-dards and Technology in that it has only one primary customer—the CIA. The report of the independent panel that reviewed this joint venture identifies several advantages resulting from In-Q-Tel's status as a private entity:

- It can make equity investments in private entities.
- It has a flexible deal structure modeled after commercial investment vehicles.
- It has fewer bureaucratic constraints, both in terms of civil-service employee limitations and administrative red tape often attached to government grants and contracts.
- It can obligate funds in multiyear increments.
- It is not required to comply with Federal Acquisition Regulations requirements.[20]

This flexibility has produced results. Since 1999, In-Q-Tel has reviewed more than 7,500 business proposals, engaged more than 4,500 technology companies, invested in more than 160 companies, and delivered more than 300 technology solutions to the intelligence community. One of In-Q-Tel's more high-profile successes was its investment in Keyhole, which provided satellite-mapping capabilities and, after acquisition by Google, ultimately became Google Earth.

New Markets Tax Credit

The New Markets Tax Credit (NMTC) program is administered by the Treasury Department's Community Development Financial Institutions (CDFI) Fund but through private-sector intermediaries. The program was created in December 2000 to address the persistent challenge of revitalizing impoverished, low-income communities that often lack access to credit and capital. The program provides tax incentives to attract private-sector, market-driven investments in businesses, economic development, and real-estate development projects located in low-income urban and rural communities. Former Treasury official Cliff Kellogg said the program is intended to expand "the range of what's 'investible' by providing slightly more return when investors are balancing the risk-return tradeoff."[21] In other words, the NMTC encourages investors to "take a second look" on investment opportunities that they might otherwise pass.

The program works by allowing individual and corporate taxpayers to reduce their tax liability by 39% of the amount of the investment over a 7-year period in exchange for providing capital to vehicles known as community development entities (CDEs), which in turn invest in low-income communities. Investors typically use two investment structures: direct investments to CDEs and tiered investments, which can involve equity investments or leveraged investments (an investment structure where a portion of the investment amount originates from debt and a portion from equity).

The CDE plays the role of intermediary in allocating federal investment. A CDE can be either a for-profit or nonprofit entity, as long as it can demonstrate a primary mission of serving—or providing investment capital for—low-income communities. The CDE has 1 year to place most of the investments into qualified low-income community investments, which typically are:

- Loans to, or investments in, qualifying businesses or real-estate projects
- Loans to, or investments in, other CDEs
- The purchase of loans originated by other CDEs
- Counseling to low-income community businesses

To date, the CDFI Fund has made 386 awards totaling $21 billion, through six different allocation rounds. More than $13.7 billion of private funds have gone into CDEs, which represents more than 70% of the NMTC allocation authority awarded to CDEs through 2008. Demand for NMTC allocations far exceeds availability. To date, CDEs have requested a total of $202 billion in allocation authority since 2003, a demand of more than seven times credit availability. According to the U.S. Treasury Department, for every $1 in credited taxes under the NMTC program, more than $14 is being invested in community projects.[22]

The program has enjoyed bipartisan support, including from both the George W. Bush and Clinton administrations. The NMTC program was also named as one of the Top 50 Government Innovations as part of the Harvard Kennedy School's 2009 Innovations in American Government Awards. A Government Accountability Office (GAO) review concluded that "investors indicated that they have increased their investment budgets in low-income communities as a result of the credit, and GAO's analysis indicates that businesses may be shifting investment funds from other types of assets to invest in the NMTC."[23]

The program has also been a lifeline to the charter school community by attracting more private capital to help finance charter facilities. For example, the Charter School Development Corporation, led by City First, has provided financing to a number of Washington, D.C., charter schools, including $21 million for the E. L. Haynes Public Charter School. Ánimo Watts Charter High School in South Central Los Angeles, which serves 400 students, received a $9.1 million investment from the program.

NMTC could serve as a model for attracting investments into the education community by using a similar framework but adjusting the terms and eligibility. For example, instead of just providing financing to entrepreneurs who start small businesses in low-income communities, it can offer financing to education entrepreneurs who are providing services to low-income, low-performing schools, or charter schools.

THE CASE FOR GREATER PRIVATE-SECTOR INVOLVEMENT

Advocates for greater federal policy support for private-sector entities argue that assistance is needed to help accelerate new-technology adoption, make riskier investments more attractive to the private sector, attract entrepreneurs to address urgent social challenges, or scale innovations that face entrenched incumbents. Advocates use the scope of the problem, such as climate change, or the urgency of the challenge, such as better equipping the intelligence community with new capabilities, to underscore the need for public support of these private ventures.

For example, advocates argued that the ATVM program was needed because of the large amount of capital required to retool facilities or bring new energy-efficient cars to market. These are capital-intensive businesses facing entrenched competition from incumbents, which has created numerous barriers to new entrants introducing alternatives. Fuel-cell innovator Bloom Energy has required $250 million in capital thus far, 10 times as much as other startup ventures, and is still approximately 2 years away from an initial public offering. In comparison, it took Google only $25 million of venture capital investment to get to initial public offering.

Entrepreneurs entering the education sector face the similar challenge of requiring substantial capital to scale their solutions. The regulatory environment, particularly with its lengthy procurement processes, can require providers to spend months devoting substantial resources in staff time and funding to responding to complicated request for proposals, many of which will not result in a sale. Many incumbents, particularly large publishers, have armies of sales staff and long histories with district personnel, which makes it even more difficult for disruptors to secure opportunities. President Obama's Council of Economic Advisors released a report that noted, "Selling an educational product to a school district may require substantial contact with a diverse set of actors, including state and local procurement officers who oversee funding streams, academic consultants who advise districts, key school board members, and principals and teachers in individual schools."[24]

Proponents of greater private-sector involvement also argue that companies can achieve greater efficiencies, leading to lower costs for the government agency and taxpayers. Private-sector entities are freed from many of the bureaucratic restrictions and processes that can bog down even the best-intentioned government agencies. This flexibility not only allows innovators to be more nimble, but also allows government agencies to focus on their core competencies. The SpaceX story exemplifies this not only in terms of significant cost savings, but also in the reframing of a government entity's mission to support private-sector innovation through longer-term research while focusing on near-term safety and quality with its contractor partners.

The pay-for-performance systems NASA is using can also help save funds by paying only for the achievement of verifiable results. This stands in contrast to typical government programs that often run over on both costs and schedule. A 2002 study looked at 258 government transportation projects in the United States and around the world and found that 90% of the projects examined had cost over-runs, with an average overrun of 28%. The study concluded that many public officials have sought to ignore, hide, or otherwise leave out important cost and risk information to make total costs appear lower and gain approval.[25]

Private enterprises also have a greater incentive to invest in R&D as they seek ways to provide better services, different solutions, or lower costs. Public-sector investment in education R&D, although difficult to estimate, is about 0.03% of the overall public-sector budget, while private-sector firms often spend, on average, 100 times that percentage.[26] Rebecca Henderson and Richard Newell researched innovation trends in other sectors and the public policy's contribution in accelerating those innovations. They found:

> In every one of the sectors explored here, rapidly growing demand triggered both extensive private sector investment and extensive diffusion of new technology. . . . Accelerating innovation requires increasing both the supply of and the demand for new technologies. Beyond supply and demand, however, the theme that emerges most clearly from our histories is the important role that public policy has played in fostering vigorous competition and "markets for technology" in each industry and the centrally important role that this competition has played in accelerating innovation. Here again our histories suggest that there is no single policy or set of policies that is always appropriate, but that policy design must be actively tailored to the structure of the industry and the particular circumstances of the market. They focus attention on three policy instruments in particular: antitrust, intellectual property and support for public open standards.[27]

In other words, public policy helped create a supportive regulatory and financial ecosystem that encouraged, rewarded, and protected private-sector innovation and R&D.

More recently, calls have come from the business community for the government to simply create a more balanced regulatory environment that allows companies and private solutions to compete fairly with one another and other providers. These regulatory policies range from telecommunications to trade, where even minor changes in regulations can result in favoring one industry, company, or country over another. Entrepreneurial activity does not occur in a vacuum. Government regulatory policy can unleash innovation just by creating an environment in which new ventures can thrive and the playing field is level.

Education regulations also stifle innovation. Blended learning and online learning models can often progress students to higher-level grade work but are held back because of regulations that require credit to be awarded based not on demonstrated mastery, but on seat time. Higher education has also seen an uneven application of regulations over the past 4 years. For example, the gainful employment regulation applies only to for-profit institutions instead of holding all higher education institutions accountable for ensuring that students persist through a program and graduate with a manageable debt. The Department of Education also issued a sweeping regulation in 2010 that required distance education programs to secure permission to operate in every state in which they enroll at least one student. Instead of promoting distance education as increasing access to courses and lowering costs, the regulation did the opposite. It generated such a significant outcry that the Department eventually announced that it would no longer enforce the requirement. The response hardly provides the legal certainty providers needed to invest in building out programs.

Some states are adopting reforms that allow them to grant flexibility to innovative programs. For example, Ohio allows school districts to request a waiver for an innovative pilot program to be exempted from specific laws or rules. Their Credit Flex program also offers high school students the chance to earn credit in three ways (entirely or in combination): by completing traditional coursework; by testing out or otherwise demonstrating mastery of the course content; or by pursuing one or more "educational options" (e.g., distance learning, educational travel, independent study, an internship, music, arts, afterschool program, community service or engagement projects, and sports). In 2005, the New York City School District launched an Empowerment Schools initiative through which principals have greater autonomy in exchange for agreeing to take on greater responsibility for raising student academic achievement. The approach was also proposed for states by the reform group Chiefs for Change, which proposed an "earned autonomy" approach be included in the reauthorization of the Elementary and Secondary Education Act (ESEA). As schools and districts meet academic targets and raise student achievement, they would earn flexibility and autonomy.

CAUTIONS FOR GREATER PRIVATE-SECTOR INVOLVEMENT

All federal programs are proposed with best intentions that often fall short during implementation, particularly as unintended consequences emerge. For example, while many of the U.S. Department of Energy programs are intended to stimulate innovation, there is growing concern that the programs distort the market in such a way as to discourage innovation and risk-taking.

Many government innovation programs often place government in the position of picking winners and losers. Winners are usually picked through bureaucratic processes rather than by new idea–chasing venture capitalists whose technical and investor expertise helps allocate scarce capital to the most promising ventures. In these cases, politics often influence decisions, rather than rigorous analysis and due diligence.

For example, members of Congress sought to have ATVM loans used as part of a bailout of U.S. auto manufacturers when the Obama administration deemed the TARP program an inappropriate vehicle for such investments. Instead of supporting innovation, ATVM was being used to support the status quo. Another example is Solyndra, the solar energy company that received a loan guarantee and then filed for bankruptcy in September 2011. Several inquirers were launched, including a criminal investigation. Republican lawmakers have criticized the decision process that led to the loan guarantee award. At best, this is an example of the government's picking the wrong winner without careful due diligence and a system to enforce conditional awards. At worst, depending on the outcomes of the investigations, it illustrates how these policy levers can be used to reward political allies and donors. However, it is important to stress that there are problems with selection process with any number of federal programs that award grants to nonprofits or private entities. For example, a TNTP analysis (The New Teacher Project, 2010) of the U.S. Department of Education's Race to the Top program highlighted "concrete examples of how reviewer subjectivity, score inflation, and inconsistent scoring across applications yielded a winners' circle that excluded some states whose proposals appeared to most closely reflect the stated goals of the program: to build consensus behind bold reform."

Darryl Siry, the former chief marketing officer of Tesla Motors, noted in *Wired* magazine that venture capitalists are accounting for several factors when valuing a company, including how much more capital the company will need to get to market or another investment transaction that would provide a return for the venture capitalist.[28] U.S. Department of Energy loans and loan guarantees have amounted to free leverage for the investor's bet, with little to no downside. The upside is multiplied and the downside remains the same because the most the equity investor can lose is the original investment. As a result, the agency's programs have distorted the capital markets, as venture capital firms now prefer to back a company that has received a loan or loan guarantee, rather than a company that has not. In other words, the Department of Energy is influencing private-sector decisions and selections—perhaps unintentionally, but nonetheless, the result is still the same. The Department of Energy's loan-guarantee program has both supporters and detractors no matter where it focuses investments. If it backs untested projects to provide financing where private investment is lacking, it gets criticized for putting taxpayer funds at risk. If the program backs established and proven technologies, it is criticized for competing with banks and distorting the marketplace.

This market distortion will have a stifling effect on innovation as private capital chases fewer deals and companies that do not have government backing have a harder time attracting private capital. A survey of cleantech executives conducted in April 2010 by Deloitte confirmed that this concern was widespread. The study found that 73% of respondents were concerned that the government was influencing the competitive landscape of the industry with the stimulus funding.[29]

These concerns illustrate the challenges of establishing government programs that support private-sector entities. However, the point of debate for many of these sectors is not whether the government should help private enterprises but rather which policy levers and tools best support private enterprises. Concerns about market distortion are legitimate, but excluding private-sector entities—as federal education policy has done—also creates significant distortions in a market. Any federal program will have its strengths and weaknesses, and some should be discontinued because of lack of effectiveness. But these concerns do not outweigh the benefits of having a thriving marketplace of private-sector entrepreneurs tackling social challenges, particularly in education.

THE RELUCTANT EMBRACE OF PRIVATE COMPANIES IN EDUCATION

Private-sector companies are involved in nearly every area of K–12 education, from managing schools to developing textbooks and online learning courses. However, federal policy toward private-sector education companies lags compared with other sectors. As a result, education remains one of the only public policy areas where private companies have difficulty entering and thriving. Although outsourcing services such as transportation to a private company is relatively uncontroversial, turning over school management to a service provider is still seen as taboo. Engaging a nonprofit professional development provider is viewed with less suspicion than if the district entered into a similar arrangement with a for-profit provider.

We rarely see a government leader embrace private companies the way officials do in other sectors. For example, NASA Administrator Charles Bolden made an appearance at the FAA conference focused on space commercialization where he remarked, "We cannot survive without you. I can't tell you any stronger. We are big fans of commercial, we are huge fans of commercial space."[30] It would be difficult to imagine a secretary of education making similar remarks to for-profit professional development providers, charter school operators, or online providers.

An inherent apprehension about the motivation and behavior of profit-seeking businesses in education remains. The most prominent concern voiced by opponents of for-profits in education is that these businesses will divert resources and tax dollars from services for students to profits for the firm. The skepticism surrounding for-profit entities in education manifests itself in laws, funding programs, and regulations. As a result, investors' risk is increased, which in turn decreases the amount of private capital that would otherwise be available to fund and scale education entrepreneurs. For example, private investment in cleantech surged from $1 billion in 2001 to nearly $4.5 billion in 2008 due largely to what investors saw as a more policy-friendly environment. However, during that same period, the education industry attracted only $560 million, most of which was in postsecondary education. Joseph Keeney and Daniel Pianko observed, "Huge flows of private capital fund promising companies through the formal venture capital market and informal angel investment market every year, but very few of those dollars flow to the K–12 sector because of its limited potential for radical innovation."[31] And Silicon Valley blogger Sarah Lacy noted, "I've spoken to many venture capitalists who say they'd love to use technology to change education, but few think they can make money at it."[32] One reason is that somehow it is acceptable to make a profit by reducing greenhouse emissions but not by reducing dropouts.

Whereas other federal policy areas seek to attract private-sector entities to bring their entrepreneurial thinking to various social issues, federal education policy often establishes barriers that result in discouraging private-sector involvement. ARRA authorized the $650 million i3 fund to "accelerate the creation of an education sector that supports the rapid development and adoption of effective solutions." The competitive grant competition was structured to provide grants that expand the implementation of, and investment in, innovative and evidence-based practices, programs, and strategies. Secretary Duncan said, "We're looking to drive reform, reward excellence and dramatically improve our nation's schools."[33]

There was a caveat, however. Instead of casting a wide net to identify successful solution providers, Congress limited eligibility to only local education agencies (LEAs) or partnerships between a nonprofit organization and one or more LEAs. The U.S. Department of Education further narrowed the definition by also restricting the eligibility of subgrants to only LEAs and nonprofits. This essentially tilted the competition toward nonprofit entities, even if for-profit entities provided similar services. For example, ETS and Pearson are direct competitors in assessment design, development, and implementation. ETS, however, could directly apply for i3 funding or form a partnership with an LEA because of its nonprofit status, whereas Pearson would need to go through a competitive procurement with an LEA after the grant was funded.

Another example is the Obama administration's regulations related to for-profit higher education institutions. These for-profit colleges play an important role in our diverse system of higher education by offering flexible course schedules and pioneering the use of online technologies to meet the unique needs of working adults, single parents, and other nontraditional students. Critics of for-profit colleges, however, are quick to point out that while they account for only 10% of students enrolled in higher education, these students receive 23% of federal student loans and grants and are responsible for 40% of all student loan defaults.

The administration's regulations evaluate programs essentially based on the "gainful employment" of students through a series of tests and formulas to ensure that the debt a student assumes is reasonable relative to how much he or she can expect to earn upon graduation. Protecting students and taxpayers from low-quality programs and unwieldy debt burdens should be a priority, but these are issues we face across the entire system of higher education. Many community colleges struggle with low completion rates, yet are exempt from the administration's proposed regulation. Even Harvard Medical School would fail to meet the proposed loan repayment standard. If the administration sincerely wanted to protect students and taxpayers, then it would apply the gainful employment test to all institutional programs, regardless of their tax status.

A WAY FORWARD:
CREATING A HEALTHY, COMPETITIVE EDUCATION ECOSYSTEM

Given the scope and urgency of improving the country's system for educating its citizens, it makes little sense to limit solutions and entrepreneurial spirit to only some groups based on their tax status. Federal policy can replicate successful models used in other sectors to support innovation in education with safeguards to protect teachers, students, and parents.

Adopting this approach would require thinking of education less as an institutional system and more as an ecosystem of various providers and consumers characterized by a welcoming policy environment to all innovators, shared risk to help attract investors to incubate promising ventures, supportive funding and regulations that allow innovations to grow, and incentives that reward quality and results (which can also be used as part of transparent reporting initiatives to provide increased consumer protections). To be clear, an entrepreneurial education landscape is not one in which the government or foundations simply pick winners and losers. Rather, it is one in which these entities help remove barriers to entry for quality providers and think deeply about the impact their policy or philanthropic decisions will have on the broader educational marketplace and potential investors or entrepreneurs in the field. Absent that, venture capitalists and investors will simply seek out other sectors that have more supportive policy and regulatory environments for their investments. At a time of declining state and federal revenues, policymakers should be stimulating, not stifling, the influx of private capital to our education system.

To be sure, it is easy for the government to overstep its bounds and squander its investments. But learning from past efforts in other sectors can help inform the design of policies that promote more entrepreneurial activity in education. Education would benefit from adopting private-sector engagement strategies used by agencies such as NASA, HHS, and Energy. At a minimum, this would entail expressing a clear policy of intent toward attracting new entrants and entrepreneurs who are thinking of creative ways to solve new problems or address stubborn ones that have perplexed those in our education system. This would not preclude other experts from nonprofits and universities from working on solutions; it would simply bring more of our best and brightest to solving some of our most difficult education challenges. It would also attract talent and promote labor mobility within the education sector by encouraging entrepreneurs to take their experiences and apply them to new ventures and endeavors. Education's challenges are unique in some ways but remarkably similar in others to the challenge of scaling health reform across our fragmented health-care delivery system.

Finally, a crucial part of creating a thriving ecosystem is for government to strive to provide a level playing field for providers. The Obama administration used the Race to the Top competition to encourage states to create level playing fields for charter operators. As a result, states passed laws eliminating caps on charters or providing equitable funding between public schools and charters. A similar approach is needed to reduce barriers to not just for-profit providers, but also new models of education such as full-time virtual and blended models. Waivers are needed for models that want to measure student achievement based on competency, not seat time. Only with this regulatory flexibility can innovators truly enter markets and disrupt a system of entrenched incumbents.

Our country can no longer afford to raise academic expectations for children while simultaneously shutting out an entire group of providers who can help parents, students, teachers, and school leaders reach those expectations. Ultimately, our public policy should urgently seek to better educate our children by any means necessary. When it comes to other crucial challenges our country faces—creating a more reliable health-care system, finding efficient sources of clean energy, or improving space exploration—policymakers do not ask whether they should engage for-profit companies, but how they should. It is time for education policymakers to follow suit. We need to embrace a quality revolution that focuses solely on holding organizations accountable and responsible for improving student outcomes. Those that do should be rewarded and scaled so that we can ensure that students receive the education that they deserve using the entrepreneurial spirit and genius that have made America so great.

CHAPTER 7

The Role of For-Profits in K–12 Online Learning

Michael B. Horn

For decades, the role of for-profits in K–12 public education has been relatively well established. For-profit companies have long provided critical products and services to public education—from classroom products like technology devices, textbooks, and chalkboards to supplemental services like transportation. The number of schools that for-profit companies run and the direct provision of education that they provide, however, has remained relatively small. With the rapid rise of online learning, this is changing, as for-profits are increasingly playing a role as an education service provider, for example. Online learning represents unprecedented opportunities not just for innovation in education, but also for an expansion of for-profit providers' involvement. Indeed, for-profits have taken on a more significant share of the online learning market, which has allowed them to transition into the direct provision of teaching and learning.

Online learning's inherent scalability—which is distinct from the traditional provision of education—coupled with for-profits' more natural ability to scale influences their ability to dominate the online learning market. Although there are a significant number of nonprofit and governmental players in online learning, a greater number of for-profit companies are leading the charge in the field. As these for-profit companies amass scale, they can then use their increased capital to invest significant sums in research and development to improve online learning, as well as to invest in advocacy that simultaneously increases the reach of online learning in K–12 education and benefits their own companies.

Because of the ever-changing policy landscape, some stakeholders question if this new dynamic of for-profit dominance will persist. As online learning has scaled, so too have new for-profit providers scaled. Unlike in other sectors of education, the policy landscape has largely not discriminated against for-profits any more than it has against their nonprofit and governmental counterparts. As for-profits continue to attract more attention, however, and as education as we know it continues to change with online learning's ascent, this trend is not guaranteed to continue.

THE NUTS AND BOLTS OF ONLINE LEARNING

Contextualizing for-profit's place in the online learning world requires understanding the components that comprise online learning. A complete online learning program must have four essential components: technology platforms and infrastructure, people and pedagogy, assessment, and curriculum and content.[1] Within this framework, many types of online learning models—offered by for-profit, nonprofit, and government organizations—have emerged in the last decade. Some of these models encompass nonprofits and governmental organizations that act as state online schools offering à la carte courses to students, such as Michigan Virtual School, a nonprofit, and Florida Virtual School, a government entity. Many nonprofit and for-profit online organizations, from the VHS Collaborative to Apex Learning, have emerged to play a similar à la carte course role in a variety of ways.

Still other online learning organizations offer full-time virtual schools for students. Both districts and virtual charter schools run these models and often subcontract their operation to for-profit online learning providers. The virtual school solutions market includes both education management organizations (EMOs) that operate full-time virtual charter schools as well as the for-profit online learning providers of curricula, content development tools, technology platforms, and technology infrastructure.[2]

Other organizations play a wide range of miscellaneous roles in online learning. These include developing curricula, digital lessons, modular curricula, and whole courses, as well as instructional materials that range from test-prep software to tutoring services. Some organizations—again, both for-profit and nonprofit—offer a variety of technology platforms that do such things as host whole courses, provide tools for authoring content and adapting instructional materials, manage interactions with students and instructors, capture data electronically, keep track of student progress in grade books, and offer assessments. Newer technologies offer mobile learning solutions and social networking tools for both learning and collaborating. Still other companies consult with schools, districts, and states to help them implement online learning in a variety of forms and serve students in both blended-learning settings in bricks-and-mortar schools as well as in full-time virtual schools.

A staple of all these environments when they come together to create a learning solution for students is the four components mentioned above, which can be distilled into a simple acronym—TPAC—standing for Technology, Pedagogy, Assessment, and Content (see Figure 7.1).[3]

Figure 7.1. TPAC for Online and Blended Learning

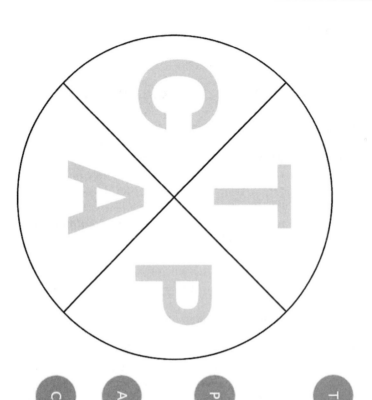

T

TECHNOLOGY & PLATFORMS
• Enterprise Architecture
• Learning Management system/virtual learning environment
• 1:1 Computing
• Broadband Internet infrastructure
• Need new SIS models for standards-based and new competency-based approaches

P

PEDAGOGY / PEOPLE / PD
• Teachers need new skills to teach online
• Administrators need new skills to manage online programs
• New Response to Intervention (RTI) models through blended

A

ASSESSMENT
• Online / Adaptive
• Personalization engine
• Performance-based

C

CONTENT & COURSES
•Online content & courses
•Dual enrollment
•Credit recovery
•Common core curriculum

142

Three of these components—pedagogy, assessment, and content—are so routine as to be nearly unremarkable in an educational environment. But the first component—the technology platforms and infrastructure—is a required part of online learning, and represents a critical difference from traditional learning environments. Technology platforms and infrastructure are what give online learning a unique place in the education field. It may also help explain why for-profits are playing a larger role in the development of online learning at this point than they play in other educational settings.

THE SCALE FACTOR

In many instances, experience in producing a good or service allows the producer to realize where they can reduce costs and improve yields. Most industries—but certainly not all—have some sort of scale economies so that unit costs decrease as they make more of the offering. When no technology enabler exists that allows people to reduce costs dramatically and improve yields as they produce more, there tend to be limited benefits to achieving scale. The provision of education has historically been one such sector—consider the way that the ratio of teachers to students is watched so closely. Technology and experience may have changed the way that teachers work, but they have not reduced the amount of time a teacher has to work to produce a similarly educated class of students.[4]

For the first time, however, online learning has given the provision of education a technology that enables it to scale. This can be seen in the rapid growth that online learning has achieved, as well as the rapid and unprecedented scale that education organizations powered by online learning have attained. In higher education, people once thought that schools like Arizona State University, with 55,000 students enrolled on the Tempe campus, were large. At its peak in 2010, the University of Phoenix enrolled nearly 600,000 students.[5] Sebastian Thrun, a former Stanford professor and the founder of Udacity, which offers massively open online courses (known as MOOCs), famously enrolled more than 160,000 students in a free online learning course on artificial intelligence for Stanford.[6] Indeed, Arizona State University is now using online learning to scale enrollment rapidly. Its educational mission is "to establish ASU as the model for a New American University, measured not by who we exclude, but rather by who we include" with goal number one being "quality and access for all."[7]

The same dynamic has been true in the K–12 world. In the past decade, the number of K–12 students enrolling in at least one online course has grown rapidly. Although estimates vary widely, most suggest that growth is at least 30% per year and that the students enrolled in online courses number in the millions now. KIPP, a network of charter schools that was founded in 1994, began earnestly scaling beyond its original two schools in 2000. At about the same time, K12 Inc., an online learning company, was founded; the company officially offered its first classes in September 2001. In the 2011–12 school year KIPP served just over 39,000 students, whereas as of June 2012, K12 Inc. served 147,728 full-time equivalent students.[8] Its growth continues at a breakneck pace, with enrollment in 2012 up 46% from the previous year.[9] Florida Virtual School, Florida's state online learning entity founded in 1997, serves more than 148,000 students, mostly in à la carte courses. The Khan Academy, a nonprofit that offers online lesson videos, assessments, and teacher and student dashboards, had roughly 5 million unique users per month at the end of the 2012 school year, up from 3 million in December 2011.[10]

THE IMPACT OF THE "SCALING FACTOR" ON INDUSTRY DYNAMICS

Because online learning relies on easily scalable technology, many of its costs are fixed and frontloaded, which can require a substantial initial capital investment. For example, it costs Florida Virtual School roughly $300,000 to develop a course, but, generally speaking, once a full online learning course is launched, the only real variable or marginal costs are the costs of labor.[11] After the upfront investment, the physical infrastructure necessary to scale is considerably less expensive than in a traditional bricks-and-mortar learning environment.

This fact creates an advantage for for-profit companies because—as other chapters in this volume explore—compared with their nonprofit and governmental peers, for-profits have an easier time gaining access to capital in a reliable and expedient manner. Why? For-profits have owners—or shareholders—which nonprofit and governmental entities do not have. In a viable market, for-profits can naturally attract capital from owners who seek investments that will realize returns. By not having shareholders, nonprofit organizations lack this natural pathway. As a result of these dynamics, for-profit companies spend $2 to $4 raising capital for every $100 they bring in, whereas nonprofits spend $10 to $24 for every $100 they raise.[12] Operating in an environment with significant potential for economies of scale seems to advantage for-profits.

Although significant nonprofit and governmental online learning organizations—like the VHS Collaborative, Michigan Virtual University, and Florida Virtual School—do exist in K–12 education, it is safe to say that for-profit entities have dominant market share across much of the online learning landscape. Where nonprofit and governmental entities have built significant scale, it is often because they have established a coherent business model that mirrors a for-profit's business model. Such a model allows them to scale with additional revenue as they serve additional students, as opposed to a model reliant on grants or fixed governmental appropriations. For example, the Florida Virtual School does not receive its revenue from a fixed government appropriation, but instead earns money based on the number of students who enroll in and successfully pass its courses.

Again, one noticeable exception is the Khan Academy, which has attracted significant philanthropic support and is continuing to grow rapidly. That said, because of the way the Khan Academy constructs most of its online learning content—through simple lesson videos as opposed to integrated courses—its fixed and frontloaded costs are lower than those of more established and older online learning players, even as it is now investing more heavily in its analytics platform, for example. Khan Academy also does not itself pay teachers to work with students, so its variable costs are essentially zero as it scales. This suggests that the dynamics in the nascent and fast-evolving field of online learning may be in the process of changing yet again such that this analysis of how the current dynamics present some advantages for for-profit entities may become dated.

As mentioned earlier, for-profit online-learning companies currently provide two types of general services. The first service for-profit online companies provide involves supplying states, districts, and individual schools with a variety of online-learning solutions, including curricula, instructional systems, data, and talent management.[13] In this role, for-profit online-learning providers are not too different from other for-profit entities in education, such as textbook companies, which have contracted with public school districts for decades. Interestingly, for many years, the textbook business has been one component within K–12 education with access to significant economies of scale. For this critical reason, in today's mature industry, there are three dominant for-profit textbook providers in K–12 public education with massive reach and scale.[14]

The second service that for-profits provide is, in essence, as education management organizations (EMOs) that operate full-time online schools. EMOs are for-profit companies that provide "whole-school operation" services to public school agencies. Like school districts, they receive public funding that follows the student. States or districts will typically contract with an EMO to provide all the curricula, teachers, administrative services, and materials (computer, Internet connection, and manipulatives) to students enrolled in full-time online schools. In this scenario, EMOs perform functions not unlike those of a school district or a nonprofit charter management organization (CMO).

The world of charter schools provides a telling case study of how online learning has advantaged for-profit providers. In the "traditional" bricks-and-mortar schools in the charter world, for-profit EMOs manage only 12.5% of schools (or 20% of the total number of students enrolled in charter schools).[15] CMOs and so-called mom-and-pop independent organizations run the vast majority. In the full-time virtual charter school world, the story is almost the exact opposite. EMOs enroll roughly 75% of the total student enrollment in full-time online schools across the nation.[16] Four for-profit companies dominate this landscape today: K12 Inc., Connections Education (which is owned by Pearson), Advanced Academics (which is owned by DeVry University), and EdisonLearning. Although these companies also offer individual courses, their core businesses have been in running full-time online schools. K12 Inc. currently serves 147,728 full-time equivalent students, although it serves 105,912 full-time unique students in its managed public schools, which it operates in 29 states and the District of Columbia.[17] Connections Education expects to serve more than 45,000 full-time unique students in its 24 public schools in 22 states as well as its national, tuition-based, private virtual school in the 2012–13 school year. In the prior academic year, Advanced Academics served more than 23,000 unique students in 30 states, with about 70% of courses serving full-time students.

What's remarkable about this is that these providers are operating in a nearly identical regulatory framework as their counterparts in the traditional charter school space. Neither in the traditional school model nor in the newer online learning model are there any policies that specifically incentivize the involvement of for-profit companies. In both cases, most states have prohibited for-profits from directly opening and operating charter schools. Instead, nonprofits must apply for the charter and then may contract with a for-profit company to run the school. And yet the major for-profit EMOs in K–12 online learning have figured out how to dominate the market. It would seem that the scale economies they derive from the online technology—coupled with their easier access to capital—is a relevant factor.

Figure 7.2 below gives a rough picture of how economies of scale work for online schooling; the graph depicts how K12 Inc.'s operating expenses have changed in correlation with the expansion of full-time unique student enrollment. Since K12 Inc.'s public filings only extend back to 2004 and the company offered its first class in 2001, this graph misses any economies of scale that the company realized in its initial years of operation. The company likely experienced some of its biggest

Figure 7.2. K12 Inc.'s Economies of Scale, 2004–2011

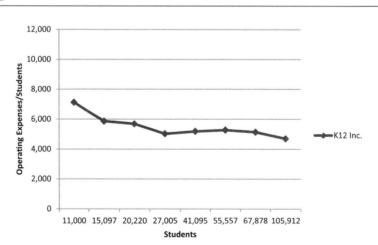

Figure 7.3. Aspire Public Schools' Economies of Scale 2000–2011

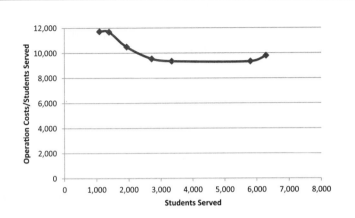

gains in economies of scale in these early years—growing from zero students to 11,000—as the company likely invested a lot of money up front in developing its products and services. Despite this missing information, the graph shows that K12 Inc.'s operating expenses per student have fallen nearly $2,500 from 2004 to 2011, when it served nearly 95,000 more full-time students.

Take Aspire Public Schools, a traditional CMO that operates primarily in California, as a comparator. Historically, the CMO has not leveraged online learning or blended learning (although this is changing) and, unsurprisingly, its economies of scale (Figure 7.3) are smaller. Here, a fuller picture emerges that places K12 Inc.'s economies of scale in better context. Like K12 Inc., Aspire has realized lowered expenses per student as it has grown to serve just under 8,000 students over a decade. Their savings per student, however, are just under $2,000—and again, the biggest fall in expenses per student for K12 Inc. is almost certainly not captured in Figure 7.2. In its first few years of operation, K12 Inc. grew to an enrollment similar to Aspire's enrollment levels after a decade in operation.[18]

THE IMPLICATIONS OF SCALE

As an organization scales both in terms of the numbers of people it serves and its corresponding revenues, it can use a portion of its revenue to invest in significant research and development (R&D) that furthers innovation, or in advocating for improvements or changes to public policy. For-profits possess a dominant market share in the online-learning world due in part to their ability to scale rapidly. It is no surprise, then, that for-profits also spend significantly more than nonprofit and governmental organizations to support R&D and advocacy efforts that benefit the company individually, and improve the online-learning environment more broadly.

Of course, the nonprofits that have been able to scale in this field also have the ability to spend their revenues on R&D and advocacy to benefit themselves—and often the online-learning field more generally. That said, for-profits often have an advantage here; as they establish themselves, on average they have an easier time raising further capital that they can invest in these areas. Nonprofits can do this, too, but it is more difficult.

R&D

One way that for-profit companies are advancing K–12 online learning is by investing in R&D—both their revenues as well as investment dollars—to increase curricular offerings, create better products and services, and build new technology platforms. Given the rapid pace of development in social networking tools, collaboration software, digital instructional materials, technology platforms, and mobile devices, the market for educational resources has become much more complex than it was in the late 1990s when online programs were first being launched. As a result, it is more crucial than ever for online-learning providers to create new and innovative products that reflect recent technological advancements.

K12 Inc., a publicly traded company, provides a case in point. As the largest provider in K–12 online learning—helped in part by its ability to scale—the company has invested large sums in R&D. As mentioned, the company has scaled to serve more than 140,000 full-time equivalent students—meaning well over that in terms of unique students, as the students taking individual courses are not disaggregated in this number—through its various services. Its yearly revenue has scaled in concert with enrollment increases; in 2011, its annual revenue was $522.4 million—up from $384.5 million in 2010. Because of this scale, K12 Inc. has been able to invest significantly in its products and services. Its 2011 annual report states that the company has invested over $240 million over the lifetime of the company "to develop and, to a lesser extent, acquire curriculum and online learning platforms that promote mastery of core concepts and skills for students of all abilities."[19] Today, the company boasts more than 600 e-learning courses.

Although it is difficult to ascertain the exact amount of R&D in which K12 Inc. invests on an annual basis, its annual report provides some clues. The company spent roughly $16.3 million in product development costs in 2011—or roughly 3% of its revenues.[20] This figure, however, does not perfectly represent the development costs that would fall under R&D. According to its filings, "Product development expenses include research and development costs and overhead costs associated with the management of both our curriculum development and internal systems development teams. In addition, product development expenses include the amortization of internal systems and any related impairment charges."[21] Some small subset of its instructional costs and service expenses—roughly $307 million in 2011—is also devoted to R&D, as its annual report explains by saying that these "development costs may include instructional research and curriculum development."[22] It also had available R&D tax credits of $3.3 million and $2.2 million—a further indication of its R&D activity.[23] Last, the annual report gives some clues as to what the company will be investing in from an R&D perspective, as it says the company plans "to invest in additional curriculum development and related software in the future, primarily to produce additional high school courses, world language courses, and new releases of existing courses and to continue to upgrade our content management system and online schools."[24]

Connections Education similarly invests significant sums in R&D. Although the company serves fewer students than K12 Inc.—and therefore has less revenue to invest—it still invests a few million dollars each year in R&D, based on discussions with management over the years. The for-profit company Pearson, a longtime leader in the textbook industry that spans many verticals in education, recently acquired Connections Education. Given Pearson's prominent leadership role in digital learning resources, it is a reasonable guess that significantly more R&D resources will go toward bolstering the company's products and services in the years ahead.[25]

Nonprofits and governmental organizations that scale are also able to use their revenues to invest in R&D to benefit both themselves and the field of online learning more broadly. For example, FLVS spends significant sums on R&D annually, which has gone to develop such groundbreaking courses as its Conspiracy Code online video game–based courses—including an American history one and an intensive reading one—and to continue to investigate more constructivist and competency-based approaches in online learning.[26]

But in keeping with the notion that for-profit companies have an easier time raising capital, which can go toward furthering their products and services through R&D, K12 Inc. yet again demonstrates this point. In April 2011 the company raised $125.8 million in capital from the private placement of 4 million shares of restricted common stock at $31.46 per share to Technology Crossover Ventures.[27] To those alleging that for-profits are always taking money out of their product development to return money to shareholders, K12 Inc. has not pursued this path, as it has yet to pay a dividend to its shareholders.[28]

Advocacy

Advocacy is another key way that for-profit companies are advancing student access to online learning. Today there are a number of policies that place barriers on the growth of online learning, such as seat-time constraints, a lack of true teacher-licensure reciprocity from state to state, enrollment caps, and limitations on geographical reach, among others. Whether students have access to publicly funded online-learning opportunities rests largely on the policies in place in their state. In 2005, for example, there were only 11 states with policies to support full-time online schools and only 8 states with full-time online schools. Just 6 years later, 30 states offered students access to full-time online schools. The growth of full-time online schools in those states has resulted in significant innovation, as districts have in turn innovated to better serve the needs of students through the creation of their own array of online programs, either through full-time online schools or a variety of blended-learning options from the perspective of the student.

These policy restrictions often—but not always, as discussed below—affect for-profits, nonprofits, and government organizations equally. As a result, all organizations are motivated to advocate for policy and regulatory changes, but on average, because of their scale, for-profits have significantly more capital to do something about it. Indeed, if a policy or regulation stands in the way of a for-profit's efforts to achieve scale, then it has significant motivation to advocate for a policy change. Nonprofit and government organizations may not naturally possess this motivation unless the policy affects their ability to gain or maintain prestige.[29] In some cases, governmental online organizations are also restricted in their capacity to scale outside of their own states and therefore the advocacy roles they can play are limited.

Again, for-profits' motivations for advocacy are captured in K12 Inc.'s annual report. The company stresses the importance of things such as "regulations restricting virtual public school and hybrid school growth and funding," two factors that inhibit the growth of online learning.[30] Furthermore, K12 Inc. supports policies that help its nonprofit partners secure federal and state grants.[31] Last, the company highlights the impact of the judicial process in opening up or restricting access for students to publicly funded online-learning options.[32]

These interests are often aligned with the broader online-learning movement's interests, to which K12 Inc.'s annual report attests. For example, the company pays attention to how "the poor performance or misconduct by operators of other virtual public schools, public school district virtual learning programs, or hybrid schools could tarnish the reputation of all the school operators in our industry, which could have a negative impact on our business."[33]

To further these aims, K12 Inc. spends money on a variety of advocacy-related items. Because K12 Inc. is not large enough to staff individuals in state capitols across the country—as are organizations like unions and school board associations—the company engages in direct advocacy in the form of paying lobbyists around the country. In addition, the company engages in a secondary line of advocacy, which involves funding various stakeholder groups across education. Parent organizations receive much of this support, but the company also supports candidates from both sides of the aisle who advocate for a broad set of education reforms, even when those policies do not directly affect K12 Inc. Indeed, CEO Ron Packard and others with the company often say that advocacy on behalf of education reform and expanded opportunities for parents and kids is a core principle— or competency—of K12 Inc.

According to the *New York Times*, for example, K12 Inc. has spent roughly $681,000 on lobbying in Pennsylvania since 2007, and had contributed nearly $500,000 to political candidates around the country from 2004 to 2010.[34] Connections Education has similarly spent in the millions on advocacy—both in direct advocacy in the form of lobbying and in the form of supporting various grassroots groups. According to the Center for Responsive Politics, it spent $120,000 on actual lobbying expenditures in 2010 and roughly $90,000 in 2011.[35]

Nonprofits and governmental organizations also work to alter online-learning policies and regulations. As Andrew P. Kelly wrote, in higher education, despite the attention paid to the lobbying activities by for-profit universities, the top lobbying nonprofit and public universities actually outspend their for-profit counterparts. For example, the Apollo Group, which owns the University of Phoenix, does not even crack the top seven in higher education lobbying spending when nonprofits are included, according to Kelly's examination of data from the Center for Responsive Politics.[36] Nonprofit and governmental online-learning organizations also spend dollars on advocacy to advance the field and their interests. For example, the Florida Virtual School spent just under $50,000 on actual lobbying expenses in 2010 and $24,000 in 2011, according to the Center for Responsive Politics.[37] Although this number does not include general advocacy expenditures, it appears that their scale has enabled the for-profits to spend more to advance the field in K–12 education.

Historically, education has been governed based on regulating inputs such as spending, rather than measures of student outcomes growth. The question of whether the existing online-learning players—including the for-profits—will advocate for a system that is strict on outcomes-based accountability remains open. They could merely advocate for opening up students' options and focus their efforts less on academic quality, which would arguably be dangerous to scaling quality educational options.

Signs of Shifting Regulatory Environment?

As discussed in other chapters in this volume, the government has often created an advantage for nonprofits in education by barring for-profits from having access to certain governmental funds, as in the Investing in Innovation (i3) program. At this point, such efforts have largely not affected the online-learning field.

Regulations in the online-learning sector have generally not discriminated in overt ways against for-profit providers. As discussed, most states bar for-profit providers from directly receiving the charter to open new schools. But this policy is not unique to the world of online learning, and full-time virtual school for-profit providers have been able to contract with the nonprofits that hold the on-line charters and scale rapidly.

Often run by governmental organizations, statewide online schools that pro-vide à la carte courses have to some extent crowded out the growth of both online-learning for-profits and some online-learning nonprofits.[38] This policy is not a direct policy against for-profits per se, but it does create a "most-favored nation" type status within these states, as the statewide online schools possess some scale and adoption advantages over their online-learning course provider counterparts. For example, the majority of states that operate statewide online-learning pro-grams fund them based on a state line-item appropriation. From the perspective of school districts that generally do not have to pay for the service, it is free for students to take these online courses.

The flip side of this, however, which works in the favor of the for-profit online learning companies, is that the enrollment and growth of these statewide online schools is capped based on available funds. Even then, a small number of the state-wide online-learning programs—like the Florida Virtual School—automatically receive per-pupil funds based on the number of courses students take. This gives FVS a decided advantage over other online-learning providers that compete in the state, as districts are not allowed to bar their students from taking these courses.

Given the minimal discrimination against for-profits in the online-learning space, many—although not all—of the advocacy efforts by the for-profit online-learning providers have pushed for policies that advance the field of online learning more broadly, not policies that specifically benefit for-profit providers. Neverthe-less, the increasing visibility of for-profit providers in public education has led to a backlash against some of them as of late. News organizations—both national and local—have reported several stories in recent months that raised questions about the quality of the for-profit full-time virtual schools as well as questioned the validity of having for-profits participate in the provision of public education.[39] As a result, shareholders have filed lawsuits against K12 Inc. and some states have conducted audits and hearings to investigate their practices.

In K–12 education, public, private, and nonprofit operators of public schools have for the last decade been held accountable for performance. But the signs point to increased scrutiny for proprietary firms, especially those with online and blended-learning models. This is partly because of more general questions about how well full-time virtual schools can educate children, partly based on the fact that in some states reimbursement rates for full-time online schools are compa-rable to those for bricks-and-mortar schools despite lower costs, and partly based on general resistance to new teaching and learning models. In any case, this in-creased scrutiny points to an even greater emphasis on evaluation and outcomes for proprietary K–12 operators in the future.

The for-profit online-learning companies—particularly those that directly provide education—have taken note. In K12 Inc.'s annual report, for example, it mentions several ways the regulatory framework could shift to crack down on for-profit firms specifically, as it draws a direct comparison to what has unfolded in the past couple of years in higher education where federal policymakers have instituted regulatory changes that disproportionately affect for-profit colleges.[40]

That said, what this statement also points to is that it would likely be significantly harder for the government to crack down on K–12 for-profit online-learning schools compared to how the government has targeted the for-profit postsecondary schools. In the postsecondary sector, the vast majority of for-profit institutions were receiving large portions of their revenue from one source—Title IV funds regulated by the federal government. The distribution of these funds already distinguished for-profit institutions and their career college counterparts from traditional higher education institutions. As the note in K12 Inc.'s annual report states, however, for-profit online providers in K–12 receive the majority of their revenue from a number of different states. The federal government therefore has significantly less ability to limit their right to participate in providing education, and the chances of all of the states that have full-time virtual schools cracking down on the proprietary providers is unlikely.

That said, as the K12 Inc. annual report also implies, because "the schools we contract with and serve are governed by independent governing bodies that may shift their priorities or change objectives in ways adverse to us, or react negatively to acquisitions or other transactions," continued negative press could cause these entities to stop contracting with for-profit providers.[41] If that were to happen, then the state laws that prevent for-profit providers from directly receiving the charters to operate schools could become a much bigger deal than they are today.

CONCLUSION

Ultimately the discussion of the role of for-profits in K–12 online learning is less about for-profits versus nonprofits and more about the innovation of what is possible for delivery in new models of learning versus the forces of the traditional model and the ability to change. That said, because online learning presents an unprecedented opportunity for economies of scale in education, online learning advantages for-profit firms because of their more natural—although certainly not exclusive—ability to scale. Scale in turn means the ability to increase revenues and spend more money investing in R&D and advocacy for the field. As a result, for-profit players are playing a major role in all facets of online learning and in the direct provision of education in a way that has not been true in other sectors. Policy, to this point, has largely not discriminated against them in favor of their nonprofit or governmental peers.

CHAPTER 8

Philanthropic Dollars in Commercial Markets

Blessing or Curse?

Stacey Childress & Tamara Butler Battaglino

Most people associate philanthropy with social purposes not well addressed by markets. These include programs for disadvantaged children and youth, homeless shelters, food banks, and disaster relief, as well as civic organizations such as museums, symphony orchestras, and historical societies. Americans are uniquely generous in their support of such efforts.

But less familiar is philanthropic funding for projects that operate in commercial markets. Although markets are not perfect, they are good at allocating investment capital to the most promising opportunities and then fueling their growth when they serve their customers well. The exchange between buyers and sellers can be an engine for innovation, quality, and long-term viability, including for activities that generate public good along with returns to investors.

The K–12 public education system is a great example of a sector in which public, philanthropic, and commercial capital sometimes interact. Most K–12 education spending pays for employee salaries and benefits, but districts and schools also buy all sorts of things core to their academic purposes, such as curricular materials, professional development services, and instructional technology. The vast majority of this spending is funded with their per-pupil revenues from public sources, but philanthropists subsidize district and school purchases, too. Donors also fund the development of instructional products and services that education institutions buy (or use for free). So, whether or not they realize it, philanthropists sometimes play on both the demand and supply sides of K–12 markets.

Donors often support organizations and leaders who inspire them and demonstrate promising results, but might not focus as deliberately on how those projects fit into the overall market landscape. In some areas of giving, certain kinds of projects can influence markets in ways that increase performance and promote scale and sustainability while others might actually interfere with well-functioning markets.

Markets—which often include for-profit and nonprofit suppliers—can be a lever for the scale and sustainability of solutions that help drive better learning outcomes for students through offerings such as curriculum, assessments, or professional development services. For-profit companies spend billions on R&D, marketing, and distribution of these products and services, some of which can drive better outcomes for students. Even though philanthropists have natural affinity with nonprofits, for-profit providers are important actors in the ecosystem and can be instrumental in reaching philanthropists' goals, too. Philanthropists should be on the lookout for opportunities to strengthen market incentives that drive innovation and performance. They should also avoid weakening such incentives where they exist. In other words, philanthropists should strive to be more aware of and deliberate about the effects their giving can have on functioning markets.

To better understand how they can have an impact on market scale and sustainability in a more intentional way, philanthropists should ask if their donations:

- Increase the capacity of schools and districts to make good buying
  decisions in the long term by helping them identify and express
  their needs more effectively and by creating better, more transparent
  information about the performance of products and services
- Support innovation and increase the quality of offerings over time
- Make it easier for providers to achieve scale and sustainability, including
  the ability to attract capital and talent to grow efficiently over time

In this chapter, we outline a point of view about the intersections between philanthropy and markets, propose a draft framework for analysis and decision making, and provide some noneducation and education examples to help illuminate our emerging thinking. The ideas are still in the early stage of development, so our goal is to provoke reflection and discussion rather than provide a definitive blueprint for action.

DOES PHILANTHROPIC CAPITAL STRENGTHEN OR WEAKEN MARKETS?

In our work at the Bill and Melinda Gates Foundation and The Parthenon Group, we try to make sense of the interaction between philanthropy and commercial markets particularly in K–12 segments such as digital content and adaptive courseware, which combined represent approximately $1.3 billion in revenue. These segments are poised for rapid growth and increased attention from commercial investors and philanthropists. They are part of the broader $8 billion curriculum and instructional materials market, which is dominated by for-profit companies but includes some nonprofit players. Market dynamics are well established even though incentives are not always aligned to reward suppliers whose products improve results for students or offer higher-quality services at affordable prices. Procurement and adoption cycles are often long, and demand is fragmented across 15,000 school districts that sometimes have difficulty precisely identifying and articulating their needs. For-profit companies respond to market incentives to serve their customers and generate a return for their investors. They invest in R&D, allocate resources to attract and reward talent, and market their products to grow their market share. When this cycle is successful, they have access to more capital for innovation, quality improvements, and growth.

The commercial capital markets have a clear structure that philanthropic capital markets lack. There are well-established categories that match the lifecycle of businesses—angels, early-stage venture capital, mezzanine investors, with continued success leading to large private placements, strategic acquisitions, or public offerings. Throughout the cycle, the capital providers require their companies to develop and refine their business models so that they generate the expected returns. Because the philanthropic capital markets lack this structure and discipline, nonprofits that operate in the same market spaces as for-profits usually don't have similar pressures to develop sustainable business models. They have some advantages because customers often perceive them to be more driven by social purposes because they do not have the same profit motives. Occasionally, a nonprofit creates a strong business model and as a result becomes less reliant on philanthropy and government for growth and sustainability, but this is rare. When a nonprofit that operates in commercial markets performs well and creates buzz around its offerings, it can attract significant philanthropic dollars, at least for a time. Some philanthropists ask their grantees to develop sustainable business models, but few donors have the relevant expertise or support structures that commercial capital brings to bear on its investments. Without a relentless focus on business-model questions (e.g., who are our customers, what do they need, what is their willingness and ability to pay, how will we reach them, and so on), philanthropic funds can weaken the long-term viability of an organization by removing pressures that would force it to build a more efficient cost structure or better serve its customers in order to generate sufficient revenues to cover costs. Because even the largest strategic foundations rarely have interest in funding projects in perpetuity, if nonprofits operating in commercial spaces do not hone their business models, most of them face long-term challenges to scale and sustainability.

Some thought leaders and commercial providers argue that philanthropy can actually hamper the ability of for-profit companies to get traction and effectively serve students with business models that are more sustainable for the long haul.

One frequently cited example is the rise of charter management organizations (CMOs) around the same time as for-profit school operators were beginning to emerge. The argument goes something like this: By creating a nonprofit alternative to for-profit school operators backed by commercial investors, philanthropists provided communities with a less threatening alternative. This made it even more difficult for commercial providers to grow market share to levels attractive to commercial investors, thereby weakening incentives enough that the segment never realized the aspirations of early players. Because it is impossible to prove a counterfactual, the validity of this argument is unclear. There could be other reasons why for-profit operators did not become the dominant school management model, including the weak performance early on by some operators, the political opposition that mobilized against high-profile providers in some cities, and legitimate philosophical questions about the appropriate role of for-profits in direct delivery of social services. But we do know that a decade later, a number of nonprofit CMOs are serving a small percentage of the nation's students well but face significant scaling and financial sustainability challenges because of their reliance on episodic government grants and philanthropic organizations, which are subject to changes in leadership and strategic priorities.

It is worth noting that the CMO example is materially different from the market segments we focus on in this chapter. In the K–12 sector, more than 85% of schools are run by local governments with the majority of the remainder connected to religious institutions or organized as nonprofits. This means for-profit operators were trying to break into a market space largely unaccustomed to commercial providers. After 20 years, the entire charter sector only serves about 4% of all U.S. public school students, and the for-profit providers account for approximately 12.5% of the total (in other words, about 0.5% of all public school students). The segments we focus on in our work (and in this chapter) are *already* dominated by for-profit players, with nonprofit providers making up a very small portion of the market. Nevertheless, the same arguments made about the dampening effects of philanthropy on the commercial opportunity in the early days of the CMO movement are being made now about the curriculum and instructional materials market, especially as it transitions from print to digital offerings.

Hindsight has its limits, so we instead are attempting to develop some forward-looking hypotheses about how philanthropy might interact with existing market dynamics. What follows is our early attempt to create a frame for grantmaking decisions. The ideas we describe are our own and should not be interpreted as the official institutional stance of our two organizations.

We developed a two-by-two to visualize the interaction between supply and demand. The vertical axis represents the level of economic incentives for suppliers. The horizontal axis illustrates demand by estimating the level of addressable demand for a product or service. Figure 8.1 is a snapshot of the framework.

Figure 8.1. Visualizing the Intersection of Supply and Demand Characteristics

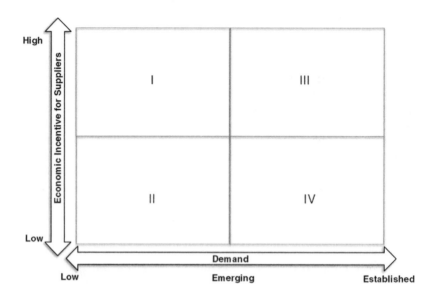

- In quadrant I, economic incentives are high for suppliers, but demand from buyers and/or users is low.
- In quadrant II, economic incentives are low for suppliers, and demand from buyers and/or users is low.
- In quadrant III, economic incentives are high for suppliers, and demand from buyers and/or users is established.
- In quadrant IV, economic incentives are low for suppliers, but demand from buyers and/or users is established.

What are some implications for philanthropy in each of the quadrants? We propose that in general, a good role for philanthropy is to help jumpstart activity or reshape incentives where there are gaps in supplier activity, with a particular focus on strengthening the demand side's ability to articulate its needs and evaluate solutions. In segments that are "functional," philanthropists should be especially careful about their role. By "functional," we mean the market has a large addressable customer base and suppliers can make money, which will motivate them to invest in the development, distribution, and maintenance of product and service offerings.

Sometimes K–12 market dynamics do not provide the appropriate incentives for the existing market leaders to innovate on their current product and service offerings. Purchasers might not yet recognize emerging user needs, they might have a pain point but struggle to articulate it in an RFP, or they might know what they need but be risk-averse in pursuing an as yet "unproven" strategy. In the absence of clear and compelling demand, established players have little economic incentive to assume the increased risk of innovating on existing products. Meanwhile, entrepreneurial upstarts have trouble breaking through the regulatory and procurement maze to challenge incumbents' hold on the market. This misalignment of incentives leads to the perpetuation of the status quo in the markets, which all too often lack sufficient focus on student performance as a key metric. This presents an opportunity for philanthropy.

Ultimately, sustainable markets require long-term commitments of significant resources to innovate, market, distribute, and support products and services. Philanthropists should invest directly in the supply side only when there are insufficient economic incentives for vendors or commercial investors to do so themselves. Even in these circumstances, donors should consider the ongoing marketing, distribution, and R&D required to sustain solutions in a healthy marketplace, not just the short-term investment required to create something new. Where sufficient economic incentives exist but are misaligned with learning outcomes, philanthropists should consider alternatives that might reshape incentives toward performance rather than only pursuing direct investments in new solutions.

NONCOMMERCIAL FUNDING TO STRENGTHEN MARKETS: EXAMPLES OUTSIDE OF EDUCATION

We share our emerging thoughts on how these ideas apply to K–12 markets later in this chapter. But first, this section describes some familiar examples outside of education to help illuminate the framework.

The Evolution of the Internet

In the 1970s and 1980s, scientists and computer experts had a way of communicating with one another through their computers.[1] At the time, this was a relatively niche interest and the nature of the opportunity for the commercial sector was unclear. The networks that enabled the connectivity were developed over time through a mix of private, government, and university funding. Packet switching, developed at MIT and government labs, was a foundational innovation that contributed to DARPA's creation of ARPANET, which connected the computer networks of university and government research labs. Later, the National Science Foundation's NSFNET provided access to supercomputer sites from research and education organizations.

Together, ARPANET and NSFNET provided backbone infrastructure that eventually led to the commercial Internet as we know it today. They were funded by noncommercial capital. Eventually, as more businesses and households bought personal computers, the interest in connecting to services and other users grew. Commercial Internet service providers began to emerge in the late 1980s and early 1990s. It remained unclear for a period of time whether there was much opportunity for commercial investors and companies, even as consumer demand grew for access to the Internet and the World Wide Web. Government and philanthropic support acted as a bridge between an unclear commercial opportunity and the incredible explosion of value that occurred as the Internet transitioned to a ubiquitous utility that catalyzed a technology revolution.

One inflection point was the development of the Mosaic browser at the National Center for Supercomputing Applications, funded in large part by the National Science Foundation. The browser drove enormous value creation and provided a free user-friendly tool for the general public to take advantage of the power of the Internet and World Wide Web. The Mosaic source code was used as the base for early commercial browsers such as Netscape and Internet Explorer in the early 1990s. Even though commercial players eventually captured large market shares, the nonprofit Mozilla.org continues the Mosaic tradition of innovation with a range of open software applications such as the Firefox browser (which they now operate through a for-profit subsidiary). The attempt to meet customer needs with free offerings sometimes raises user expectations of commercial offerings and leads to innovation across a product segment.

Once the commercial potential of the Internet became clearer, the need for noncommercial investments in infrastructure to support it diminished rapidly. ARPANET was decommissioned in 1990. The Internet was essentially commercialized in 1995 when NSFNET was decommissioned, removing the last restrictions on the use of the Internet to carry commercial traffic. Figure 8.2 illustrates how noncommercially funded activity shifted from the lower left to the upper right over the last 20 years as the supply-and-demand dynamics changed.

We are not suggesting that noncommercial funders were acting purposefully to strengthen market incentives in the lower boxes of the framework—the activity evolved organically alongside influxes of commercial capital that spurred innovation in areas such as the router technologies necessary to connect networks of computers. Once the market took off, the noncommercial activity in the top-right box became more deliberately focused on standards and quality. Open software applications are intended to give consumers high-quality alternatives to commercial offerings. W3C and ICANN are standards-setting bodies that govern the issuance of domain names, among other activities.

Challenge of Vaccines in Developing Countries

Sometimes donors take more deliberate action to strengthen and harness market forces for social purposes. Vaccines in the developing world are a good example.[2] Many children in developing countries do not have access to vaccines that—if

**Figure 8.2. Noncommercial Funding During Market Evolution
of the Internet and World Wide Web**

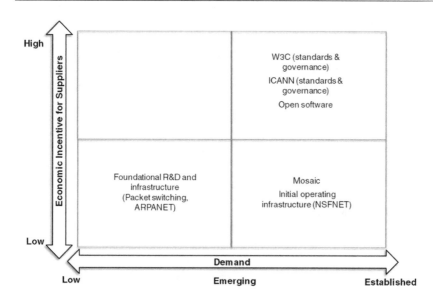

available—could save millions of lives every year. There are no vaccines for some of the diseases that cause the greatest burden of sickness and death in developing countries—including malaria, tuberculosis, and AIDS. For other diseases, safe and effective vaccines already exist, but may need to be adapted to resist extreme temperatures or to protect against a particular disease strain that is common in a given region. In some cases, the high costs of vaccines and other legal and clinical barriers have delayed access to new vaccines in poor countries by 20 years or more.

A group of developed countries and philanthropists have created a new mechanism called an Advanced Market Commitment (AMC) to spur vaccine development or adaptation in ways they hope can be economically sustainable over time. AMCs have the potential to stimulate the development of vaccines for developing countries. Because these countries often have little ability to pay, manufacturers give priority to providing vaccines for industrialized markets where their investments can be recouped more quickly. AMCs for vaccines provide the prospect of sustainable markets in developing countries and initial sales prices that allow vaccine makers to recover their original investment. This provides vaccine makers with incentives to invest in manufacturing plants needed to develop these vaccines and produce them on a large scale. It also gives developing countries the purchasing power to buy vaccines at prices they can afford over the long term, thereby creating an addressable and sustainable market for the vaccine makers.

One of the first AMCs is focused on vaccines for pneumococcal diseases, the leading killer of children worldwide. Pneumococcal vaccines do not exist because the diseases mostly occur in developing countries that cannot afford to pay the same price as developing countries. Therefore, pharmaceutical companies lack sufficient incentive to support the R&D necessary to create new vaccines. In order to address this market challenge, the Bill and Melinda Gates Foundation and five national governments—Italy, Canada, Norway, Russia, and the United Kingdom—have committed $1.5 billion for an AMC to purchase pneumococcal vaccines once they have been developed.

Although vaccine development is important, even when they exist at affordable prices (creating the kind of incentives suppliers need to focus on the market), many developing countries need financial support to plan and implement large-scale immunization programs in order to increase the reach and effectiveness of the vaccines. When philanthropists fund these types of planning and implementation activities that are usually outside the scope of commercial capital, they help strengthen the market for the long term, even when suitable economic incentives for vaccine purchases already or will soon exist. Philanthropic investments focused on the development of high-quality vaccines are necessary but not sufficient. Investment in strengthening the capacity for delivery of the vaccines is important to achieve the intended impact of preventing diseases, even when economic incentives for vaccine development are in place. Figure 8.3 illustrates these approaches. Product development alone is far from sufficient. Philanthropists should consider all aspects of a system, including the marketing, distribution, and ongoing R&D efforts that are required to ensure the intervention's long-term scaling and sustainability.

Applying the Ideas to K–12 Education Markets

What can education philanthropists take from these examples to inform their work? How might they approach commercial segments of the K–12 education markets so that over the long term, incentives support high-quality offerings that improve learning outcomes? There is no magic formula for figuring out how to strike a productive balance. In fact, because markets are by nature dynamic, the best answer today might become outdated quickly. But it can be helpful to have some guiding principles. Our approach is to start broadly by analyzing the dynamics at the segment level (e.g., instructional materials) rather than the specific opportunity (e.g., a specific digital math product). This helps inform a larger view of what is happening for many buyers and sellers, rather than focusing solely on whether a particular product or service needs philanthropic funding to develop or grow. Figure 8.4 is an overview of our proposed approach.

**Figure 8.3. Philanthropic Activity Aimed at Strengthening
  Vaccine Markets in Developing Countries**

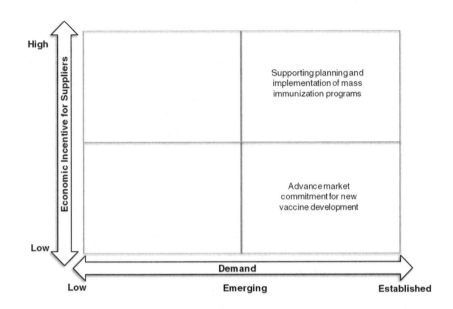

**Figure 8.4. Proposed Approach to Philanthropic Investments
  in Each Quadrant**

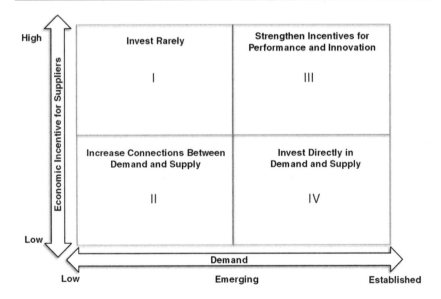

Our goal in this section is not to be comprehensive or overly analytical, but rather to introduce some early ideas as clearly as possible. With this in mind, rather than provide examples from multiple K–12 markets, we stick to one large market space and work through some relevant segments to illustrate key concepts. What follows is a way of thinking about philanthropic investments in K–12 curricular and instructional content and delivery, a space that is gaining increasing attention from customers, suppliers, and commercial and noncommercial investors due to factors such as broad adoption of Common Core State Standards and the shift from print to digital. Many (though not all) examples of specific investments are from the Gates Foundation's Next Generation Models (NGM) team. This is simply because we know them best, not because they are better than other examples that might be familiar to readers.

Quadrant I: High Economic Incentive, Low to Emerging Demand. Where *economic incentives are high for suppliers but demand is low,* philanthropists should invest rarely and then only to support demonstrated demand. The primary examples of this kind of opportunity are large, single-site custom technology projects. We are not implying that these projects are unimportant or misguided—just that they meet the needs of a limited user base, and suppliers are usually sufficiently rewarded for meeting those needs because buyers have or can mobilize public resources to fund them. Occasionally, a project in this quadrant might still make sense for strategic philanthropists. Perhaps the project is too risky to justify spending public dollars and/or too expensive to be covered fully by onetime state and federal grant programs. Occasionally, a pioneer in this situation might need capital to try something that could create a new paradigm or a proof point to catalyze broader market solutions.

In 2011 and 2012, the Gates team worked with a CMO on a project that initially fell in this quadrant. As a blended-learning pioneer, this CMO rapidly increased the number of digital curricular products in its instructional program over a few years. Quickly, the number of applications with different logins and approaches to identity management coupled with distinctive data formats became a barrier to their ability to manage the personalized instruction they were trying to deliver. Every great new learning product they wanted to add made the problem worse. Their initial funding request was for an in-house custom-built platform to serve their data integration and application interoperability needs. They had scanned the market and were not convinced that the leading vendor doing similar work for school networks could meet their needs, but they did not want to go through another school year with a manual approach to their problem. As an investor, the Gates team was reluctant to fund a single-site custom solution given the trends it saw toward broader market solutions to the problem over the next few years, but the team also generally agreed with the school operator's assessment of the current state of the market.

In the end, the Gates team challenged the operator to find at least two more like-minded school networks who would agree to use a common, temporary platform that could meet their shared needs while waiting for other market activities to shake out over a couple of years. They did, and Gates funded the development of custom software for application interoperability and the cloud-based hosting service necessary to operate it as a shared service for multiple school networks. It was just good enough, not a technological breakthrough.

Over the following year, the market accelerated much faster than the CMOs or the Gates team predicted. Many high-profile charter networks began to move more rapidly toward blended models, a number of new blended school operators emerged, and public dialogue about blended learning grew in school districts. As a result, more entrepreneurs responded to the opportunity. After the first school year of operation, a number of new providers had entered the space with cost-effective solutions. After significant scenario analysis, all involved agreed the best path forward was for each CMO to issue an RFP articulating their interoperability and integration needs and to retire the temporary solution earlier than planned. The school operators had developed a much more concrete and sophisticated understanding of their needs and were able to clearly articulate them in a consistent way, even though they issued separate RFPs. The RFP responses included the leading provider from the year before, as well as entrepreneurs who had launched companies since then.

In the end, it is impossible to know how much the decision to support a consortium of CMOs on a temporary common platform helped accelerate more entrepreneurial activity to address the attractive market opportunity, but had the Gates team funded an expensive, long-term, custom solution for a leading blended CMO, we would have taken one of the most sophisticated customers out of the market for several years. This most likely would have had dampening effects on the incentives for innovation on the supply side at the very beginning of a new market opportunity.

Quadrant II: Low Economic Incentive, Low to Emerging Demand. In the lower left quadrant, *where economic incentives are low and demand is low,* philanthropists occasionally have an opportunity to fund projects that strengthen market dynamics. This could help some solutions eventually meet the needs of a larger customer base so that sustainable business models can be built around them. We call this approach "improving connections between demand and supply." Instructional tools that customers usually build in-house are a good example. A teacher or IT staff member in a school or district might create an instructional module that meets a local need. Economic incentives for suppliers are low because it seems like an isolated or unique need to the customer, who creates it from scratch. Because of this, these types of applications usually don't attract much attention from vendors, even though they might already have or could build a solution to meet the need in a cost-effective way. But what if it were possible to make demand for these kinds of products more visible and solutions easier to find and implement across many customers? This could help buyers realize that some of their needs are not so unique and encourage them to try existing offerings rather than creating duplicative tools from scratch. Funding application and content aggregators like PowerMyLearning can make such offerings more widely accessible and interoperable with one another. PowerMyLearning has aggregated more than 300 learning applications—quickly building toward 2,000—and is mapping them to Common Core, then making them available on a destination website. Creating a one-stop shop for relatively low-demand resources could help shift buyer behavior toward using existing resources more often. Of course, there are a growing number of for-profit providers of this service, so nonprofit offerings like PowerMyLearning will have to deliver superior service and develop a sustainable business model in order to create long-term value for customers.

Another current example of a segment in this quadrant is adaptive literacy products for blended schools. These schools, which aim to integrate technology in their curricula to personalize learning for students, seek adaptive courseware that allows students to operate autonomously in either a "learning lab" environment or within in-class rotations, typically in 30- to 60-minute blocks. Although many school leaders seem relatively satisfied with the available math products, they are not satisfied with the flexibility or performance of the available literacy products. Because this is still a relatively small market, and given the high fixed costs of developing such tools, vendors have not yet made sufficient progress in defining and developing new products.

What is the role for philanthropy in such a case? Are there options other than investing directly in a developer to create a point solution and hoping it meets all customer needs? Over the long term, it is better for schools, teachers, and students if many high-quality providers are competing to meet their needs. One approach would be to help a number of blended schools clearly articulate the problem they need a product to solve, then use philanthropy to fund a prize to spur product development activity among vendors to address the problem. Mobilizing many innovators to create solutions generates far more investment than the cost of the prize, and highlighting the accomplishments of winners can send strong signals to the market about what products that meet customer needs look like. A slightly different approach could be supporting a buying consortium of blended schools to issue a joint RFP for a product that meets certain criteria. The schools would commit to buying the product that best meets the RFP criteria, thereby creating a sufficiently large and well-defined market to elicit investment from prospective vendors.

Over time, strategic philanthropic investments in this quadrant could move some activity toward the upper right quadrant (III), where economic incentives and demand are high, thereby driving innovation, affordability, and sustainability.

Quadrant III: High Economic Incentive, Established Demand. What is a productive role for philanthropy *where demand is established and economic incentives are high?* Because this is part of the market that works relatively well, donors should tread very carefully in this space. As mentioned earlier, opportunities exist to reshape incentives to focus on outcomes, including improvements in student performance. Although economic incentives can be high in certain K–12 market segments, demand is sometimes ill-informed or not well articulated, resulting in weak expectations and metrics for performance. Commercial suppliers will respond to demand and deliver against baseline customer requirements, but not overinvest in innovation ahead of demonstrated demand, given pressures to deliver returns to shareholders. Philanthropists can partner with buyers and sellers to strengthen incentives for innovation and performance but must be careful not to erode positive economic incentives in the process. Opportunities that fit this area include better market information, stronger incentives for performance, and a limited number of content and distribution exemplars.

Increasing the transparency and quality of information about the performance of products can be a valuable role for philanthropists. One way donors can do this is to fund rigorous evaluations of the effectiveness of products. Another is to support efforts to make customer information more visible. EdSurge, a new entrant into the education media landscape, is developing a set of reviews and ratings for education technology products by starting with the content and applications most used by the emerging blended model schools. By incorporating the voices of teachers and school leaders who actually buy and use these products, this kind of effort has the potential to create much stronger customer-focused and performance-based incentives for suppliers by organizing and distributing reviews through a trusted channel.

Investing directly in supply through content exemplars presents a dilemma. The instructional materials market segment has large revenues and healthy margins and is experiencing a transition from print products to a mix of print and digital. Although it can be valuable for philanthropy to help really innovative solutions get traction to push a new vision, too many philanthropically subsidized providers could dilute economic incentives and drive out commercial capital. Over the long run, a vibrant ecosystem of providers needs commercial capital and for-profit players. If philanthropists make it harder for companies to compete because of an abundance of free or below-market-rate offerings, commercial investment becomes harder to attract. This places the burden largely on philanthropy and government to support ongoing innovation, scalability, and sustainability through nonprofits. Given the relative strengths of commercial and noncommercial investors and the amount of risk capital they have at their disposal, this outcome would be suboptimal.

When considering an exemplar strategy, philanthropists should try to clarify their underlying assumptions about the impact an exemplar is designed to create. Some topics to consider are:

- *Market need:* Do customers lack a clear sense of what they need or are they simply having trouble articulating it in an actionable way? Do vendors lack the capacity to drive innovation in a particular area or are the incentives weak or misaligned such that they are hampering innovation? Is there an existing solution available that could meet the need well if customers knew about it or if the provider improved it based on feedback from buyers?
- *Business model:* If development is funded by philanthropy and it is available for free, how will quality and distribution be sustained over time? If created in partnership with a revenue-generating nonprofit or for-profit, how will intellectual property rights work? Are there different pricing models for different users depending on the funder's mission? What implications does this have for the offering's long-term viability?
- *Time frame:* Is the goal to create a new offering that establishes itself as a long-term part of the market, or is it more important to put up an early example of what is possible to create new demands from customers that existing or emerging suppliers can respond to and innovate against over time?
- *Path to market impact:* What is the hypothesis about how the offering will influence the trajectory of a market segment? What is the likely competitive response from existing players? Are there opportunities to partner with one or more suppliers to leverage their existing distribution channels to scale the exemplar if it proves more effective in driving student achievement than existing options?

One well-known example in this category is Khan Academy, a nonprofit that is helping to shift the public's idea of how short video lessons and learning analytics can be used by students and teachers for personalized learning, in and out of classrooms. A great, free solution can help shift entrenched ideas about teaching and learning and thereby open up new opportunity for lots of players. These types of offerings can also raise buyers' expectations, which can push developers of premium products to meet or exceed the features and performance of the free option. A push of this nature can help shape incentives for innovation and quality as providers attempt to grow or sustain revenue.

But there are potential downsides to free exemplars, even if there are only a few in a market segment, especially if they begin to capture significant market share without evidence of superior performance or a clear plan for financial sustainability. When purchasers face shrinking budgets, it's possible for a popular free offering to claim market share and reduce the ability or willingness to pay for products that might actually perform better. Given education markets' weak performance signals, over time this can dilute incentives for innovation and quality in unhealthy ways. The $8 billion instructional materials and assessment markets likely can include a healthy mix of free and premium offerings from established and emerging players, but regardless of their corporate form or pricing strategy, all should be evaluated based on results for learners with their effectiveness data made available broadly. However, if too many free offerings drive out commercial investment, the weak track record of sustainable nonprofit business models means that the capital requirements for long-term innovation and quality are much larger than philanthropy or government can sustain successfully.

Ultimately, some philanthropists will continue to fund exemplars to demonstrate new possibilities in certain market segments, but these investments should be pursued with a clear understanding of the broader market dynamics. This will help maximize the short-term and long-term positive impact of the exemplars and at the same time minimize the potential for negative impact on functioning markets.

Quadrant IV: Low Economic Incentive, High Demand. Philanthropy can play an important role in the lower right quadrant, *where economic incentives are low but demand is high.* In other words, even though plenty of demand exists for a product or service, something about the way the market works is creating barriers for suppliers. These factors include market fragmentation and procurement policies that make it difficult to aggregate demand. Market segments that are in transition to new customer expectations can also create demand that is out of sync with existing economic incentives. In this quadrant, philanthropists should consider careful direct investments in demand and supply with an eye toward shaping incentives to help activity move toward quadrant III where demand and economic incentives are both high.

On the demand side in quadrant IV, philanthropists can fund proof points and growth of effective blended school models to expand demand for great personalized learning tools by enlarging the customer base. Donors can also help groups of schools and districts join forces to better understand their shared needs and practice smarter demand by more effectively articulating their requirements for higher-quality solutions at more affordable prices. In this spirit, the nonprofit company Digital Promise has assembled a "league of innovative schools" that will serve as a test bed and demand consortium for innovative learning technologies.

Disconnections between user needs and purchasing decisions can also create incentive mismatches. In K–12, the decision maker is usually a district administrator, committee, or school principal. In some states, these buyers are required to choose from a list of suppliers or products approved by a state board or department of education, which are even further removed from the daily work in classrooms. Teachers occasionally have input into school and district curricula planning discussions, but rarely participate in the actual purchase decision. This creates a gap between the needs of teachers and students as users and the decisions made on their behalf. One promising idea on the horizon is to put resources into the hands of teachers through "electronic wallets" so they can directly purchase learning applications for their students. Merging the buyer/user role more tightly should create much stronger market signals about what teachers and students need and which products and services meet those needs. This also gives philanthropists a way to fund demand that strengthens market incentives for innovators. With a subsidized demand activity like this, the goal should be to test its effectiveness, then help it migrate to regular district and school budgeting processes through reallocation of curriculum from other procurement mechanisms.

Direct investments in supply in this quadrant should only be pursued in close partnership with buyers. For example, nine states and a philanthropic alliance that included Gates and Carnegie Corporation formed the Shared Learning Collaborative (SLC) in 2011 to create a shared open-source infrastructure for data integration and application interoperability. The market is moving quickly to data-rich learning applications that have the potential to transform the learning trajectories of millions of students. One barrier to their full potential in terms of market penetration and student outcomes is the difficulty teachers and students face in making all of these great tools and applications work together to create a full picture of student learning. This is a large-scale manifestation of the same problem faced by the CMO in our quadrant I example.

Addressing this challenge could create enormous value for product segments in quadrant II and III. Because of the historical fragmentation of the K–12 markets, data integration and application interoperability costs are currently so high that they either go unmet or pull scarce resources from other priorities. Educators are faced with the challenge of trying to make the various data-rich instructional tools they use work together effectively for their students. As more appealing and effective instructional solutions become available, the bigger the burden on teachers.

No proprietary player has sufficient incentives or legitimacy to address the problem in the near term in ways that support a more open and competitive marketplace. And K–12 education does not have government agencies such as DARPA to make significant R&D and infrastructure investments.

The SLC partnership between states and philanthropic funders is designed to help state, district, and school investments in learning technologies work better together through a catalytic infrastructure investment. Existing and emerging suppliers can leverage the SLC's open-source infrastructure to serve their customers better and invest more of their R&D dollars in making their products better rather than solving interoperability and integration challenges over and over.

The nine participating states have the potential to aggregate demand for innovative solutions, learn from one another about how to articulate clearly their needs in RFPs, and hold suppliers accountable for delivering against those needs. This has the potential to enable a multistate performance-driven marketplace for applications, content, and tools from many providers—for-profit and nonprofit,

Figure 8.5. Illustrative Examples of Investment Types in Each Quadrant

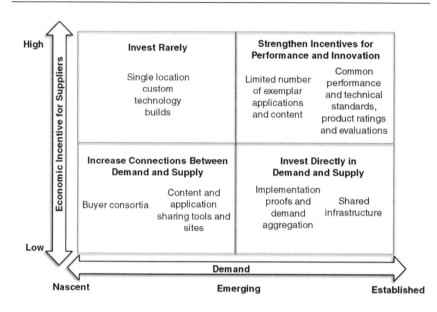

existing and emerging. In February 2013, the SLC transitioned to inBloom, Inc, a new nonprofit charged with stewarding the underlying technology. Over time, the project should strengthen performance incentives and drive value in the upper right of the framework by making it easier to evaluate products based on their performance and by aggregating sufficient demand for more breakthrough innovation in learning applications.

It is possible the market will move in ways that eventually make inBloom's shared infrastructure unnecessary. If this happens, the decommissioning of ARPANET and NSFNET provide good historical examples of the graceful retirement of catalytic infrastructure investments that outlive their usefulness. Figure 8.5 illustrates some of the examples discussed in each of the sections on the four quadrants.

CONCLUSION

Philanthropists who fund projects that operate in commercial markets have an opportunity to deploy their scarce capital in ways that strengthen the overall market, thereby leveraging commercial investment and for-profit activity to achieve their goals. In this chapter, we have proposed a way of thinking about how to do this.

Because incentives are a powerful tool, philanthropists should think carefully about how to strengthen them to meet their goals and avoid creating unintentional consequences. Donors should be cautious in segments where economic incentives are high by investing rarely and with the specific goal of shaping incentives for innovation and performance. Except in rare instances, we believe aggregating demand, helping buyers better express their needs, and making those needs more visible to suppliers will be more promising than investing directly in products. In segments where economic incentives are currently weak, philanthropists can invest more directly to help jumpstart market activity and serve as a bridge to healthier ecosystems with better choices for buyers and users in the long term.

Because our thinking is still evolving, the framework we propose is not intended as a prescription for donors or a comprehensive explanation of the Bill and Melinda Gates Foundation's current approach to giving in these areas. Rather, we aim to document our early thinking about how philanthropic dollars and projects interact with K–12 commercial market segments and what the implications might be. As the ideas are discussed, debated, reshaped, and put into practice, they should become more practical and useful. We hope they evolve into a guide for donors who see promise in harnessing the power of commercial markets for positive social impact.

CHAPTER 9

Between Efficiency and Effectiveness

Evaluation in
For-Profit Education Organizations

Matthew Riggan

My research team huddled around a speakerphone in a small conference room. On the other end of the call was the leadership team of an education firm that had developed an intervention we had studied and were preparing to release findings on. The study was not a summative evaluation—we were not looking at test score data or graduation rates, for example—but its findings nonetheless raised concerns. Overall, implementation of the intervention appeared to be weak and inconsistent. And research tells us that even the best interventions have little effect when implemented poorly.

The discussion that followed was awkward and at times a bit surreal. The company's leadership took an aggressive tone with us yet did not substantively challenge our findings. Instead, they argued that we had misunderstood the intervention and what it was designed to accomplish. It was neither fair nor reasonable, they suggested, to expect the level of organizational impact that we had indicated was missing. Further, they argued that we had conducted our fieldwork in sites with known implementation problems, implying that we would have seen a different picture had we looked elsewhere.

We were disconcerted. The company itself had nominated the sites. We had asked for best-case scenarios—places where things seemed to be going particularly well. And our expectations for impact were considerably *more* conservative than the claims made by the company in its own promotional materials. At the outset of the study, company leaders had pressed us to take a closer look at quantitative outcomes like test scores, confident that we would find evidence of impact on student learning. Now a kind of amnesia had appeared to set in. What happened?

Our findings certainly supported the idea that the company had overestimated its influence on schools, but a lot of other factors may have come into play as well. Schools and districts change quickly. The difference between being an exemplar and a cautionary tale can be as small as a leadership change, and it is not at all hard for a school to make that jump over the course of a few years. On top of that, reform gets harder as scale increases. Rapid growth almost always means greater variability in outcomes and often leads to quality-control issues.

In sum, the context in which school change happens can shift, often dramatically, in a short time. A research study designed at the beginning of that period is unlikely (and often unable) to adapt to those changing conditions. Yet findings from the study will be published nonetheless.

Such is the dilemma of independent, third-party research. Once the evaluation genie is out of the bottle, it is awfully hard to get it back in. As researchers, our job is to have some distance from the interventions we study. Our task is to present findings—good, bad, or in between—based on our best analysis of the evidence. But for the interventions we study, those findings can have real consequences. The findings may be picked up by the media, influencing public perceptions. They can be taken into account by funders or investors or become the subject of political debate.

This is especially true for for-profit education firms. Although some such companies, such as textbook publishers, have operated comfortably in the field for decades, relative newcomers such as proprietary colleges, online learning ventures, and education management organizations have encountered skepticism, scrutiny, and outright hostility. They are also much more sensitive to the market because their revenue comes from investors, shareholders, and customers rather than grants or categorical funding streams. Public perceptions can seriously impact the bottom line, and evaluation findings can certainly shape public perceptions. When the *New York Times* ran a story questioning the performance of online schools operated by K12 Inc., the company's stock price plummeted 34%. A subsequent shareholder lawsuit alleged that the company misrepresented the performance of its schools, and it is not implausible that the outcome of the suit will hinge at least in part on the credibility of the performance data the company presented to investors.[1]

In this chapter, I examine the current state of evaluation practices among proprietary organizations in K–12 and higher education, with a specific focus on organizations whose work bears directly on student outcomes. I describe how these organizations view evaluation work, what they choose to focus on and why, the assets and capabilities they bring to the work, and the challenges they face. From a policy perspective, I explore the question of how to encourage transparency and rigor in the evaluation practice of private enterprises while allowing them to do what they do best—innovate and attract investment. I argue that for-profits in education tend to do two things especially well: use customer feedback to drive improvement and monitor outcomes in light of resource allocation. On the other hand, there remains a lack of rigorous, third-party evaluation of most for-profit institutions and the products or services they offer. I argue that this is primarily because in education little overlap has existed between the concerns of shareholders and of policymakers. I conclude the chapter with general suggestions for how policymakers might address this disconnect. As preceding chapters remind us and I demonstrate, for-profits are only superior when incentivized to improve educational services.

OPPORTUNITIES AND SCRUTINY FOR FOR-PROFITS

A better understanding of evaluation practices among proprietary education firms is important for two reasons. First, the role of these firms is steadily expanding. In higher education, the number of students served by for-profit colleges and universities has exploded over the last decade, though this group still comprises a small share of the total student population.[2] Meanwhile, private-sector involvement in K–12 education stands poised for similar expansion.

For-profit firms have always held an established and recognized place in the public education infrastructure, frequently receiving contracts for security, information technology, food service, textbooks, and curriculum materials. Recent federal policy has created increased demand for supplemental services, many of which are provided by for-profit firms.[3] For example, the 2001 No Child Left Behind (NCLB) legislation dramatically increased demand for providers of supplemental education services (SES), such as tutoring and remediation, which underperforming schools are required to offer their students. The market for these services—funded through Title I dollars—is now estimated at $2.55 billion, up from $1.75 billion in 2001.[4] In 2003–04 alone, the number of approved providers for SES increased 90%, and for-profit firms comprised half of all providers at the time.[5] NCLB also led to the unbundling of many comprehensive school reforms (which themselves had been developed in response to the availability of federal funds) into curriculum or professional development initiatives.

More recently, the Obama administration's focus on turning around low-performing schools has created a large and growing market for school turnaround specialists. School improvement grants account for about $3.5 billion in the Title I funding states receive, and school turnaround models are prominently featured in the Race to the Top initiative. Further, adoption of the Common Core State Standards by most states will profoundly impact the curriculum, textbook, and assessment markets. Each of these initiatives has presented new opportunities for both for-profit and nonprofit firms.[6] New standards require new assessments, which in turn require new (or updated) curricula, programs, and supplemental materials or services. Aided by both Race to the Top and influential philanthropies, a push toward expanding charter schools (both virtual and bricks-and-mortar) and even voucher programs has further expanded the window for private-sector involvement in the management of K–12 institutions. Between 1998 and 2010, the number of public (district or charter) schools operated by for-profit firms grew from 131 to 739, and these schools now serve around 353,000 students.[7]

Second, opportunities for expanded private-sector involvement in education at all levels have prompted concern, criticism, and calls for closer scrutiny of the practices of these firms. In higher education, this has led to congressional inquiries and investigations and drawn the attention of the U.S. Department of Education. In particular, proprietary colleges and universities are now regulated based on the amount of debt their students incur relative to what they can expect to earn as a result of obtaining a degree.[8] Institutions that fail to meet this "gainful-employment" standard no longer qualify as institutions where students can spend federally subsidized loans or grant funds. (Given that in some schools these dollars account for 90% of all revenue, this effectively constitutes a death sentence.) Additionally, proprietary colleges have been required to curb aggressive recruiting practices and awarding bonuses for recruiters based on the number of enrolled students.

These changes, coupled with a weak economy and some bad press, have contributed to dramatic declines in enrollment in proprietary colleges during 2011.[9] Although these measures arose from concern that some institutions were placing an unsustainable debt burden on their students while failing to prepare them to get and hold jobs, they effectively imposed a standard (for both performance and reporting) considerably more demanding than that used to judge public institutions of higher learning.

In K–12 education, public, private, and nonprofit operators of public schools have for the last decade been held accountable for performance. But signs point to increased scrutiny for proprietary firms, especially with regard to online and blended-learning models. This is due partly to general questions about how well virtual schools can educate children, partly to the fact that in some states reimbursement rates for virtual schools are comparable to those for bricks-and-mortar schools despite lower costs, and partly to general resistance to new teaching and learning models. In any case, this increased scrutiny points to even greater emphasis on evaluation and outcomes for proprietary K–12 operators in the future.

THE ROLE OF RIGOROUS EVALUATION

Evaluation can be formative or summative. Formative evaluation focuses on feedback to drive improvement, while summative evaluation focuses on generating evidence of impact or lack thereof. As University of Illinois, Urbana-Champaign evaluator Robert E. Stake puts it, "When the cook tastes the soup, that's formative;

when the guests taste the soup, that's summative."[10] Each plays a critical role in the lifecycle of any intervention. Research and development efforts rely heavily on formative evaluation, while the long-term success and growth of an intervention often hinges on whether evidence of its effectiveness can be supported by summative evaluation.

Formative Evaluation and R&D

Every education intervention is intended to solve some kind of problem or address some kind of need. Some needs are educational (teaching and learning problems) while others are organizational. What kind of problem an organization is trying to solve shapes the role of research and formative evaluation in product development and field testing. As is the case for most academic work, products and services that private companies develop are informed by research on particular topics. As such, the research and development (R&D) process begins with learning from existing research rather than designing new studies.

The focus of this preliminary research takes one of two main forms. One branch starts from an established need (for example, delivering effective professional development in mathematics) and seeks to use existing research to identify an effective response to that need. For example, the READ 180 program was developed by researchers at Vanderbilt University based on their work exploring factors associated with reading difficulties among older students.[11] The lead researcher, Ted Hasselbring, partnered with Scholastic to further develop and refine the model to bring it to market.

The second branch is more market-focused. It seeks to identify a size and type of need (for example, "nontraditional" college students or home-schooled children) and determine the extent to which currently available products or services are addressing that need. To borrow from Michael Horn's discussion of the role of "disruptive innovation" in education, the former might be viewed as research on "sustaining innovations" (doing something we already do better), where the latter would be more disruptive (serving a need or market that does not fully exist yet).[12] Online-learning systems offered by companies like K12 Inc. and Kaplan fall into this category, as they seek to fundamentally reconfigure (and in some cases even replace) the basic organization (resources, staffing, time, and physical space) of schools and classrooms. This type of preliminary research focuses more on emergent demand, along with prospective changes in the policy climate (the expansion of voucher legislation, for example).

Formative evaluation plays a critical role in the R&D process both before and after products or services are brought to market. While still in development, products are evaluated using focus groups and field testing coupled with user feedback. An interesting aspect of this stage is the importance of qualitative research methods and approaches focused on how consumers use a product or service, their satisfaction with it, and the degree to which they report it as benefiting them. Asking teachers about the utility of a given curriculum and its impact on their teaching plays an important role in understanding whether it is likely to gain traction in the marketplace, even though such self-reported measures are considered weak in traditional research and evaluation. For example, the design research team at Pearson Education created a "usability lab" in which users of products in development can interact in real time with research staff while the research team observes their use of, and response to, these products.[13]

Once products are brought to market, utilization and implementation become central to formative evaluation. The implementation challenge is something of a chicken-and-egg problem. We are more likely to see impacts where implementation is the strongest, but weaker implementation often indicates design problems rather than user error. Part of the purpose of formative evaluation is to improve the ability of all customers to utilize the product or service to produce results. Doing so successfully both expands the base of potential customers and improves satisfaction. Not surprisingly, then, companies go to considerable lengths to learn how broadly and well their products are being used and to collect feedback on problems or possible improvements. In summative evaluations, these customers (teachers, for example) are in effect mediating variables—the means through which a product might achieve an outcome. In formative research, they are part of the field testing process. For example, Scholastic and K12 Inc. both solicit real-time feedback from users of their online products, including reporting problems or glitches but also ease of use and overall utility. In addition to embedded feedback, formative evaluation also relies on more traditional measures such as user surveys and focus groups. And because the materials are online, the companies can revise them in real time to respond to this feedback.

Summative Evaluation: Generating Evidence of Effectiveness

In 2001, the U.S. Department of Education's Office of Educational Research and Improvement was renamed the Institute for Education Sciences. The name change signaled a pronounced shift in federally funded education research: Descriptive, process, and implementation studies (along with virtually all qualitative methodology) were out, and randomized, controlled trials were in. How reforms were conceived, designed, and implemented became ancillary questions. What really mattered was "what works," with "working" defined primarily as showing significant effects on standardized tests compared with a randomly assigned control group (or some approximation thereof). This shift has pressured reformers to demonstrate that their initiatives are effective based on these criteria. Doing so could open new markets for providers, especially where supplemental services or school turnarounds (both of which require schools or districts to adopt evidence-based practices) are concerned.

It is perhaps surprising, then, that the narrow focus on test scores and experiments appears to be considerably less prevalent among private firms in K–12 education than in the policy and research communities. To date, very few products or services owned or operated by for-profit companies have been evaluated using experimental (or even rigorous quasi-experimental) methods. Among the ten largest for-profit education management organizations (EMOs), for instance, not one independent, third-party evaluation is publicly available, nor do research articles about any of these firms appear in peer-reviewed journals.[14] For curriculum and professional development providers, the record is slightly more substantive, with a handful of products or services offered by private firms subjected to rigorous evaluation. These remain the exception rather than the rule, however.[15] Several reasons exist for this, most deriving from the unique position that for-profit firms occupy in the education marketplace.

HOW THE PROFIT MOTIVE SHAPES EVALUATION PRACTICE

In many ways, for-profits and nonprofits are quite similar in their approaches to evaluation. Both use it to drive program improvement, seek positive findings to bolster their reputations and drive growth, and worry about the impact of negative findings. But they differ in two important ways, each of which influences their relationship to evaluation. First, whereas many nonprofits and public agencies operate on a fixed revenue model, for-profits do not. Second, for-profits operate, well, for profit: Either they earn more than they spend, or they go out of business.

Funding to provide education products and services can come from three basic sources. First, an organization can receive funding to provide services or products to a given population. The population that receives those products or services does not purchase or contract for them directly, and the revenues themselves are fixed. School districts and nonprofits that award grants use this model. Second, an organization can receive revenue in exchange for services or products provided—for example, tuition. In this case, the recipient of services purchases them directly from the organization, and the total revenue earned is a function of the number of paying customers. Third, an organization can benefit from investment that produces future financial returns. Such a model is possible only when revenues are not fixed.

As school choice (in its various forms) becomes more prevalent in the education landscape, some nonprofits are moving toward the customer-focused approach, making them less dependent on grant funding and more dependent on attracting and keeping customers. The reverse is decidedly not the case: For-profit companies do not function on a fixed revenue model. The fact that their revenue (and, consequently, their ability to attract investment) depends on engaging and retaining customers—and that it must exceed their expenses by some margin—significantly influences their relationship to evaluation work.

The "Best-Foot-Forward" Problem

For reasons both obvious and understandable, firms are cautious about proceeding with rigorous, third-party evaluations until they are confident positive outcomes will be found. In practical terms, this means that the product or service must be extensively refined and field tested prior to evaluation and the research must be conducted in sites where implementation is known to be fairly robust. Implementation research is exceedingly complex, however. It is not simply a matter of knowing whether formal program components are in place; those components must be used in a way that is consistent with the intervention's intent. And for all of the long-term focus on it, documenting changes in instruction or leadership remains time and resource intensive and is still an inexact science. Companies try to measure implementation in a variety of ways, including site visits, teacher surveys, and tracking use of online resources. All of these contribute to an enhanced understanding of how much variation in fidelity may exist, but they remain indicators rather than precise measures.

Uncertainty about implementation limits the ways rigorous impact studies can be conducted. For example, a research design in which schools are randomly selected to receive an intervention does not ensure implementation fidelity. On the other hand, randomly assigning students to a school or program already known to be strong can raise vocal objections from parents and educators not assigned to the program who are advocating for students who are not selected for the program. Reformers face a catch-22 situation: Rigorous, third-party evaluations are only desirable under ideal conditions, yet those same conditions tend to thwart rigorous evaluation.[16] Given this context, the scarcity of such studies is not surprising.

One strategy some companies adopt is to contract with lesser-known evaluation firms and keep their research in-house. If the results appear positive, they provide an initial basis for claims of effectiveness that the company can publicize. If they show little or no impact, the company can use them internally for program improvement without damaging its reputation. Larger companies may also pursue a similar strategy with their own research staff, conducting rigorous studies in sites where their products are being used but limiting dissemination of findings.

To be sure, the best-foot-forward problem applies to nonprofits as well. Negative evaluation findings can certainly undermine future fundraising efforts. But the link between the two is far less direct. It is exceedingly rare for a funder to terminate a grant early based on evaluation findings, for example. On the other hand, widely publicized research questioning the quality of a school or other intervention can have an immediate impact on student recruitment, enrollment, and retention, and could also have a chilling effect on investment. For both nonprofits and for-profits, damning evaluation findings can be harmful. But they can do more harm more quickly to for-profits.

If the Incentive Is Not There . . .

Although some firms may shy away from third-party evaluation because the stakes are too high, others may do so because the stakes are too low. Even for those for-profit companies that operate closest to the accountability press faced by schools, it is not always clear that rigorous, third-party research is required to be successful. A recent Government Accountability Office report on the What Works Clearinghouse (WWC) found that only 42% of surveyed districts had even heard of WWC, and those that had used its products to a "small to moderate" extent in making decisions.[17] (To date, no analysis of the impact of WWC findings on financial performance of education organizations has been conducted.) Accountability may be very real, but that has not necessarily led districts to clamor for better research.

Similarly, it remains unclear how important a company's track record of increasing performance is to state or district contracting or procurement decisions. For example, textbook adoption processes vary by state and are subject to an array of political and institutional pressures.[18] Performance data may or may not be a factor. Similarly, professional development contracting tends to be based more on local relationships than on academic performance criteria. As one executive I interviewed put it, "That's not how the [professional development] market works. The market purchases on an individual basis from the retired teacher that they know. And while it may be a $4 billion market, there might be 40 million providers." Getting a seal of approval from a third-party evaluator may well help in marketing and selling a product, but it is unclear that the absence of approval really hurts. For private enterprises in particular, if the customer does not demand something, it is difficult to see why firms would spend money and time delivering it, especially considering the risk that evaluation findings could harm the company. There may simply be more to lose than to gain.

This differs markedly from nonprofit organizations. For for-profits, the metrics that are most central are the ones that relate to profitability. Whether their customers are families or state departments of education, there is no reason to invest in rigorous research without demand for it. For nonprofits operating on a fixed revenue model, the exact opposite is true. Their customers are their funders. And funders, especially for large grants, demand independent, third-party evaluation.

The Market as Evaluator

Whole sectors of the education marketplace exist where schools orient to a completely different set of accountability pressures. Many privately owned, nonpublic schools serve middle- and upper-middle-class populations, relying primarily on tuition dollars for revenue. Their success depends on a steady stream of families who want to enroll their children. As such, they are judged primarily by the degree to which they provide students entry to higher (and more exclusive) levels of schooling. For elementary and middle schools, high school placement is a major outcome of interest; for high schools, college and university matriculation counts most. Such outcome measures require neither rigorously constructed comparison groups nor external evaluators. Schools that send their graduates to elite secondary or postsecondary schools will be in high demand. The market serves as the evaluator.

For for-profit firms, students, their families, and (in the case of curriculum or professional development) teachers are their customers. Thus, they direct an enormous amount of effort toward the question of whether the customers are happy and satisfied because this satisfaction directly impacts their bottom line. As I noted, these efforts often rely on more qualitative or self-reported measures that may be less valued by the research and policy community but are more closely attuned to what the firm cares most about: whether customers are satisfied, whether their expectations are being met (or exceeded), and whether they are likely to recommend the firm to others.

The preference for "voting with your feet" and customer satisfaction metrics over more traditional outcome measures in some sectors of the education market raises the question of where and under what conditions this preference is warranted or appropriate. If customers are exercising a choice and if they are happy, do we need more rigorous forms of evaluation? The answer depends on whom the product or service is serving and what the expected outcomes are. If the purpose of a mathematics program is to change how math is taught and thereby improve student achievement, whether or not the program makes teachers happy is only indirectly related to the outcomes of interest. In that case, the outcomes of greatest interest to the company providing the service and those of greatest interest to the public would appear to diverge. Similarly, it is common to find charter schools that fare no better than their noncharter counterparts using conventional metrics such as test scores, attendance, or even teacher qualifications yet are oversubscribed and boast high levels of student and parent satisfaction. Again, this would seem to be a case where more informal outcome measures miss the mark, since it is likely that widespread access to better evaluation would affect both enrollment and satisfaction.

A Focus on Measures of Efficiency

For-profits orient toward attracting and retaining customers because their revenue depends on it. But their financial success depends not only on revenue, but also on efficiency. It is not merely a question of what outcomes are produced, but of what level of resources is needed to attain them. Because education for-profits view outcomes in light of investment and resource allocation, they focus attention not only on getting better, but on finding more efficient ways to achieve a given result. This is most apparent in the case of higher education, where the performance of proprietary colleges and universities has primarily been judged from the stand-point of traditional financial metrics such as business performance, value of the enterprise, and stability of earnings.[19]

The emphasis on business performance necessarily focuses attention on re-source utilization. Taking their cue from management practices, most proprietary colleges establish key performance indicators focused on the relationship between investment and results, such as number of students per course or revenue per staff member, and track expenditures in all areas—from staff salaries to recruitment to energy use—closely. The image of bucolic, sprawling campuses may still reflect the university ideal, but for-profit colleges analyze the square footage per student when examining resource allocation. Students are the primary revenue source for these schools, and after staffing, facilities are their second biggest expense. Among large institutions, costs for new campus construction or return on invested capital may be factored in as well. These schools set specific goals for each of these metrics and evaluate managers based on whether or not those goals are met.

The same incentives apply to for-profit EMOs, often leading them to a more flexible view of how resources should be allocated. Although virtual schools have attracted the most attention (and controversy), in reality blended-learning models are much more common among for-profit EMOs. In these schools, resource al-location decisions are made based on whether students need close interaction with a teacher to achieve a given result or whether working individually with interactive software would achieve the same ends.

Investors in proprietary institutions (K–12 and higher education) use the lens of outcomes to differentiate strong education models from weak ones. But the companies that are most attractive to potential investors are those that achieve good outcomes but are not operating efficiently as they could be. These compa-nies can generate significant returns by improving their business processes and efficiency while maintaining education quality.

Contrast this with public education institutions, which operate in an envi-ronment where both revenues and resource allocation are constrained. One con-sequence of this basic fact is that the relationship between inputs and outcomes in public institutions is less direct than in the private sector. A school district is capable of raising additional funds when needed through tax increases or bond initiatives, but these are increasingly politically difficult to push through and can be time-consuming. And when such revenue increases are approved, it is almost always on the grounds of need (for example, responding to population growth or change), rather than performance. Budget-cutting battles are fought along the same lines. Further, extensive regulation coupled with contract provisions limits the flexibility of public institutions when it comes to resource allocation. Less flex-ibility and control over revenues and expenditures leads to less emphasis in the public sector on the link between investment and results.

In a recent paper focused on how state systems can encourage schools to make better use of scarce resources, Karen Hawley Miles and colleagues noted several problems with how states and school systems allocate and use resources. Rigid requirements focused on class size and student–staff ratios, compensation systems based more on longevity than performance, cumbersome and procedural tenure and dismissal processes, seat-time requirements for credit accrual, and in some cases contractual provisions limiting classroom support for teachers all result in schools that have little room to maneuver in seeking to improve performance or use resources effectively.[20] A recent analysis by the Center for American Progress found large discrepancies in spending among districts that achieved similar results and served students with similar demographic characteristics.[21] The report concluded that how education dollars are invested could potentially mean the difference between progress and stagnation.

Under these conditions, districts have far less incentive to operate efficiently. Nonprofits operating on grant funds are often not permitted to run surpluses of any significant size, while public entities that do so run the risk of appearing to receive too much funding and thus exposing themselves to cutbacks. The lack of focus on efficiency has created an asymmetry in the amount and quality of data available in public, and some nonprofit, organizations. An extensive and growing body of data is focused on outcomes, but few if any clear, transparent metrics exist to track resource allocation.

Reputation and Competitive Advantage

Although formative evaluation is critical to the development of some products or services, for some firms it can also be perilous. This type of evaluation involves identifying what is not working in order to fix it. Perhaps more important, it involves documenting those shortcomings, in the form of either quantitative outcomes or customer feedback. The intense scrutiny some private firms face—in some instances extending all the way to the subpoena of emails and internal documents—has made them reluctant to engage in this process for fear that both internal and external formative evaluation results will be interpreted and used in a summative manner, hurting both their reputations and bottom lines.

Another concern among for-profit companies relates to intellectual property. These companies compete with both public-sector institutions and with one another. Just as conducting formative evaluation requires firms to generate data about what is working and what is not, analyzing outcomes relative to investment requires documenting what data are collected to conduct those analyses and how the analyses are conducted. If profitability is based on not only outcomes but also efficiency, sharing information—voluntarily or not—about how efficiencies are achieved amounts to surrendering competitive advantage.

In each segment of the marketplace, for-profit companies may view evaluation differently depending on the degree to which they believe they can benefit from it (or conversely, the degree to which it can harm their competition). Whether in K–12 or higher education, supplemental services or school management, companies with established track records or strong evaluation capacity tend to see opportunity in increased accountability. Provided that the playing field is level, they see evaluation as a way to differentiate themselves from their competition.

In K–12 education, organizations such as America's Choice, which boasts a strong evidence base for the effectiveness of its programs, use evaluation results to great effect in their marketing materials. America's Choice prominently features research findings about its various products (school design, literacy, and mathematics programs) on its website, focusing specific attention on results demonstrated through independent research and evaluation efforts.[22] Similarly, the website for Scholastic's READ 180 proclaims, "READ 180 is now the most thoroughly researched reading intervention program in the world. Hundreds of studies, peer-reviewed journals, and the federal government's What Works Clearinghouse have all documented its effectiveness on student reading achievement."[23] To support this claim, the company publishes a compendium of research focused on the intervention and links to all of the reports and research it cites in making claims of effectiveness.[24] Pearson Education highlights its history of commissioning independent, third-party evaluation for its curricular products and routinely releases summary reports from these studies.

In higher education, proprietary colleges seeking to claim academic effectiveness aggressively publicize data related to learning and career outcomes in marketing and communications materials. For instance, the University of Phoenix publishes an Academic Annual Report focused on student learning outcomes using a variety of measures.[25] The report provides data on student and alumni satisfaction, student engagement, self-reported learning outcomes, information literacy skills, academic proficiency, and degree completion rates. Similarly, Capella University devotes significant space on its website to learning and career outcomes, as it reports faculty ratings of student skills, student and alumni satisfaction, and self-reported learning and career impacts.[26]

The profit motive influences the types of evaluation that for-profits deem necessary and the types of data they collect as a result. But it also influences the degree to which they use evaluation findings to make decisions. Since the late 1960s, analyses of policy and program improvement have shown that evaluation findings have little influence.[27] Many reasons exist for this (politics not the least among them), but the underlying structural problem is that evaluation work is loosely coupled with program design and decision making. Put another way, evaluation is traditionally driven more by demands for technical sophistication than by the questions that planners and practitioners actually need answered. The result is that most evaluations are underused or ignored altogether.

For-profits are certainly subject to the same internal political and organizational dynamics that can compromise the use of evaluation findings. But they also have certain structural advantages that make it less likely that the findings will not be useful. The focus on efficiency (outcomes attained relative to inputs) is based on the assumption that changes will increase profitability. To borrow a phrase from Michael Quinn Patton (2002), this type of evaluation is designed with explicit attention to "intended use by intended users." This focus, coupled with the flexibility that for-profits have to quickly reallocate resources, creates a much tighter loop between evaluation and management than is normally the case in the nonprofit or public sectors.

FOR-PROFITS, NONPROFITS, AND
THE ACCOUNTABILITY LANDSCAPE

Without question, changes in the education policy environment are raising the profile of evaluation work focused on the private sector. How this shift is perceived depends a lot on what kinds of products and services a company offers, as well as its position relative to its competition.

When it comes to private-sector engagement in education, significant differences exist between types of companies. Supplemental service providers compete with one another, but they rely on the public school system for revenue. Tension often exists between such providers and school districts. No Child Left Behind stipulates that parents can choose which providers to use for their children and that the districts must pay for those services. Providers therefore have an incentive to recruit students, while districts have an incentive to restrict that recruitment to limit the damage to their bottom line.[28]

For all of this competition, however, these providers are decidedly *not* trying to put school districts out of business, nor do they pose any real threat to established interests in the field, such as school boards or unions. Not surprisingly, these enterprises respond to the same accountability pressures that drive public education institutions. In many cases, the products and services they offer are tailored to help schools (and in some cases, parents and families) respond to these very pressures.[29] When No Child Left Behind legislation called for districts to offer students in low-performing schools access to SES such as tutoring, it also stipulated that those providers demonstrate evidence of student improvement within 2 years. Providers were quick to claim such benefits (with varying degrees of credibility), presenting themselves as helping schools respond to a federal mandate. These organizations (both for-profit and nonprofit) designed and marketed services intended to complement traditional reforms rather than replace them. In these instances, little difference exists in the treatment of for-profit and nonprofit organizations within the marketplace, since they both occupy a similar position within the accountability landscape.

By contrast, enterprises that actually seek to operate schools (whether in K–12 or higher education) compete directly with public school districts or state colleges and universities. Although many private higher education providers argue that they serve a segment of the student population the public system neglects, they also recognize that, appropriately or not, the public sector does not regard them as benign, and they see increased (and in some cases special) scrutiny at least in part as a response to the perception that they are a threat.

For-profit involvement in the management of K–12 schools is newer, and though it has expanded quickly, less than 1% of K–12 students are educated in public schools run by private companies. But the development of online and blended-learning models in K–12 education, coupled with an increase in privatization of public schooling (through vouchers, charter schools, and other initiatives), is creating a range of new opportunities for such providers. These developments stand to eat away at district budgets and weaken the influence of school boards and unions. Coupled with political and philosophical concerns about whether private companies should be running schools, this has prompted stiff resistance and calls for increased scrutiny similar to that experienced by higher education providers.

Private enterprises attempting to push into the traditionally public sphere may view calls for greater accountability and evidence of effectiveness with a jaundiced eye. In higher education, research showing comparatively higher tuition rates and debt loads for students in proprietary colleges has been decried as unfair because most public institutions are subsidized with taxpayer dollars.[30] Similarly, efforts to ensure that student loan debt is in line with projected earnings based on degree attainment and choice of field are viewed as cumbersome regulations.

The adoption of the gainful-employment standard certainly appears to create a different set of accountability measures for for-profit colleges. Before the ascent of proprietary colleges, public colleges and universities had little accountability for student performance, in part because there is still no real consensus about how to measure college and university performance. As noted in a recent *Chronicle of Higher Education* report, a lack of clear standards, criteria, or even guidelines for determining what type of work merits college credit creates myriad problems, including systemwide devaluation of credits and an inability to distinguish between high- and low-quality institutions.[31]

Why the double standard? Ironically, proprietary colleges' focus on efficiency may be partly to blame. Institutions operating on fixed revenue may have little reason to become more efficient, but by that same measure they have little incentive to cut back on resources invested in students' education. The perception—warranted or not—that proprietary colleges seek to cut corners is part of what justifies the double standard for evaluating them.

More recently, the use of a different standard for proprietary colleges has come under some scrutiny. An interesting—or disturbing, depending on one's point of view—byproduct of the push to examine returns to education for students in proprietary colleges has been a groundswell of interest among some states in conducting similar analyses. As Kevin Carey wrote in the *Chronicle* report,

> The "gainful employment" regulations that the Department of Education is working to impose on for-profit colleges are nothing less than a repudiation of traditional higher-education quality control. . . . How long will it be before politicians who see higher education as nothing more than a way to train future workers simply cross out the "for profit" limitation on the gainful employment measures?[32]

There are early indications that this is already happening. As states face pressure to reduce budgets, they have begun asking which aspects of a college education are most likely to benefit their economies. Florida governor Rick Scott was roundly criticized for questioning whether having so many students majoring in psychology or anthropology would benefit either them or the state. Yet states need as many gainfully employed professionals as possible to sustain or grow their tax base. Like it or not, it is not hard to see why a governor would wonder whether some fields of study might do more to achieve these ends than others.

This in turn has implications for secondary education, for which the primary outcomes of interest in recent years have been 11th-grade test scores and graduation and postsecondary matriculation rates. Adding the question of what going to college actually does for a student economically casts a different light on what it means to be "college-ready," opening up new lines of research and evaluation. Indeed, in addition to online and blended-learning models, some investors in proprietary schools have suggested that career and technical education—high schools focused on career preparation, much like current offerings for associate degrees—may represent a significant market opportunity.

Among conventional bricks-and-mortar schools, we see little difference in the accountability pressures that public, nonprofit, and for-profit institutions face. All public schools are accountable under federal law, all are required to test students annually and disaggregate the results by subgroup, and all face sanctions for repeated failure to meet performance expectations. Among private schools, all are judged by their ability to provide students with access to more and better educational options at the next level (either high school or college), and all are accountable to the families of their students.

Among schools that adopt nontraditional models, the accountability picture is more complex. Online, blended, or self-directed learning models use more flexible pacing than traditional approaches and thus may be ill-suited to high-stakes annual assessment. Echoing an argument made by proprietary colleges, companies that operate or support such schools note that they tend to appeal to students who have struggled in traditional environments and thus serve populations that perform well below grade level in core subjects. Further, participation in these schools tends to be more fluid, with students moving in and out of them more frequently than is the case in traditional schools. Some of this is likely because high-need students are also highly mobile or because online schools simply do not work for everyone. But in some cases it is also by design, with students rotating through online programs for remediation, enrichment, or credit recovery purposes. Given this fluidity, assessments administered annually—snapshots, essentially—may not effectively capture the impact of these schools on student learning from the time they enroll to the time they exit. This is similar to the challenge some alternative schools face; these schools also serve high-need populations, depend less on the traditional school calendar, and are more likely to base progress on mastery (demonstration of required skills and competencies) rather than number of years in the system.[33]

USING EVALUATION TO PROMOTE EFFICIENCY AND EFFECTIVENESS

When it comes to evaluation, this analysis suggests the profit motive presents both significant opportunities and barriers. In addition to individual firm characteristics, for-profits' approach depends on which sector of the education market they occupy (K–12 or higher education; supplemental services, operations, or some combination of the two). However, two common characteristics do appear across most companies in terms of what they choose to measure and how. First, for-profits in education focus heavily on the customer experience and prioritize customer satisfaction. The result is an evaluation approach that emphasizes ongoing user or customer feedback that can drive product improvements or management decisions. In current research and evaluation circles, such indicators would be considered weak—potentially helpful for contextualizing other outcome measures but of little use on their own. Conversely, it appears that although at least some for-profits are adept at exploiting positive evaluation findings when they have them, they do not have an overriding concern with justifying their products or services using rigorous third-party evaluation. This may be because such evaluation is related only loosely to the financial performance of a given product or service. Second, academic performance—however it is measured—is analyzed alongside other organizational performance indicators related to operational efficiency. For-profits use evaluation to identify how they can get better results for their students, but they also consider whether they could get the same results with fewer resources.

In an era when schools, districts, state universities, and community colleges face relentless pressure to cut budgets and where public disaffection with schools is high, we can learn something from these two areas of emphasis. Although many large school districts administer parent surveys, few would argue that they prioritize customer service or that they are particularly responsive to user (in this case, teacher and principal) feedback. This more developmental, formative approach to evaluation, focused on improving the user or customer experience, would be a welcome change in the field of education. Similarly, measuring performance as the relationship between inputs and outcomes rather than simply the outcomes attained would appear vital to getting the most from the dollars available to education institutions.

On the other hand, the lack of rigorous, third-party evaluation of many for-profit operators raises concerns about how prospective consumers should make informed decisions about whether to purchase their products or services and about whether the claims made by such companies in marketing materials are justified (though we should note that these concerns are not confined to the private sector). Among some critics, such concerns are compounded by the profit motive. Clearly, it would be nice if a large evidence base existed for a wide range of educational institutions, products, and services. But historically there has been little reason to think that the outcomes of primary concern to policymakers and regulators in education overlapped with those of shareholders.[34] Good evaluation is time-consuming and costly, and investment in it does not guarantee that the client will like the results. It is therefore only reasonable to expect the prevalence of rigorous evaluation to increase if the policy climate creates incentives for that to happen.

The adoption of the gainful-employment standard hints at what is possible when education performance metrics become more closely aligned with financial ones in the sense that it is causing proprietary colleges and universities to play close attention to the indicators it effectively enshrines. But it also highlights the challenges inherent in trying to encourage such alignment. In seeking to address concerns about profit motive trumping other outcomes, the government has effectively established a performance standard for proprietary colleges that does not exist anywhere else and has dictated that one particular indicator (projected earnings relative to debt) is more important than others—including the degree to which a student makes real learning gains while in school. This is an exceedingly blunt instrument.

So what can policymakers do to promote evaluation—both within and outside the for-profit sector—that retains a focus on efficiency while more fully addressing questions of effectiveness? The first step relates not to evaluation per se, but to the flexibility of schools and school systems to manage resources well. Establishing performance indicators and operational metrics linking resource allocation and other outcomes is of little use if leaders do not have latitude to redeploy those resources when the data indicate that it would be prudent to do so.

A second step would be to find ways to more closely align incentives for educational and financial performance. At the postsecondary level, this would require working toward greater consensus around a set of minimum performance standards for colleges and universities. This would be, by definition, reductive—one would not expect all colleges to do the same thing. For many occupations, these standards already exist in the form of certification or licensing requirements. In other cases, establishing them would involve identifying a small number of things that one could reasonably expect every college and university to do, such as teaching students how to write well. Whatever these measures are, they should be proximal to the educational work of universities rather than tied up in long-range labor-market outcomes over which schools have limited control.

At the K–12 level, this would mean rewarding schools more for performance than for enrollment. The phenomenon of oversubscribed but underperforming charter schools suggests the need for either greater accountability in how they are monitored (revoking charters for schools that fail to meet performance targets) or greater incentives for meeting performance goals (having a tiered system of per-pupil reimbursement depending on performance). Neither of these would be easy to implement, but both would go a long way toward aligning public and private goals and desired outcomes for education.

Finally, policies could be developed to encourage states and school districts to weigh rigorous evidence more heavily in decisions about resource allocation and contracting. Done correctly, this could tighten the coupling of educational and financial outcomes. Taken together, policies such as these would increase both the quality and use of evaluation data in and outside the education private sector.

CHAPTER 10

Would Steve Jobs Be a Hero if He Had Built an Education Company Every Bit as Good as Apple?

Chris Whittle

When newspapers report on Starbucks, Singapore Airlines, or tens of thousands of other companies, the headline does *not* begin with phrases like "the for-profit coffee company" or "the for-profit airline." That these entities are organized with earnings as one objective is assumed and accepted without controversy. To call it out would be viewed as redundant, similar to saying "vote-seeking congressman runs for election!" However, when the media covers a proprietary education enterprise, it is virtually a sure bet that the headline will include the words *for-profit* (such as "for-profit school seeks to . . ." or "for-profit college announces that . . ."). It is as if the media want to flag that there is something different or new or, I'll go ahead and say it, perhaps *bad* about these organizations. And then, in the reader's mind, the questions, thoughts, and—most important—emotions begin. Is a for-profit school right? If profit is flowing away from a college, isn't the quality of the college compromised? Isn't there an inherent conflict between shareholders and the interests of children? Shouldn't schools be just like charities?

As founder and CEO of two proprietary education entities (Edison Schools, the company generally viewed as having played the leading role in the early days of the charter school movement, and Avenues: The World School, a new global schooling initiative with campuses planned in the world's leading cities), for over 20 years, I have fielded these questions from reporters, critics, parents, and faculty. I have discussed them across hundreds of dinner tables with friends and family. When AEI asked me to write about this topic, I jumped at the opportunity. Far from a chore, the assignment provided an opportunity to catalog, organize, and— most important—interpret hundreds of discussions about a topic that is likely to be a growing theme in education circles around the world in the century ahead.

As the organization of this chapter will soon reveal, I confess to writing with a strong point of view. Do I believe for-profit organizations are messiahs that will singularly solve the world's educational problems? No, I do not. Rather, I think that much of the discourse on this topic is and has been ideological and/or emotional in nature, sometimes skillfully nudged in that direction by opponents of the private sector, many of whom have different kinds of profits of their own to protect. Logic and a grasp of how business and economies actually work have largely been absent from the commentary.

This chapter explores the emotional logic behind knee-jerk reactions to for-profit status; such is the natural starting point for a volume that seeks to provide context to the for-profit debate. Part I of this essay recaps frequently raised questions and arguments about this issue and my responses to each. As you will see, although I understand how these concerns can be raised, I don't believe they have much merit. Differentiating based on tax status makes little sense when the goal is to provide a high-quality education. Part II notes questions that are almost never asked, as these are revealing in their absence. Part III attempts to address this question: If there is little logic in the typical questions and concerns, then why do they continue to be raised?

PART I: ALL THE ARGUMENTS, NONE OF THE REAL REASONS

The Flawed Theory of Singular Motivation

When campaigning, labels matter. Think, for a moment, about the words *for-prof-it*. When one hears "for-profit education company," what does the reference evoke? For one thing, it sends the signal that profit is what the organization is *all* about. I cannot count the number of times that I've heard something along these lines: "A for-profit company is about one thing: producing returns for its shareholders. Nothing else matters." Ask yourself: Would anyone say that Steven Spielberg, a spectacularly successful producer of movies that have made billions in profits, is "only about profit"? In making *Schindler's List*, did he not have something else in mind beyond earnings?

Some people espouse the theory that quality education cannot be achieved unless an organization and its employees have only one motivation: providing quality education. To them, the introduction of a second motivation, such as producing a return for capital that has been deployed to provide quality education, pollutes the purity of an "education-only" mission and thus reduces the quality or efficacy of a school or college.

There are so many flaws in this theory that it is hard for me to know where to begin, but I will rest my case by discussing just one. Specifically, virtually all actions of individuals and organizations have multiple causes. So if this issue exists, then it exists in virtually *all* matters. Very few actions in life have a single motivation, regardless of the person, the organization, the tax status, or the field. Let me just point out a few examples to make the case, some from the field of education and some not. As you will see, there is no attempt to be politically correct here.

Do you believe that our best elected officials run for office *solely* on the basis of serving the public? For sure, it may often be their primary motivation, but other factors invariably come into play. Some *also* desire and enjoy the fame and the credibility that comes from effective service. (It never hurts to begin a meeting with "when I was governor"!) Others *also* want and like the power. Some are *also* campaign junkies. A few may even see it as the best-paying job they can find!

Do you believe that great newspapers are *solely* interested in providing "all the news that is fit to print"? That is certainly why many news vehicles were created, but virtually all of them *also* want to increase their circulation in order to produce more subscription revenue and advertising sales.

Do you believe that heads of excellent public school districts care *solely* about education? It may well be what drives them most, but they may *also* care about the great retirement benefits, see the post as a stepping-stone to higher office, and/or want their contract renewed in order to put bread on the table for their families.

And, do you believe that the sole motivation of nonprofit teacher unions is to improve schools? You'll find the mission statement of the American Federation of Teachers (AFT) interesting in that it contains a long list of motivations, with improving the lives of its members (teachers) listed first and "strengthening the institutions in which we work" (that would be schools) listed third.

The point? Lincoln, Roosevelt, and Kennedy all wanted to do good things for their country and the world, but they *also* needed to win elections to do so. The AFT does care about children in schools, but it *also* wants to maintain and grow its membership in order to generate dues. A school district superintendent wants to improve schools, but she *also* wants to keep her job. No differently, Steve Jobs wanted to create the greatest computers and devices in the world, but he *also* tried to produce profits in order to build value for his shareholders and himself.

Very little in life is motivated by a single desire. Individuals trying to lead good lives or leaders trying to build organizations that provide something useful must balance multiple objectives in order to do something for the greater good. Producing profit (like winning votes, getting your employment contract renewed, or increasing membership dues) is just another objective to be managed. The presence of a profit objective does not mean that a for-profit school or college cannot *also* be the best educational institution in the world. (Nor does it guarantee it.) Most important, it doesn't preclude leaders of for-profit educational institutions from placing educational quality at the very top of their priorities or simply using profit as a tool to help fund their mission. Simply stated, a company can have a cause, and the best ones usually do.

An Imaginary War: Profit Motive Versus Educational Quality

There are those who believe that if you introduce a profit motive into education the institution will make decisions to achieve profit at the expense of educational quality. Again, this is one of those views that, unexamined, seems plausible, but when truly considered is highly simplistic.

To begin, let's test the validity of this "worry" by seeing how it applies to the most important "connect point" in education: the teacher and the student. How would the behavior of a teacher be any different in a nonprofit institution versus in a for-profit one? I can't think of one example. The actions of teachers in a classroom (methods of instruction, classroom management, and caring for children) are completely independent of a school's tax status. If the relationship of a teacher to a student is unaffected, then that is a huge step toward demonstrating that a profit motive and educational quality can coexist. Teachers are, we should remember, the most important determinant of educational efficacy.

Some might say, "All right, I'll take your point that it doesn't change how teachers behave, but the leadership of the school might make lots of profit-driven decisions that could negatively impact educational quality. For instance, they could hire less experienced teachers at lower salaries, increase class size, or decrease the quality of facilities—all in an attempt to reward shareholders." In some theoretical debate, that might be right, but in the real world, it isn't. The last thing the leader of a proprietary school wants to do is decrease the quality of education. Parents choose a school for its educational quality, and they can see when quality is being impaired. A good proprietary educational leader looks for savings *in things that don't matter educationally*, just as a thoughtful leader of an airline would never look to save money by cutting safety. Just one small example: Many private schools in highly urban settings buy up expensive contiguous real estate (often homes) in order to expand. It is very easy to spend $1–2 million per classroom going down this road—and the achieved classrooms are often subpar because the homes were never meant to be schools. The better plan: Build a school from scratch or find a large building that is suitable for conversion to a school. The result: *better* classrooms at perhaps 30 to 50% of the cost. Far from negatively impacting education, such a decision delivers a better educational result while also producing shareholder returns.

Looking at What Goes Out and Forgetting What Comes In

Imagine two private schools, each with a $20,000 per year tuition. School A is set up as a nonprofit and School B as a for-profit. Which one is better?

The first thought that sometimes goes through the mind of a parent or reporter or critic when contemplating the above is this: "If School B, the for-profit one, has money *flowing out* to investors, then it has less money to use for students and thus must be worse than School A."

Seems logical, right? However, it is not even close to correct. Although perhaps understandable as an initial reaction, that this thought might linger in the mind of a modern-day college graduate is a condemnation of not only the economic education our country provides but of how well we are doing in developing critical thinking skills. Why? Two big reasons.

First, profits do not flow out of many for-profit entities. Apple is, on a given day, the most valuable company in the world and clearly one of the great business successes. And yet it has not consistently paid dividends. Although a dividend is expected to be declared soon, the last one was paid in 1995. So what happens with all that cash? Apple reinvests it in different ways to accomplish its central mission: making highly innovative technology products. How, then, do its shareholders make money? On the value of their shares, not by profits "flowing out of" Apple.

Second, and perhaps more important, the above knee-jerk reaction leaves out fully half of the equation that should be considered. It focuses entirely on what supposedly "flows out" of School B and does not address "what flows in" to School B. We've already established that what "flows out" is more theoretical than actual. What "flows in," on the other hand, is very real. The definition of capitalism includes the word *investment*. If School B is a well-conceived for-profit school, then it is the beneficiary of the other half of the equation: capital. Before profits are ever taken out of a school, capital is invested into it, often for many years. Although many people view profit as a "drain on school resources," it in fact "buys" something for a school: capital. Think of profit as nothing more than the rent payment on capital. And does capital investment make a difference? Count the ways. It can be the difference in whether something even exists. It can be the difference in whether something is done well. And, most important, it can be the difference in whether something is changed for the better.

This piece is not an advertisement for a particular organization, and thus I'm hesitant to bring into the discussion something I'm presently involved in, but Avenues: The World School is a hugely relevant example of all of the ways capital can make a difference.

Leading cities around the world are starving for high-quality education options. For instance, *The China Daily News* recently reported that in Hong Kong waiting lists for private schools have reached record highs. In fall 2011, *The New York Times* reported that one top private school in New York had so many applications that it accepted only 2.4% of nonsibling applicants for its kindergarten grade. Harvard accepts 6% of applicants for its freshman class! Why is there such a shortage? In a sentence, to start a significant, top-flight private school in a major metropolis today can easily require $50 million to $100 million of capital. (Point of reference: Avenues raised $75 million just to launch its New York campus.) Without significant funds, you simply can't start a major, important school. Capital can thus determine whether a great new school even gets to open.

Next, capital can determine whether you are able to do something right. I see this every day that I go to work. Well before the first Avenues campus opened, there were more than 40 full-time team members working away on every aspect required for opening day—from faculty recruitment to curriculum design to construction management. Only someone who has been around a typical school launch knows that having a large number of "advance" people is important to a successful school opening. A typical new school might have three or four people on staff a few months before opening day and open with a classroom or two in highly limited facilities without the resources its founders would like. The difference: the amount of capital available.

Finally, capital is often the engine of change. It takes time and talent to figure out how to change schooling for the better (this is called research and development)—and time and talent cost money. At Avenues, we're looking to improve every aspect of schooling, and we are lucky to have the investment capital to do so. As just one example, because we want to be the best foreign language school in New York City, we plan to require students to begin a half-day immersion program in either Mandarin or Spanish at age 3 and to continue such a program for their first 7 years at our school. Hiring immersion consultants, visiting successful immersion schools around the world, and recruiting capable immersion faculty (all of whom must be bilingual) are innovations made possible by capital. And the impact of capital does not stop once an entity is created. Continuing reinvestment is an important part of any for-profit model.

There's No Free Capital—Not Even for Nonprofits

Reading the above, some might say, "But nonprofits can get the benefits of capital, and they don't have to pay for it." Wrong. Free capital is just as rare as a free lunch.

A couple of years ago, I was recruiting a CFO who worked at a nonprofit school. The candidate happened to mention that his school had about $40 million of debt. That's capital, and just like equity, it has a cost. That cost is called *interest,* and unlike equity, which can wait years for its reward via share price appreciation, interest is typically paid currently, usually monthly. It *is* something "flowing out." Counterintuitively, while most for-profit entities are not being "drained" by having to pay out cash to equity shareholders, significant numbers of nonprofits are actually paying out ongoing costs for their capital in the form of interest payments!

But, some might say, "Why don't we just set up a nonprofit that gets philanthropic contributions and has no debt?" Isn't that completely "free" capital? No. Gifts come with three kinds of costs. First, it costs money to raise the gifts—and sometimes real money, such as the salaries and expenses of development functions. (The next time you visit an Ivy League school, stop by the development department to get a sense for exactly how much.) Second, the greater cost is in the bandwidth from the organization's leadership needed to raise philanthropic funds. How many "nonprofit" college presidents have said off the record that they spend too little time on the academic aspect of their institutions because they are so consumed with fundraising? And, third, if debt has interest as its cost, the "strings attached" for gifts are the equivalent of interest payments. That's why every nonprofit prefers a gift to "the general fund" versus one that provides for a specific use, sometimes a use that is not the primary mission of the institution.

There are other issues related to using philanthropy as a capital source: Is there enough of it? Is it scalable? Can it be done everywhere, and is it sustainable? Regarding there being sufficient philanthropy, the Foundation Center reported less than $1 billion in total K–12 philanthropy in 2010 out of the $650 billion total K–12 sector expenditures. That means all current philanthropy runs U.S. K–12 schools for less than 1 school day. As another reference point, it is less capital than just one significant initial public offering (IPO). Regarding scalability, it is one thing to raise philanthropy for a single college or school. It is quite another to raise it for hundreds of schools, an issue that many nonprofit charter school entities are struggling with today. This is not the case with capital raised by for-profit entities. If an entity demonstrates that it can produce returns in a few situations, its access to capital increases and becomes simpler to raise. Regarding using philanthropy everywhere, it is one thing to raise philanthropic capital in a society that has a long legacy of doing so and quite another to attempt this in cultures where charity is viewed very differently. For example, there are colleges and schools all over the world that offer little or no financial aid (something that would be scandalous in America). Similarly, few colleges around the world enjoy the enormous endowments seen here in America. Finally, regarding sustainability, philanthropic funds are often linked to families or individuals who can change their minds, run out of money, or suddenly take leave of life. Philanthropic capital is one of the great goods of our society, and this is in no way an argument against it. It is simply a statement that it has its limitations and thus should not be the single source of capital for something so large and important as education.

There Is One Right Way—A False Dichotomy

Opponents of education provided by for-profit organizations like to frame the argument in a way that forces a reader or listener to choose between for-profit and nonprofit operation. "Do you want to get rid of *all* the nonprofit public schools?" "Do you want *all* of our schools to be run by corporations?" (To be fair, zealots of for-profit education can sometimes do the same arguing that the world would be better off if *all* schools were operated for profit.)

Who said there had to be "one best way" to provide schools? Forcing a choice that doesn't need to be made may be effective sloganeering, but it is not a good method of building a stronger educational landscape. What builds a better educational world is a panoply of educational options, all trying to be the best at what they particularly do. What the world needs is a "mall" of educational possibilities, not some Soviet-era arrangement where there is a single option. That's called monopoly, and it is one reason educational quality in the United States suffered in the last century. Sure, there were some religious and private schools in certain communities (although not often in smaller towns), but for the most part, there was a "single brand" of public schools. Two decades ago, the introduction of charter schools and the expansion of public school choice challenged that notion. Today there is a more vibrant educational setting. We are a long way from the highly differentiated world we see in other sectors, but one can now imagine a day when educational consumers will have dozens of schooling options from private to public, from nonprofit to for-profit, from bricks-and-mortar to hybrid to virtual. The idea that there is "one right way to do schools" should soon be a thing of the past.

Another Kind of "There Is Only One Way" to Do This

As noted above, many see the idea of profit in education as "draining away" resources from a school. Implicit in that point of view is the thought that there is only one way to run a good school, that there is some universal and ideal "cost structure" that produces an ideal education. Tampering with that single ideal (by inserting profit, for example) dilutes results. In what other sector is there only one way to do something well? Shouldn't it be at least conceivable that there are ways to redesign schooling for the better and that there might be some profit left for the capital that made the redesign possible?

Note: "There is only one way to do it" thinking is jingoistic as well. If the only way to run a good school is to spend $10,000 per year or more per pupil (roughly the average per-pupil spending in U.S. public schools today), then are the private school operators in India that provide it for $2 a month *all* wrong? If the only way to run a good school is to be small, then are the leading high schools of China (many with 4,000-plus students) *all* wrong? If the only way to run a good school is to have class sizes below 20, then why is most of Asia (with class sizes in some cases over 50) beating our pants off in international testing?

It Is Okay for the Parts to Be For-Profit, Just Not the Whole

In the late 1990s in a Duluth, Minnesota, school board meeting about the school district recruiting a for-profit company to run one of its schools, the superintendent presented members of the school board with a list of more than 100 "for-profit" entities with which the school district did business. They ranged from school bus services to dairies to computer manufacturers to textbook companies to, literally, the contractors that built the school building. He made the point, quite compellingly, that since schools are filled with products and services provided by for-profit entities, having a for-profit company run the school should not be a big deal. If so many of the parts are provided so nicely to schools by for-profit entities, then why could "the whole" not be?

The apparent logic of his position is so convincing that I find it hard even to theorize what argument someone might make to oppose it.

PART II: THE QUESTIONS NEVER ASKED

Could Proprietary Education
Be a Superior Alternative in Some Cases?

If those interested in this topic were being objective, wouldn't we hear the above question more often? Given that for-profit entities are the quality providers in virtually every other sector, isn't it strange that this question is largely absent from the discussion? Think about it. Have you even heard of a nonprofit airline? (There's one I can recall. It was Aeroflot, and it had one of the worst safety records on the globe. A friend of mine reported passengers bursting into applause upon safe landings.) Do you know anyone who owns a nonprofit car? (Do you really believe a nonprofit car manufacturer could compete with the likes of Mercedes or Honda?) Have you ever stayed in a nonprofit hotel or bought nonprofit shoes? If you think for-profit fast food is bad, can you even imagine a government-run McDonald's? The point: We look to the private sector for goods and services in virtually everything, and we are generally happy with what we receive. Why, then, would it not be the same in the world of education? That we don't quickly make that presumption is telling.

And Who Has Been Raising Education Prices
to Nosebleed Levels for Decades?

One possible reason to be against for-profit entities in education might be "Oh, they'll just gouge us to death in order to make a profit. If profit is included, then education will have to be more expensive." Hmmm. Let's ask ourselves this: What kind of entities have been raising educational pricing at breakneck speed for decades? Answer: *nonprofits.* The price of entry into *nonprofit* education has skyrocketed in the past 30 years. Tuition at America's colleges and universities (which are completely dominated by nonprofits) has risen dramatically, well over the increase in noneducational goods and services (most, by the way, provided by for-profits!). It is actually much worse than those figures indicate. The reason: Tuition is simply one way consumers pay for nonprofit private education. How about that annual gift that you are expected to give to your nonprofit college or school? When you factor that in, the true cost of nonprofit college and schooling has mushroomed at an unbelievable rate. (And the huge increase is one key reason students are being saddled with huge debt for college.)

The reality is very clear: The educational sector, dominated by nonprofits and government entities, has been raising prices at a much faster rate than those sectors where for-profits are the primary players. Would you not expect the reverse? What is going on?

Where Are the For-Profit Heroes?

What popular educational heroes are leaders of for-profit entities? Odd that I can't quickly name one! How are heroes made these days? Well, I think most of us would agree that the media play an important role—and there has certainly been no rush to lift up leaders from the for-profit education sector. Perhaps that's because there aren't any. Maybe it is because they've all been chased away! Or perhaps it simply isn't politically correct to recognize the good work of those in the for-profit education sector.

What we know is that there are plenty of press-made heroes in *other* for-profit categories. The late Steve Jobs surely leads the list, but he is not alone. The entertainment and sports industries are filled with popular heroes making millions, from Lady Gaga to Lebron James. And there are many completely deserving nonprofit educational heroes, from Wendy Kopp at Teach For America to Joel Klein for his leadership of the New York City schools. So why, in the hundreds of proprietary entities, large and small, in the educational space do we struggle to name one? Could it be that it is simply politically incorrect for the media to champion such an organization or individual? (An interesting "test case" will be to see if Joel Klein, a hero to many in the media when he was in the public sector, is bestowed that same honor when he undoubtedly advances education while at News Corp.)

Why Is There Less Debate on
For-Profit Education in India, China, and Brazil?

In India, educational entrepreneurs abound, often filling the very gap caused by the shortage of public schools. In China, there are more than 100,000 private schools (more than all the public schools in the United States—and large numbers of these are family-owned enterprises). Throughout Latin America, many college and universities are proprietary. Roughly 80% of the schools in the UAE are private—and most of these are for-profits. Even Sweden, certainly a left-leaning country, has instituted a national voucher system that allows children to attend for-profit private schools at government expense, and Kunskapsskolan, a for-profit provider, has now become the largest private schooling entity in Scandinavia. Why is the rest of the world "ahead of" the United States in this regard? How strange that "capitalism" in education is still somewhat controversial in the capital of capitalism!

PART III: THE REAL REASONS FOR RESISTANCE

As the above hopefully demonstrates, when discussion turns to the intersection of education and capitalism, the weaknesses in the arguments most often raised, as well as the questions left unasked, point to this conclusion: *Factors below the surface of this argument are more important than those being consciously debated.*

My original plan for this essay was to puncture the standard arguments and then hold forth with, as therapists say, an interpretation—a description of what was really going on. I had high hopes. I hate to disappoint you, but the second part of my mission has been far more difficult than originally predicted. Try as I might (and I did!), conclusively finding the *real* reasons for resistance to profit in the education sector has eluded me. At least to me, they remain mysterious.

So, I am left to share with you some intuitive guesses as to what dynamics might be driving the heat around this topic. Here are three thoughts for your consideration:

1. The Free Enterprise System in General Has Long Suffered from a Bad Rep— and That Continues Today. Putting aside the debate on the private sector in education, capitalism/free enterprise has a host of detractors in a much broader sense. Surely this is no news flash, as Occupy Wall Street and any presidential debate will indicate. The issue has been with us for a long time—the popularity of socialism among intelligentsia in this country many decades ago being a prime example. The extremes (such as income disparity) that free enterprise can produce, the harshness that many experience from it (such as the loss of their jobs), and its almost Darwinian nature make the ongoing unease understandable. However, objectively there is no doubt that it is the best economic system the world has yet seen. America is the largest economy on Earth, and no other country of our size enjoys our GDP per capita. The century-long, control/test experiment of America and the Soviet Union made a point we should not forget. That point was accentuated with China's clear success when it moved toward America's economic approach versus following that of the Soviet Union. Like the saying on democracy goes, "It is an awful system, but it is the best one we know." Still, the broader debate implicates materially the discussion within the education sector.

2. Our Children: The Last Stronghold of Innocence. Elongating the innocence of childhood is an objective of many, perhaps most, parents. Their feelings go something like this: "Why submit our children to the rough-and-tumble realities of the world any sooner than need be?" What does that have to do with this discussion? There may be some subtle transference of that feeling to this particular topic. A parent might think that a child being in an institution that has as one of its objectives a return on capital is some kind of innocence lost. There is not, in my view, much rationality to that position, as I would doubt that most children within a proprietary school even know that it is proprietary, but I can imagine how this might be a factor in how people process the topic. When critics of proprietary education have used the slogan "our children are not for sale," it would seem they are pulling on this particular heartstring—and with substantial emotional effect. Understandable as this feeling might be, *that does not make it right.* As noted above, it is hard to find any evidence that the caring nature of a student–teacher relationship is impacted at all by how a school's finances are organized. To make the point further, I would suggest that by far the greatest loss of innocence occurring within educational institutions today would be in the thousands of *nonprofit* public schools that education reformers have labeled "dropout factories." Though sentimentalism is completely understandable when it comes to our children, they need our tough-mindedness—particularly on matters that are critical to their well-being—as much as our love. Proprietary schools are not the only route to superior educational quality, but maligning them is likely to lead to a weaker educational world, and that's not good for anyone's children.

3. We're Being Cleverly Manipulated. Profit comes in many forms. Some consider profit to be self-interest. People and institutions have lots of self-interests. Sometimes these are in the form of financial gains. Other times they are of a more political nature. Particularly in the world of public education (which has been one of the primary battlegrounds of this debate), many institutions (from unions to school districts to politicians supported by unions) have interests to protect. They may see the introduction of private-sector entities into education as threatening *their* status quo, and to defend it, they may stoke an argument that, as the above vignettes clearly show, is easy to oversimplify or even distort. It's called demagoguery. As we all think about this topic, we should remember that there are those who don't want much depth or objectivity in this debate.

A SHORT CONCLUSION

If I have failed to uncover the complete mystery of this topic, I hope the above has achieved two things:

1. An understanding that this topic is a complex one. Beware of those bearing easy answers. They may not have thought about this much, or they may have thought about it a great deal and are not telling you all that you should know.

2. The agreement that there is no one right way. Be cautious when zealots advocate that there is one right way to do schools. There are many roads to great education. All schools are strengthened by a diversity of efforts, whether private or public, nonprofit, or even for-profit.

Conclusion

Michael B. Horn,
Frederick M. Hess, & KC Deane

In education, there's long been a tendency to correlate merit and moral worth with tax status. This shows little sign of changing. Even measured observers and thought leaders openly admit their bias against for-profit educational companies. Jay Mathews, who reports on American public education for the *Washington Post* and is a staunch supporter of reforms such as charter schools, has written, "I am biased against for-profit schools. I have long thought of them as diploma mills, without ever having visited one."[1]

The good versus evil meme characterizes the debate in Washington and the headlines of major newspapers when they report on for-profits. This can all impede efforts to deal with the more complex realities or to separate rhetoric from fact. This has stark consequences. In dismissing for-profits, educators and policymakers lose access to organizations that are uniquely agile and inclined to scale.

A more thoughtful discussion of these issues is eminently possible. President Obama's Secretary of Education, Arne Duncan, who has raised legitimate concerns about the role of for-profit colleges that fail to serve their students well, has also noted that the scaling power of for-profit universities is critical to the president's goals of boosting postsecondary attainment.

In this volume, we have not sought to "prove" or "disprove" the value of for-profit provision in the education sector. Rather, our aim has been to inform how educators, parents, policymakers, and citizens think through the thorny (and often uncomfortable) issues at play.

Although we have no illusions that readers will put down this book and come to wholly new views on the for-profit question, we do hope that it can help foster a more fruitful and constructive dialogue around the role of for-profits in education. To that end, a number of common themes emerged from the chapters that can help inform that discussion.

THE STRENGTHS AND WEAKNESSES OF FOR-PROFITS

A number of contributors explore the strengths and weaknesses of for-profit operators in today's education system—across the early child-care, K–12, and higher education landscapes. The advantages of for-profits include their ability to move more nimbly, to more readily attract capital and talent, and to scale more rapidly. The flip side of these strengths is that for-profits may be less rooted in community institutions, less stable, and more willing to cut services or personnel. Whatever the varied pluses and minuses, one of the more interesting takes may be Ben Wildavsky's observation that it's difficult to draw hard-and-fast descriptions about "for-profit" higher education versus more traditional higher education. His thoughtful reporting paints a complex picture, in which many of the casual stereotypes of for-profit providers appear upon closer inspection to be more caricature than anything else.

Ability to Attract Capital

In his chapter, Chris Whittle argues that the notion that for-profits suck money out of education is a myth; instead, he suggests the opposite is true. For-profits naturally attract capital from investors seeking to make a profit, while nonprofits—unable to promise a return on investment—more often struggle to raise funds. For-profits' ability to attract capital may be a real asset in an education sector that faces some lean years ahead.

Ability to Attract Talent

With an ability to attract capital comes an ability to attract top talent. Mickey Muldoon notes that for-profits can benefit from their tax status when it comes to attracting talent. For one thing, for-profit companies have the flexibility to actively invest their workers in the success of the company. Offering compensation opportunities such as stock options makes it possible to give employees a financial stake in the company, and to create the potential for outsized returns. Meanwhile, for-profits have far more flexibility than public systems to differentiate pay based on need and merit, and have shown more inclination to do so than have nonprofit ventures. When compensation and options are linked to individual or company performance, employees tend to feel a very direct sense of ownership in the company's success.

Ability to Scale

Because for-profits can more readily attract capital, they often have a far easier time scaling than do nonprofits and governmental organizations. Take online learning. For-profits' ability to attract capital has enabled their rapid growth in the digital environment. This in turn has allowed them to invest considerable research and development dollars into improving their products and services and advocating for the online-learning sector more generally. As Michael B. Horn points out, public policy can foster incentives that encourage for-profits to aggressively and energetically pursue socially desirable goals.

Incentive to Serve the Customer, Innovate, and Boost Productivity

Unlike nonprofits and governmental organizations, for-profits have a clear incentive to boost sales and grow profits. This creates a strong inclination to try a new model if doing so promises better success. New business practices can encourage innovation—and therefore improved learning—through a two-step process. First, if educators and parents are focused on quality learning, the need to please the customer can drive for-profits to channel their selfish energies toward finding ways to better support and promote student learning. Second, the search for profits prompts these companies to focus on efficiency and cost-cutting, whereas many nonprofit and governmental providers are much more loath to make unpopular or politically sensitive cuts. In an era of budget cuts and rising red ink, the incentive to become more productive with existing resources can be a particularly valuable trait.

The Flip Side

Of course, these dynamics all have their downsides. For one thing, for-profits are inclined to be exceedingly responsive to what customers desire. If customers want stuff that doesn't promote learning, that can be a problem. As Todd Grindal observes, many child-care programs in the prekindergarten market focus on easily observable characteristics such as cleanliness, safety, and staffing levels. These measures, however, have only a vague relationship to educational quality. Such an information asymmetry leads for-profits to invest in elements that attract customers, not necessarily those things that deliver great teaching and learning. For-profits' preference for customer satisfaction is a double-edged sword, one that proponents too rarely acknowledge.

Scaling, unless done correctly, can also present risks. Without policies that channel for-profits to deliver good instruction, they can focus on scaling via mass marketing, deceptive advertising, and cut-rate provision. In a variety of sectors, ranging from mortgages to banking, we've seen for-profits spend a lot of time and money lobbying for rules that allow them to grow in ways that are sometimes detrimental to the public interest.

In a similar vein, as Matt Riggan notes, for-profits may hesitate to commit to independent evaluation (to be fair, it's not like nonprofits or public entities have a terrific record on this count). Research carries risks: It can show that a provider is ineffective or cast doubts on a popular service or product. For obvious reasons, for-profits have special cause to be leery of such possibilities. Changes in perceived quality or reputation can quickly impact a for-profit firm's position in the marketplace. Meanwhile, the broader skepticism of for-profits, and the critical tone of much reporting, can leave providers especially gun-shy. Inaccurate or unfair interpretation of outcomes could hurt both their reputation and their financial stability.

EDUCATORS AND THE FOR-PROFIT QUESTION

In his series of interviews with actors in K–12's "new sector," Mickey Muldoon flags common misperceptions about for-profits and oft-ignored flaws of the non-profit model. Indeed, his central finding is that "neither [sector] is fundamentally more virtuous, socially valuable, or 'mission-driven.'" His interviews also surface another, perhaps surprising, conclusion. Even those comfortable with the for-profit framework in education are unwilling to fight for their expanded presence. As Richard Barth, president of the KIPP Foundation said, "You have to focus on what you want your battles to be, and this issue isn't my top priority."

Similar dynamics exist in higher education. Ben Wildavsky's interviews with for-profit administrators, board members, and instructors, all of whom have previously worked in traditional higher education, shed light on what caused these academics (a number of them accomplished and decorated) to move into the for-profit space. In particular, he sees flexibility and speed as two primary characteristics that attract new players to the for-profit sector, and argues that that traditional providers can learn a great deal from these virtues.

Wildavsky highlights the fact that individuals often enter the for-profit sector to escape the sometimes stifling organizational structure of traditional higher education. For-profit companies are generally more adaptive, Wildavsky reports, and this (while making them less stable and perhaps more "risky") is also integral to responding to the shifting circumstances and needs of the sector in general. For example, Harold Shapiro, former president of Princeton University and the University of Michigan, said of his transition into the for-profit sector, "There was a portion of the population that for various reasons was not being served by the traditional sector. I began to realize that there was potential for great social product there."

Leaving the public sector, however, comes with complications. In choosing to work in the private sector, educators report that they risk losing the respect of their former colleagues. Jorge Klor de Alva, who moved into the for-profit sector after teaching at UC–Berkeley, said of his former colleagues: "These are all people who identify what they're doing as a job to die for—how could you leave it? And yet I was putting that into question."

WHAT IS THE PUBLIC'S VIEW OF FOR-PROFITS?

John Bailey points out that the public has long supported private-sector engagement in other industries that tackle social challenges. NASA has contracted out with private companies to build space shuttles, Congress has given public funds from the American Recovery and Reinvestment Act to private firms working on renewable energy, and the military and intelligence communities utilize commercial partners in their efforts to improve operational capabilities.

Beneath the surface of the heated rhetoric around for-profits in education is also a more measured view, observes Andrew Kelly. Examining a raft of public opinion data, Kelly shows that the public is generally supportive of for-profit contracting for peripheral educational services in both K–12 and higher education, and it is comfortable with for-profit higher education institutions. Where the public is less comfortable is with for-profit management of instruction or entire K–12 schools. Interestingly, this general feeling cuts across party lines.

FOR-PROFITS AND FOUNDATIONS

In education today, philanthropy plays an outsized role in driving innovation and coloring the shape of reform. In our current inquiry, this poses a series of important questions about whether and how philanthropic investment can encourage free enterprise to invest in schooling and to devote its prodigious energies to finding quality ways to serve students and support educators.

As Stacey Childress and Tamara Butler Battaglino observe, markets have a powerful capacity to allocate investment capital in ways that fuel innovation, quality, and long-term viability. If philanthropists do too much to distort these dynamics, by channeling big dollars to the organizations and individuals who win them over with outsized passion and exciting proposals, they can give a big boost to flash-in-the-pan nonprofits that can't sustain themselves once the novelty wears off and the philanthropists decide to fund something new. Meanwhile, by elevating nonprofits that give their services away (or at big discounts), funders can undermine the ability of more sustainable and promising for-profits to thrive and succeed. On the other hand, Childress and Battaglino note that if philanthropists focus on investing in ways that jumpstart activity, set quality standards, or create common infrastructure that a variety of problem-solvers can build upon, they make it more possible to harness the creative energies of free enterprise.

LOOKING FORWARD:
MAJOR TAKEAWAYS AND POLICY RECOMMENDATIONS

Parents, educators, and policymakers have every right to be leery of for-profits in education. It's a free country, and we recognize that there are sensitive societal and cultural norms that bleed into these discussions. Indeed, some of those concerns are well deserved. Corruption and malfeasance do exist at some for-profits (though we'd note that the same is true of various nonprofit and public providers). We suggest only that it would be good for American education, for schools and colleges, and, most of all, for students, if we relaxed the reflexive vilification of for-profits and took more time to ask whether, when, and how they can help support great teaching and learning. With that in mind, we offer three quick thoughts.

First, we would do well to cease fixating on tax status as the key signifier of quality or merit. In truth, tax status says next to nothing about a company's motivations. Every venture has multiple motivations, and it seems to us unexceptional that one might be to turn a profit. That hardly seems out of place in American life, and it can (though it doesn't always) lend a healthy discipline and accountability. Rather than focusing on tax status, we should create policies that emphasize the primacy of student learning, and that deal with all providers accordingly.

Second, for-profits pose unique concerns, but they also offer unique strengths. Their sensitivity to market demand encourages greater attention to quality and outcomes. Seeking to be responsive to client needs, for-profit colleges have collected and employed data more aggressively than most of their nonprofit or governmental counterparts. Similarly, these tendencies encourage innovative practices, as for-profit companies hunt for new ways to attract new customers and remain competitive.

Third, the research community would do well to take for-profits more seriously than has often been the case. There exists only the most minimal research into the dynamics of the for-profit sector or the performance of for-profit endeavors. This is due in part to for-profits' reluctance to be studied, but also to the disinclination of many university-based researchers to study the for-profit sector. Indeed, we can testify from personal experience that a number of education researchers evince personal distaste for for-profits and thus, do not want to wade into the intricacies of these questions.

In seeking to exclude or dismiss for-profits (a tendency that is rarely observed in other public-sector endeavors), we reduce the ability of America's vibrant free enterprise engine to help tackle social ills or address critical challenges. Fields as diverse as health care, energy, defense, and space exploration all rely on for-profit participation. The federal government uses a variety of tools in these sectors to engage for-profit companies—from grants to loan guarantees and tax credits. An education space hungry for powerful problem-solvers would do well to explore the promise of such opportunities.

Today's policies do not incentivize the right things in K–12 *or* higher education. In traveling around the country, we are constantly amazed at the inability of even those working at for-profits to make a coherent case for their existence. Instead, they revert to vague claims that their venture does good and valuable work—only to prove unable to proffer any evidence to back such claims. Others just insist that for-profits aren't really any different from nonprofits, despite what policymakers and the public think, and complain that they should be treated just like everyone else. Needless to say, we find ourselves underwhelmed by such claims.

We believe that for-profits, and free enterprise more broadly, have a productive and valuable role to play in American education. But it is a role that has to be earned. Given public skepticism, for-profits need to make the case that what they offer is useful and important, and that the nation, our schools, and our students will be better if we welcome them in from the cold. We have produced this book in the hopes we can support just that kind of conversation. But it's ultimately the truth that only for-profits can make the case on their own behalf, by pushing for quality-sensitive policies, policing their own ranks for shysters and charlatans, supporting research that documents the value they deliver, and engaging in the public square.

Notes

Introduction

1. Kamenetz, 2010.
2. National Center of Education Statistics, 2011.
3. Moe & Quazzo, 2012.
4. Medina, 2010.
5. New Mexico Code, 2009, Section 22-8B-6.
6. Ravitch, 2011.
7. Harkin, 2010.
8. Samuelson, 2011.

Chapter 1

1. Petrilli, 2011.
2. U.S. Department of Education, 2011.
3. See, for example, Altman, 2010.
4. Quoted in Krigman, 2010.
5. Durbin, 2010.
6. Harkin, 2010.
7. Epstein, 2010.
8. Tom Harkin's Office, 2010.
9. *Emerging Risk?*, 2010.
10. U.S. House of Representatives, 2011.
11. Lauerman, 2010.
12. Adams, 2010.
13. Zagorin, 2011.
14. Henig, 2007.
15. See Gorman, 2004, pp. 37–62.
16. Henig, 2007, p. 73.
17. Gorman, 2004.
18. U.S. Department of Education, 2009.
19. U.S. Department of Education, 2010b.
20. U.S. Department of Education, 2010b, p. 8.
21. Henig, 2007, p. 75.
22. Indeed, the example cited on the department's website is Green Dot's "restart" of Locke Senior High School in Los Angeles, a school where teachers operate under the local union contract. See U.S. Department of Education, 2011f.

23. See, for example, National Education Association, n.d.

24. The list has since been updated to reflect electoral results, so the number of House Democrats has changed to 48 members and the number of Senate Republicans to 3. For an updated list, see Coalition for Educational Success, 2011.

25. See Cooper, 2010.

26. The Cook Partisan Voting Index uses each congressional district's past presidential vote to calculate a basic measure of how Democratic or Republican a given district is compared with the national average. See Cook Political Report, 2011.

27. Reuters, 2011; Campus Progress, 2011.

28. Lederman, 2010.

29. Kelly, 2010.

30. On the relaxing of regulations under the George W. Bush Department of Education, see Burd, 2009.

31. Lederman, 2011.

32. Senate HELP Committee, 2011.

33. The list has since been updated to reflect electoral results, so the number of House Democrats has changed to 48 members and the number of Senate Republicans to 3. For an updated list, see Coalition for Educational Success, 2011.

34. CBS News, 2009. Percentages reflect author's calculations.

35. The results of past polls are available at Phi Delta Kappa International, "PDK/Gallup Past Polls," www.pdkintl.org/kappan/pastpolls.htm. See Rose & Gallup, 2007.

36. For a snapshot of this historical trend, see Lopez, 2010.

37. Belfield & Wooten, 2003.

38. Lyons, 2002.

39. The gap between Republicans and Democrats was similarly small in 1996, though both groups were somewhat more supportive in that year: 32% of Democrats supported for-profit management of school operations, compared with 40% of Republicans.

40. See Lake Research Partners, 2009, and Americans for Democratic Action, 2009.

41. For more, see Gilroy, 2011.

42. On international comparisons, see Battaglio, 2009.

43. Schlesinger, Mitchell, & Gray, 2004.

44. The two-by-two raises the question of where early childhood education falls on the continuum. Early childhood has a large for-profit presence, which may seem to contradict the "age" dimension. However, I would argue that pre-K education is considered peripheral; it is noncompulsory, and federal money does not flow to for-profit providers. In states where public money does fund for-profit early childhood providers, however, these policies have been quite controversial, which fits with the general argument laid out here.

45. Associated Press and Stanford University, 2010.

46. Molnar, Miron, & Urschel, 2009–2010.

Chapter 2

1. For world giving amounts, see Center for Global Prosperity, 2010. For "most charitable people" rankings, which includes volunteer participation and the percentage of people who donate, see Charities Aid Foundation, 2011.

2. Center for Non-Profits, 2010.

3. See Bradley, Jansen, & Silverman, 2003.

4. For details on this reality in the public charter school sector, see Education Sector, 2009. For a more theoretical perspective, see Vander Ark, 2009.

5. Twombly & Gantz, 2001.

6. NewSchools Venture Fund, 2011.

7. Sengupta, 2012.

8. Lozier & Rotherham, 2011.

9. Wikipedia, 2013b.

10. Mathis, 2007.

11. Meier, 2011.

12. Cited in Martinez, 2010.

13. Mathews, 2011.

14. Hess, 2010.

15. Kunskapsskolan, 2010.

16. Stuit, 2010.

Chapter 3

1. Hentschke, 2011.

2. Editorial, "Rules for Gainful Education," *New York Times*, 2010.

3. For a more in-depth discussion of the theories of disruptive innovation, see Horn, Chapter 5, this volume.

4. Kutz, 2010.

Chapter 4

1. Shonkoff & Phillips, 2000.

2. Vandell et al., 2010; Vandell & Wolfe, 2000.

3. See the American Enterprise Institute's Private Enterprise Education Policy Page at www.aei.org/policy/education/private-enterprise/.

4. Phillips, Howes, & Whitebook, 1992; Whitebook, Howes, & Phillips, 1990; Sosinsky, Lord, & Zigler, 2007.

5. National Association of Childcare Resource and Referral Agencies, 2012a.

6. Mocan, 2001.

7. Morris & Helburn, 2000.

8. Hart & Risley, 2003; Shonkoff, Boyce, & McEwen, 2009.

9. Laughlin, 2010.

10. Weiland, 2011; Gormely, Phillips, & Gayer, 2008.

11. Fuller et al., 2004; Pianta et al., 2005.

12. Heckman, 2006.

13. Rolnick & Grunewald, 2003.

14. Estimates are based on data from Laughlin, 2010; National Institute for Early Education Research, 2010; and Marketdata Enterprises, 2010.

15. I exclude from this discussion care provided by nonparent family members (such as grandparents) as well as U.S. Department of Defense child-care programs.

16. Youcha, 1995.

17. Zigler & Muenchow, 1994.

18. Rose, 2010.

19. McKenna, 2010.

20. Neugebauer, 2006.

21. Neugebauer (2010) notes that of the 125 companies listed in the 1971 *Barron's* article, only 6 were still in business in 2010.

22. Marketdata Enterprises, 2010.

23. Figures are derived from data provided by Marketdata Enterprises, 2012, and Neugebauer, 2008.

24. National Institute for Early Education Research, 2003; National Institute for Early Education Research, 2009.

25. National Institute for Early Education Research, 2010.

26. Marketdata Enterprises, 2010.

27. National Association of Childcare Resource and Referral Associations, 2012b.

28. States differ substantially in their regulations regarding eligibility to serve as a CCDF- or TANF-funded child-care provider. In some states, otherwise unregulated child-care providers are required to submit to background checks and to complete training in infant and toddler CPR and first aid. In some cases, people may be eligible to receive public child-care funds with virtually no oversight from the state. Typically, states have regulations that specify a small number of the inputs associated with positive outcomes for children. For more detailed information on state child-care policies and CCDF eligibility, see Office of Planning, Research & Evaluation, 2009.

29. Bassok, Fitzpatrick, & Loeb, 2012.

30. Figures are based on estimates from Marketdata Enterprises, 2012.

31. Todd Grindal was a member of the team that founded the Franklin Montessori School, and served as its program director from 2002 to 2005.

32. Neugebauer, 2008.

33. Schulman & Blank, 2011.

34. The Florida Department of Education's State Board of Education determines readiness based on children's Florida Kindergarten Readiness Screeners. The program's "minimum readiness rate" is determined annually such that no more than 15% of all Voluntary Prekindergarten (VPK) providers would fall below the minimum rate. See the Florida Department of Education's website at https://vpk.fldoe.org/InfoPages/FAQ.aspx for more information.

35. Kirp, 2007.

36. The three benchmarks VPK programs are required to meet are: (1) the state has comprehensive early learning standards, (2) a maximum class size of 20 or fewer children, and (3) the state regularly monitors publicly funded programs. The only other state pre-kindergarten programs meeting three or fewer benchmarks were in Ohio, Pennsylvania, and Arizona.

37. See the Florida Department of Education data at www.fldoe.org/earlylearning/account.asp.

38. Kagan, 1991.

39. Helburn, 1995.

40. Mathers, Sylva, & Joshi, 2007.

41. Cleveland et al., 2007.

42. Sumsion & Goodfellow, 2009.

43. Cryer & Burchinal, 1997.

44. Morris & Helburn, 2000.

45. Although many states encourage child-care providers to incorporate assessment and observation, currently, no quality rating systems use child-level outcome data to assess reward or to penalize programs.

46. Tout et al., 2010.

47. Schulman & Blank, 2011.

48. Gormely, Phillips, & Gayer, 2011; Grindal, in press.

49. Matthews & Ewen, 2011.

50. According to the U.S. Bureau of Labor Statistics, in May 2011 (the most recent date for which data are available), the median hourly wages were $9.53 for parking lot attendants, $9.38 for animal caretakers, and $9.34 for child-care workers. See U.S. Bureau of Labor Statistics, 2011.

51. Lake, 1970.

Chapter 5

1. Harvard Business School professor Theodore Levitt is famous for his notion that customers rarely hire a specific product but instead want a solution to a problem they are facing. Levitt argued that the most successful companies are those that understand this dynamic and used the example that if the railroad companies had understood that they were in the transportation business, not the railroad business, then they could have survived and thrived. See, for example, Levitt, 1960. Harvard Business School professor Clayton M. Christensen has expanded upon this notion with the "Jobs to Be Done" framework. The fundamental notion is that jobs arise in the lives of customers and they hire products or services to do these jobs. A major reason so many new products and services fail is because companies don't understand the fundamental job to be done. Nailing the job to be done is one of the most important factors in a company's success. Christensen, Anthony, Cook, and Hall (2010) adopt the "Jobs to Be Done" language without going into a full explanation of the theory behind it.

2. For more on these flawed measures of performance in today's environment, see Christensen, 2012.

3. For the full explanation of this phenomenon, see Christensen, 1997, and Christensen & Raynor, 2003.

4. For a full discussion, see Christensen, Horn, Caldera, & Soares, 2011.

5. Christensen & Shu, 2006.

6. Christensen & Kaufman, 2006.

7. Even not-for-profits and government units have business models. In their case, the last box may be more aptly titled "Revenue Formula" rather than "Profit Formula"—as it is the funding they need to support their organization in accomplishing its mission.

8. Christensen, Grossman, & Hwang, 2008.

9. For further analysis on this, see also Johnson, 2010.

10. There is actually a reliable pattern to how this operates in regulated industries. In the early years, when technology is not good enough to deliver the public good in a reliable way, government regulation can play a critical role to promote stability and assurance. The problem comes when these rules survive long after the public need for stability and assurance has been satisfied by technological progress. Although the original intent of permits and certification is a genuine concern for the end user, the rules almost always come to be used to protect the economic interests of the existing providers—still invoked, of course, in the name of the end user (or the "public good"). The implication is that regulators must continue to change the focus of their rules as science and technology progress, but the reality is that they rarely do. Over time, this creates large and powerful companies that have a vested interest in preserving the status quo. When policymakers try to change the rules, these incumbents fall back on their arguments of stability and assurance to block the changes. See Christensen, Grossman, & Hwang, 2008.

11. Christensen, 1997.

12. Fuller, 2010.

13. When stuck in this situation, the need for disruptive innovation becomes acute. This is in part why the U.S. government has historically been so concerned with breaking up monopolies. It is interesting to see what ultimately breaks up the monopolistic practices. It is rarely the actions of the Department of Justice. Instead, it is disruptive innovation. It was not the Department of Justice that ended IBM's, Microsoft's, or Xerox's monopoly through its extensive litigation. Instead, it was the disruption pioneered by the personal computer industry, led first by Apple and later by Dell, Microsoft, and Intel, all of which made the computer much more affordable, simple, and convenient for many more people; Linux, which did the same for server operating systems; and Canon, which led a stream of new photocopying innovations that made the photocopier dramatically more accessible to many more people—all three by avoiding head-on attacks at the outset.

14. The proposed set of gainful-employment regulations has its roots in the Higher Education Act, which requires that career colleges and occupational training programs prepare students for "gainful employment" to remain eligible to receive federal financial aid. In July 2010, the Department of Education proposed a set of regulations to define gainful

employment as a measurable outcome based on student debt-to-income levels and loan-repayment rates. These regulations would apply to all programs at for-profit colleges and to occupational training programs at public and nonprofit colleges. Programs that fail to meet gainful-employment benchmarks would have their access to federal student aid restricted or completely denied. Because these regulations specifically target for-profit colleges, opponents of the gainful-employment rules say these institutions are being unfairly singled out and have lobbied fiercely to put a halt to the rules' implementation.

15. It is worth noting that just as not all for-profits define success in the same way, there are many nonprofits that do not define success in the same way. To survive, all nonprofits must perform the stated job for their customers and bring in the requisite revenue to support their business models. Beyond that, although prestige is the motivating factor for many nonprofits with large ambitions, it is not the motivating factor for all. For so-called "mom-and-pop" nonprofits, for example, pursuing prestige isn't necessarily important.

16. Kamenetz, 2010.

17. Kamenetz, 2010.

18. The U.S. Department of Education (2010c) defines high-risk students as having three of the following characteristics: delayed enrollment, no high school diploma, part-time enrollment, financially independent, have dependents, single-parent status, and working full-time while enrolled. Students with these traits map strongly to inner-city residents, low-income households, minority status, and first-generation postsecondary students.

19. Lytle, Brinner, & Ross, 2010.

20. Lang & Weinstein, 2012.

21. Horn, 2011.

22. Some recent proposals are trying to attack this problem. In K–12, two articles give some preliminary ideas for how this could work. See, for example, Aarons, 2010; and Hess, 2010. In higher education, see the discussion of the QV Index in Christensen, Horn, Caldera, & Soares, 2011.

23. Christensen & Raynor, 2003.

24. Meehan, Kilmer, & O'Flanagan, 2004. Given this fundamental difference in corporate structure, a more apples-to-apples comparison might treat the money that nonprofits raise as one source of their overall revenue and think about their expenses against that as their costs of goods sold. In this case, the funders (or customers) are in fact hiring the nonprofits to do what they deem to be an important job, and nonprofits tend to align around what their funders want, just as all successful enterprises align around their customers' jobs to be done, not necessarily the end user's. Because nonprofits do not have equity, they do not, to date, identify fundraising dollars as growth capital.

25. One problem with this is that although the cost of customer acquisition may fall because the true customers are often those giving money to the nonprofit, not the clients being served by the mission, the success of the nonprofit is in fact dependent on having customers—foundations, individuals, and so on—who are completely aligned with the nonprofits' clients' true job. That alignment is likely rarer than we might hope. Indeed, when CEOs of nonprofits complain that they are spending 65–70% of their time fundraising,

which leaves little time for actually running their nonprofit, what they often do not realize is that this is where they are leading their nonprofit. In an odd way, the original mission for the clients becomes secondary in some cases.

26. Hess, 2010.

27. For example, one policy option would be to have measures in policy that sunset a program if its outcomes do not justify the costs compared with other programs designed to achieve similar outcomes. Policies of this nature might then treat new programs not as victories in and of themselves, but instead as experiments whose perpetuation would be determined based on how they are executed.

Chapter 6

1. Obama, 2009.

2. Hightower, 2008.

3. Diamandis, 2010.

4. Kluger, 2010.

5. Foust, 2011.

6. Black, 2010.

7. American Hospital Association, 2011; American Medical Association, 2013; National Nurse Emergency Preparedness Initiative, 2013.

8. Keaton, Sable, & Liu, 2011; National Center for Education Statistics, 2013.

9. Warner, 2004.

10. RAND Corporation, 2005.

11. George W. Bush, 2004.

12. Childs, 2009.

13. Oracle Transcription, 2011.

14. Hsiao & Hing, 2012.

15. Council for American Medical Innovation, 2011.

16. "Our President on Energy and the Environment," 2010.

17. Obama, 2010.

18. U.S. Department of Education, 2010a.

19. Business Executives for National Security, 2001.

20. Business Executives for National Security, 2001.

21. Kellogg, as quoted in Armistead, 2005.

22. Community Development Financial Institutions Fund, 2009.

23. Brostek, 2007.

24. White House Council of Economic Advisors, 2011.

25. Flyvbjerg, Holm, & Buhl, 2007.

26. Hentschke, Oschman, & Snell, 2003.

27. Henderson & Newell, 2010.

28. Siry, 2009.

29. Deloitte, 2010.

30. Foust, 2011.

31. Keeney & Pianko, 2007.

32. Lacy, 2010.

33. U.S. Department of Education, 2009.

Chapter 7

1. This description of online learning borrows heavily from the work of Susan Patrick, president and CEO of iNACOL, the International Association for K–12 Online Learning.

2. Clark, 2001.

3. iNACOL uses this model to describe what online learning is. This model was adapted from the Technological Pedagogical Content Knowledge (TPCK) model from Mishra & Koelher, 2006.

4. Many cite Baumol's disease to explain this phenomenon. The basic notion is that labor-intensive industries struggle to accomplish more with fewer resources and therefore demand more and more to deliver the same product or service. Baumol famously invoked an analogy from a music performance, as he asked how one would improve the productivity of a string quartet playing Beethoven. Would you drop the second violin or ask the musicians to play the piece twice as fast? The Baumol analogy comes from Baumol & Bowen, 1996.

5. University of Phoenix, 2013.

6. Webley, 2012.

7. Office of the President, Arizona State University, 2012.

8. See KIPP, 2013, and K12 INC (LRN), 2012. From page 6 of the prospectus, K12 Inc. breaks out its student enrollment into three categories—and for the sake of counting students, assumes that four course enrollments is equal to serving a full-time student. Specifically, the document reads: "Students served through our Institutional Business and Private School offerings may enroll in a single course. For better comparability, these students are converted to full-time equivalents (FTEs) on a four-course basis. We currently exclude selected programs from our reported enrollment. For example, we do not include students in our consumer channel as we do not monitor the progress of these students in the same way as we do in other programs. We typically sell our A+ curriculum (acquired with American Education Corporation) as a site license. As these schools are not limited in the number of students who may access our curriculum, we do not include these students in our enrollment totals."

9. K12 INC (LRN), 2012.

10. Florida Virtual School, 2013b.

11. Mackey, 2009.

12. See Meehan, Kilmer, & O'Flanagan, 2004, as cited in by Horn in chapter 5, this volume.

13. Online curricula include courses, digital textbooks, games, intervention/core, online instruction, specialized/core, test-prep, and tutoring; instructional systems include learning management systems, communications, assessment systems, collaboration, social learning, and teacher tools.

14. Christensen, Horn, & Johnson, 2008.

15. National Alliance for Public Charter Schools, 2010–2011.

16. Watson, Murin, Vashaw, Gemin, & Rapp, 2011.

17. K12 INC (LRN), 2012.

18. This is a rough sketch that captures the economies of scale of K12 Inc. and is by no means a perfect diagram. K12 Inc. operates in lots of different states where they get different revenues per student, which may affect how they serve different students and so forth. This analysis does not capture any of these potential variations but instead serves to give a rough feel for the effect of scale in online learning.

19. K12 Inc., 2011.

20. K12 Inc., 2011.

21. K12 Inc., 2011. The full text of this relevant section reads as follows: "*Product Development Expenses.* Product development expenses include research and development costs and overhead costs associated with the management of both our curriculum development and internal systems development teams. In addition, product development expenses include the amortization of internal systems and any related impairment charges. We measure and track our product development expenditures on a per course or project basis to measure and assess our development efficiency. In addition, we monitor employee utilization rates to evaluate our workforce efficiency. In fiscal year 2011, product development expenses increased as we acquired the development functions of KC Distance Learning and AEC. We plan to invest in additional curriculum development and related software in the future, primarily to produce additional high school courses, world language courses, and new releases of existing courses and to continue to upgrade our content management system and online schools. We expect to gain efficiencies as we integrate the development capabilities of KCDL and AEC and leverage our collective development efforts over an increasing base of enrollment. We capitalize most of the costs incurred to develop our curriculum, beginning with application development, through production and testing into capitalized curriculum development costs. We capitalize the costs incurred to develop internal systems into capitalized software development costs." Also, see page 70 of the annual report, where it provides the following additional details and context: "*Product Development Expenses.* Product development expenses for the year ended June 30, 2011 were $16.3 million, representing an increase of $6.7 million, or 69.8%, as compared to product development expenses of $9.6 million for the same period in the prior year. The increase is primarily due to support for the Aventa curriculum acquired during the period as well as new projects including development expenses related to our financial systems implementation. Included in the $6.7 million increase in product development expenses are expenses of $1.8 million for new initiatives and ERP implementation expenses of $1.0 million. As a percentage of revenues, product development expenses increased to 3.1% for the year ended June 30, 2011 as compared to 2.5% for the same period in the prior year primarily due to the items identified above."

22. K12 Inc., 2011.

23. K12 Inc., 2011.

24. K12 Inc., 2011.

25. According to an article in the *New York Times*, Connections Education's annual revenue at the time of its acquisition by Pearson was roughly $190 million. See Saul, 2011.

26. For example, Florida Virtual School reports on its website that "Subject-matter experts from FLVS and academic scholars from the University of Central Florida were heavily involved in the development of [the Conspiracy Code American History] course. The 12 principles of brain-based learning set forth by the Caine Institute were settled upon as Conspiracy Code's educational design foundation, influencing both pedagogical and entertainment decisions. In developing the curriculum, findings from Le Tellier's work on how to strengthen/build long-term memory were also incorporated. The curriculum design team applied rigorous guidelines to ensure the academic integrity of Conspiracy Code, as well as integrate and balance the educational and entertaining aspects of the game in order to ensure it remained both effective and engaging." See Florida Virtual School, 2013a.

27. K12 Inc., 2011, p. 7.

28. K12 Inc., 2011, p. 48.

29. See Horn, chapter 5, this volume.

30. "*Regulations Restricting Virtual Public School and Hybrid School Growth and Funding.* As a new public schooling alternative, some state and regulatory authorities have elected to proceed cautiously with virtual public schools and hybrid schools while providing opportunities for taxpayer families seeking this alternative. Regulations that control the growth of virtual public schools and hybrid schools range from setting caps on statewide student enrollments, to prescribing the number of schools in a state, to limiting the percentage of time students may receive instruction online. Funding regulations can also have this effect.

"Regulations that hinder our ability to serve certain jurisdictions include: restrictions on student eligibility, such as mandating attendance at a traditional public school prior to enrolling in a virtual public school or hybrid school; caps on the total number of students in a virtual public school and hybrid school; restrictions on grade levels served; geographic limitations on enrollments; fixing the percentage of per pupil funding that must be paid to teachers; mandating teacher: student ratios; state-specific curriculum requirements; and limits on the number of charters that can be granted in a state." See K12 Inc., 2011, pp. 24–25.

31. K12 Inc., 2011, p. 25.

32. K12 Inc., 2011, p. 29.

33. K12 Inc., 2011, p. 28.

34. Saul, 2011.

35. Center for Responsible Politics, 2013a.

36. Kelly, 2012.

37. Center for Responsible Politics, 2013b.

38. Michigan Virtual University is a nonprofit organization that serves as Michigan's statewide online school.

39. For example, there have been critical reports in the *New York Times*, *The Arizona Republic*, the *Detroit Free Press*, and *EdNews Colorado*.

40. According to K12 Inc.'s annual report, 2011, "New laws or regulations not currently applicable to for-profit education companies in the K–12 sector could be enacted and negatively impact our operations and financial results.

"As the provision of online K–12 public education matures, novel issues may arise that could lead to the enactment of new laws or regulations similar to, or in addition to, laws or regulations applicable to other areas of education and education at different levels. For example, for-profit education companies that own and operate post-secondary colleges depend in significant respect on student loans provided by the federal government to cover tuition expenses, and federal laws prohibit incentive compensation for success in securing enrollments or financial aid to any person engaged in student recruiting or admission activities. In contrast, while students in virtual public K–12 charter schools are entitled to a free public education with no federal or state loans necessary for tuition, similar laws could be enacted that make for-profit management companies serving such schools subject to similar restrictions." K12 Inc., 2011, pp. 30–31.

41. K12 Inc., 2011, p. 33.

Chapter 8

1. The examples and chronology of R&D and infrastructure investments described in this section are consistent with the Wikipedia article "History of the Internet," 2013a.

2. The description of the use of philanthropy and government funds to strengthen the markets for vaccines in the developing world is adapted from the Bill and Melinda Gates Foundation, 2012.

Chapter 9

1. Tomassini, 2012.
2. Bennet, Lucchesi, & Vedder, 2010.
3. Gomez & Henstchke, 2009.
4. Heinrich, Meyer, & Whitten, 2010.
5. Burch, Steinberg, & Donovan, 2007.
6. Bulkley & Burch, 2011.
7. Molnar, Miron, & Urschel, 2010.
8. Miller, 2010.
9. Wiseman, 2011.
10. Quoted in Scriven, 1991, p. 169.
11. Hasselbring & Goin, 2004.
12. Horn, chapter 5, this volume..
13. Kids Help Pearson Design Software, 2008.
14. It is possible that private EMOs have participated confidentially in larger studies of charter school effectiveness, such as the Mathematica Policy Research analysis of charter school impacts. See Gleason et al., 2010. It is also possible that individual schools operated by these EMOs have been evaluated more rigorously, though I was not able to identify any instances where this was the case.

15. Some companies, such as Pearson, do commission third-party efficacy studies using rigorous methods. These do not appear to be subject to any form of external or peer review, however.

16. These types of studies are more feasible for some types of interventions than others. A growing body of research exists on the impact of charter schools, using admissions lotteries to randomize treatment and control groups. Such studies are possible because the school is already oversubscribed, meaning there is no added concern for withholding treatment.

17. U.S. Government Accountability Office, 2010.

18. Fordham Institute, 2004; Wiley & Barr, 2007.

19. Hentschke, Lechuga, & Tierney, 2010.

20. Miles & Baroody, 2011.

21. Boser, 2011.

22. For a full listing of research and evaluation findings, see www.americaschoice.org/resultsacschooldesign.

23. It is worth noting that the What Works Clearinghouse is reserved in its appraisal of the impacts of READ 180 on reading achievement and comprehension, noting modest effects and a "medium to large" evidence base.

24. Scholastic, 2011.

25. University of Phoenix, 2010.

26. I cite the University of Phoenix Academic Annual Report and the Capella University Learning and Career Outcome not as an endorsement of their findings but as examples of how proprietary colleges collect, analyze, and present data as a way of differentiating themselves and of enhancing their reputation and brand. Because of a lack of details regarding research methodology and reporting conventions, I cannot determine the rigor of the analyses producing the reports.

27. Patton, 2008.

28. Peterson, 2005.

29. Gomez & Henstchke, 2009.

30. Schneider & Klor de Alva, 2011.

31. Carey, 2010.

32. Carey, 2010.

33. Cable, Plucker, & Spradlin, 2009.

34. One could argue that the case of shareholder lawsuits against K12 Inc. suggests a market mechanism for promoting rigorous evaluation. Although this may be true, it is both unsystematic and expensive in practice.

Conclusion

1. Mathews, 2011.

References

Aarons, D. (2010, October 5). San Francisco creates college accounts for kindergartners. *Education Week*'s District Dossier blog. Retrieved from http://blogs.edweek.org/edweek/ District_Dossier/2010/10/san_francisco_creates_college.html

Adams, C. (2010, September 30). Debate over for-profit colleges turns partisan. *Education Week*'s College Bound blog. Retrieved from http://blogs.edweek.org/edweek/college_ bound/2010/09/debate_over_for-profits_intensifies_and_turns_partisan.html

Altman, A. (2010, September 30). A Senate spat over for-profit education. *Time*'s Swampland blog. Retrieved from http://swampland.blogs.time. com/2010/09/30/a-senate-spat-over-for-profit-education

Altwerger, B. (2005). *Reading for profit: How the bottom line leaves kids behind*. Portsmouth, NH: Heinemann.

American Enterprise Institute. (2010). *AEI survey of parents*. [Results available upon request.]

American Hospital Association. (2011, September 14). Fast facts on U.S. hospitals. Retrieved from www.aha.org/research/rc/stat-studies/fast-facts.shtml

American Medical Association. (2013). About AMA, patient FAQs: How do I find a physician? Retrieved from www.ama-assn.org/ama/pub/about-ama/patient-faqs.page

Americans for Democratic Action. (2009). Rationale for research. Retrieved from www. adaction.org.

Associated Press & Stanford University. (2010, December 14). AP-Stanford University Education Poll. Retrieved from from http://surveys.ap.org/data%5CSRBI%5CAPNational %20Education%20Poll%20Topline%20100110.pdf

Ball, S. J. (2007). *Education plc: Understanding private sector participation in public sector education*. T & F Books UK.

Bassok, D., Fitzpatrick, M., & Loeb, S. (2012, October). *State preschool crowd-out private provision? The impact of universal preschool on the childcare sector in Oklahoma and Georgia*. Paper presented at the annual meeting of the Association of Public Policy and Management, Baltimore, MD.

Battaglio, R. P. Jr. (2009, March). Privatization and citizen preferences: A cross national analysis of demand for private versus public provision of services in three industries. *Administration and Society, 41*(1), 38–66.

Baumol, W. J., & Bowen, W. G. (1996). *Performing arts: The economic dilemma*. Cambridge, MA: MIT Press.

Belfield, C., & Wooten, A. L. (2003, January). Education privatization: The attitudes and experiences of superintendents. Occasional Paper No. 70, National Center for the Study of Privatization in Education, New York, NY.

Bennet, D. L., Lucchesi, A. R., & Vedder, R. K. (2010). *For-profit higher education: Growth, innovation and regulation.* Washington, DC: Center for College Affordability and Productivity.

Bill and Melinda Gates Foundation. (2012). Advanced market commitments: Saving lives with affordable vaccines. Retrieved from http://www.gatesfoundation.org/vaccines/ Pages/advanced-market-commitments-vaccines.aspx

Block, R. (2010, December 28). Can NASA compete with SpaceX? *Orlando Sentinel.* Retrieved from http://articles.orlandosentinel.com/2010-12-28/news/os-nasa-costs-un-affordable-20101228_1_spacex-dragon-capsule-constellation-moon-program.

Boser, U. (2003, May). *Return on educational investment: A district-by-district evaluation of U.S. educational productivity.* Washington, DC: Center for American Progress.

Bradley, B., Jansen, P., & Silverman, L. (2003, May). The nonprofit sector's $100 billion opportunity. *Harvard Business Review, 81*(5).

Brostek, M. (2007, January). *New markets tax credit appears to increase investment by investors in low-income communities, but opportunities exist to better monitor compliance.* Washington, DC: U.S. Government Accountability Office.

Bulkley, K. E., & Burch, P. (2011). The changing nature of private engagement in public education: For-profit and nonprofit organizations and educational reform. *Peabody Journal of Education, 86*(3), 236–251.

Burch, P., Steinberg, M., & Donovan, J. (2007, June). Supplemental educational services and NCLB: Policy assumptions, market practices, emerging issues. *Educational Evaluation and Policy Analysis, 29*(2), 115–133.

Bush, G. W. (2004, April 26). President unveils tech initiatives for energy, health care, Internet. Retrieved from http://georgewbush-whitehouse.archives.gov/news/releases/2004/04/ 20040426-6.html

Business Executives for National Security. (2011, June). *Accelerating the acquisition and implementation of new technologies for intelligence: The report of the Independent Panel on the Central Intelligence Agency In-Q-Tel Venture.* Washington, DC: Author. Retrieved from www.iqt.org/aboutiqt/attachments/BENS%20Report.pdf

Cable, K. E., Plucker, J. A., & Spradlin, T. E. (2009, Winter). Alternative schools: What's in a name? Center for Evaluation and Education Policy. *Education Policy Brief, 7*(4).

Campus Progress. (2011). About Campus Progress' initiative on for-profit colleges. Retrieved from http://campusprogress.org/campaigns/issues/screw_u_for-profit_colleges_scamming_students_and_taxpayers_out_of_the

Carey, K. (2010, December 12). Student learning: Measure or perish. *Measuring stick,* a special report of the *Chronicle of Higher Education.* Retrieved from http://chronicle.com/ article/Measure-or-Perish/125671/

CBS News. (2009, December 17–22). CBS News poll: Satisfaction with life/parenthood. (Accessed through the Roper Center for Public Opinion Research).

Center for Global Prosperity. (2010). *Index of global philanthropy 2010*. Washington, DC: Hudson Institute. Retrieved from http://www.technoserve.org/assets/documents/index-global-philan-10.pdf

Center for Non-Profits. (2010). *Thinking of forming a nonprofit? What to consider before you begin*. North Brunswick, NJ: Center for Non-Profits. Retrieved from http://www.nj.gov/njbusiness/pdfs/ThinkingOfForming_2010.pdf

Center for Responsive Politics. (2013a). Connections education. Retrieved from http://www.opensecrets.org/lobby/clientsum.php?id=D000049657&year=2011

Center for Responsive Politics. (2013b). Florida Virtual School. Retrieved from http://www.opensecrets.org/lobby/clientsum.php?id=D000050979&year=2011

Charities Aid Foundation. (2011). *World giving index 2011*. West Malling, UK: Charities Aid Foundation. Retrieved from https://www.cafonline.org/pdf/World_Giving_Index_2011_191211.pdf

Childs, D. (2009, January 9). President-elect urges electronic medical records in 5 years. *ABC News*. Retrieved from http://abcnews.go.com/Health/President44/story?id=6606536&page=1

Christensen, C. M. (1997). *The innovator's dilemma: When new technologies cause great firms to fail*. Boston: Harvard Business Press.

Christensen, C. M. (2012, November 3). A capitalist's dilemma, whoever wins on Tuesday. *New York Times*. Retrieved from http://www.nytimes.com/2012/11/04/business/a-capitalists-dilemma-whoever-becomes-president.html?pagewanted=1&_r=0&ref=business

Christensen, C. M., Anthony, S., Cook, S., & Hall, T. (2010, August 11). Integrating around the job to be done. Harvard Business School Module Note 611-004.

Christensen, C. M., Grossman, J. H., & Hwang, J. (2008). *The innovator's prescription: A disruptive solution for health care*. New York: McGraw-Hill.

Christensen, C. M., Horn, M. B., Caldera, L., & Soares, L. (2011). Disrupting college: How disruptive innovation can deliver quality and affordability to postsecondary education. Retrieved from http://www.americanprogress.org/issues/labor/report/2011/02/08/9034/disrupting-college/

Christensen, C. M., Horn, M. B., & Johnson, C. W. (2008). *Disrupting class: How disruptive innovation will change the way the world learns*. New York: McGraw-Hill.

Christensen, C. M., & Kaufman, S. P. (2006, September 13). *Assessing your organization's capabilities: Resources, processes, and priorities*. Boston, MA: Harvard Business Press.

Christensen, C. M., & Raynor, M. E. (2003). *The innovator's solution: Creating and sustaining successful growth*. Boston: Harvard Business Press.

Christensen, C. M., & Shu, K. (2006, August 2). What is an organization's culture? Harvard Business School Background Note 399-104, 2.

Clark, T. (2001). *Virtual schools trends and issues: A study of virtual schools in the United States*. San Francisco: WestEd.

Cleveland, G., et al. (2007). New evidence about child care in Canada: Use patterns, affordability and quality. *IRPP Choices, 14*(12), 1–44.

Coalition for Educational Success. (2011). List of members of Congress registering concerns. Retrieved from http://www.ed-success.org//list-of-members-of-congress-registering-concerns.php

Community Development Financial Institutions Fund. (2009, March 31). Treasury's new markets tax credit program named one of top 50 in the innovations in American government awards competition. News release. Retrieved from www.cdfifund.gov/news_events/CDFI-2009-19-NMTC-Top-50-American-Government-Awards.asp

Cook Political Report. (2011). Retrieved from www.cookpolitical.com/node/4201.

Council for American Medical Innovation. (2011, January 12). Ours to lose: Greenberg/McInturff poll shows Americans overwhelmingly link medical innovation to job creation and reducing health care costs. News release. Retrieved from www.americanmedicalinnovation.org/ours-lose-greenbergmcinturff-poll-shows-americans-overwhelmingly-link-medical-innovation-job-creation

Cryer, D., & Burchinal, M. (1997). Parents as childcare consumers. *Early Childhood Research Quarterly, 12*(1), 35–58.

Cuban, L. (2007). *The blackboard and the bottom line: Why schools can't be business.* Cambridge, MA: Harvard University Press.

Deloitte. (2010, April 16). Deloitte/Cleantech group survey: Stimulus package will foster innovation, stimulate economic growth and create jobs. News release. Retrieved from www.deloitte.com/view/en_US/us/press/PressReleases/a958a854ba708210VgnVCM100000ba42f00aRCRD.htm

Diamandis, P. (2010, February 1). NASA embraces American capitalism and entrepreneurship. *Huffington Post.* Retrieved from http://www.huffingtonpost.com/peter-diamandis/nasa-embraces-american-ca_b_444673.html

Durbin, D. (2010, June 30). For-profit colleges and federal student aid: Preventing financial abuses. Speech, Washington, DC. Retrieved from http://durbin.senate.gov/public/index.cfm/statementscommentary?ID=2f8e0201-e43d-4dae-8013-f668e2fdb7c4

Editorial. (2010, December 7). Rules for gainful education. *New York Times.*

Education Sector. (2009). Growing pains: Scaling up the nation's best charter schools. Retrieved from http://www.educationsector.org/sites/default/files/publications/Growing_Pains.pdf.

Emerging risk? An overview of the federal investment in for-profit education, before the Senate Committee on Health, Education, Labor, and Pensions, 111th Cong. (June 24, 2010). Statement of Senator Michael B. Enzi.

Epstein, J. (2010, June 24). Bad apples or something more? *Inside Higher Education.* Retrieved from http://www.insidehighered.com/news/2010/06/24/forprofit

Florida Department of Education. (2013). Accountability data. www.fldoe.org/earlylearning/account.asp.

Florida Virtual School. (2013a). Conspiracy code—course overview. Retrieved from http://www.flvs.net/areas/flvscourses/ConspiracyCode/Pages/CourseOverview.aspx

Florida Virtual School. (2013b). Quick facts. Retrieved from http://flvs.net/areas/aboutus/Pages/QuickFactsaboutFLVS.aspx

Flyvbjerg, B., Skamris Holm, M., & Buhl, S. (2007). Underestimating cost in public works projects: Error or lie? *Journal of the American Planning Association* 68, no. 3.

Foust, J. (2011, February 14). Commercial crew and NASA's tipping point. *The Space Review.* Retrieved from www.thespacereview.com/article/1780/1

Fuller, A. (2010, May 11). Duncan says for-profit colleges are important to Obama's 2020 goal. *The Chronicle of Higher Education.* Retrieved from http://chronicle.com/article/Duncan-Says-For-Profit/65477/

Fuller, B., et al. (2004). Childcare quality: Centers and home settings that serve poor families. *Early Childhood Research Quarterly, 19,* 505–527.

Garan, E. M. (2004). *In defense of our children: When politics, profit, and education collide.* Portsmouth, NH: Heinemann.

General Social Survey. (1996). General Social Survey, 1996. Retrieved from http://www.ropercenter.uconn.edu/data_access/data/datasets/general_social_survey.html.

Gilroy, L. (2011, February 10). Annual privatization report 2010. Reason Foundation. Retrieved from http://reason.org/news/show/annual-privatization-report-2010

Gleason, P., et al. (2010). *The evaluation of charter school impacts.* Washington, DC: U.S. Department of Education, Institute of Education Sciences.

Gomez, L. M., & Henstchke, G. C. (2009). K–12 education and the role of for-profit providers. In J. D. Bransford et al. (Eds.), *The role of research in educational improvement* (pp. 137–159). Cambridge, MA: Harvard Education Press.

Gorman, S. (2004). The invisible hand of NCLB. In F. M. Hess & C. E. Finn, Eds., *Leaving no child behind? Options for kids in failing schools.* New York: Palgrave Macmillan.

Gormely, W., Phillips, D., & Gayer, T. Preschool programs can boost school readiness. *Education Forum.* Retrieved from http://nieer.org/resources/research/Gormley062708.pdf

Grindal, T. (in press). Comparing the impact of attending a school-based and non-school-based preschool on young children's cognitive skills, social behavior and approaches to learning: A propensity score analysis. *Early Childhood Research Quarterly.*

Harkin, T. (2010, December 14). For-profit education investigation. Speech, Senate floor, Washington, DC. Retrieved from http://higheredwatch.newamerica.net/sites/newamerica.net/files/articles/Harkin%20Floor%20Speech%2012%2014%2010.pdf

Hart, B. B., & Risley, T. (2003). The early catastrophe. *American Educator, 27*(1), 4–9.

Hasselbring, T. S., & Goin, L. I. (2004). Literacy instruction for older struggling readers: What is the role of technology? *Reading and Writing Quarterly* 20, no. 2: 123–144.

Hawley Miles, K., & Baroody, K. (2011). *Restructuring schools for high performance: A primer for state policymakers.* Watertown, MA: Education Resource Strategies.

Heckman, J. (2006). Skill formation and the economics of investing in disadvantaged children. *Science, 31*(5782), 1900–1902.

Heinrich, C. J., Meyer, R. H., & Whitten, G. (2010, June). Supplemental education services under No Child Left Behind: Who signs up, and what do they gain? *Educational Evaluation and Policy Analysis, 32*(2), 273–298.

Helburn, S. (1995). *Cost, quality, and child outcomes in childcare centers: Technical report.* Denver, CO: Department of Economics, Center for Research in Economics and Social Policy, University of Colorado at Denver.

Henderson, R., & Newell, R. G. (2010). Accelerating energy innovation: Insights from multiple sectors. NBER Working Paper No. 16529, Cambridge, MA.

Henig, J. R. (2007, August 24). The political economy of supplemental educational services. In F. M. Hess & C. E. Finn (Eds.), *No remedy left behind: Lessons from a half decade of NCLB*. Washington, DC: AEI Press.

Hentschke, G. C. (2011). For-profit sector innovations in business models and organizational cultures. In B. Wildavsky, A. P. Kelly, & K. Carey (Eds.), *Reinventing higher education: The promise of innovation* (pp. 159–196). Cambridge, MA: Harvard Education Press.

Hentschke, G. C., Lechuga, V. M., & Tierney, W. C. (2010). *For-profit colleges and universities: Their markets, regulation, performance, and place in higher education*. Sterling, VA: Stylus Publishing.

Hentschke, G. C., Oschman, S., & Snell, L. (2003). Trends and best practices for education management organizations. *WestEd Policy Perspectives*. Retrieved from http://www.wested.org/online_pubs/PP-03-02.pdf

Hess, F. M. (2010, October 15). Proposals for a cost-conscious era: K–12 spending accounts. *Education Week*'s Rick Hess Straight Up blog. Retrieved from http://blogs.edweek.org/edweek/rick_hess_straight_up/2010/10/proposals_for_a_cost-conscious_era_K–12_spending_accounts.html

Hess, F. M. (2010, May 24). The for-profit question. *Education Week*'s Rick Hess Straight Up blog. Retrieved from http://blogs.edweek.org/edweek/rick_hess_straight_up/2010/05/the_for-profit_question.html.

Hightower, A. M. (2008). *Seeking a human spaceflight program worthy of a great nation*. Washington, DC: Review of U.S. Human Space Flight Plans Committee, NASA.

Horn, M. B. (2011, October 24). Colorado's crummy policies lead to crummy virtual schools. *Innosight Institute*. Retrieved from http://www.innosightinstitute.org/education-blog/colorados-crummy-policies-lead-to-crummy-virtual-schools/

Hsiao, C., & Hing, E. (2012, December). Use and characteristics of electronic health record systems among office-based physician practices: United States, 2001–2012. *NCHS Data Brief*, No. 111. Retrieved from http://www.cdc.gov/nchs/data/databriefs/db111.pdf

Johnson, M. (2010). *Seizing the white space: Business model innovation for growth and renewal*. Boston: Harvard Business Press.

K12 Inc. (LRN). (2012, June 5). 424B3—Prospectus filed pursuant to Rule 424(b)(3). Retrieved from http://www.sec.gov/Archives/edgar/data/1157408/000119312512260231/d362599d424b3.htm

K12 Inc. 10-K annual report 2011. Retrieved from http://www.sec.gov/Archives/edgar/data/1157408/000119312511266919/d240743d10k.htm

Kagan, S. L. (1991). Examining profit and nonprofit childcare: An odyssey of quality and auspices. *Journal of Social Issues*, *47*, 87–104.

Kamenetz, A. (2010, April). *DIY U: Edupunks, edupreneurs, and the coming transformation of higher education*. White River Junction, VT: Chelsea Green.

Keaton, P., Sable, J., & Liu, F. (2011). *Documentation to the NCES common core of data local educational agency universe survey: School Year 2009–10*. Washington, DC: U.S. Department of Education. Retrieved from http://nces.ed.gov/ccd/pdf/pau091agen.pdf

Keeney, J., & Pianko, D. (2007, October 25). *Venture capital: Looking outside the education sector.* Prepared for the American Enterprise Institute Conference, "The Supply Side of School Reform and the Future of Educational Entrepreneurship," Washington, DC.

Kellogg, C., as quoted in Armistead, P. J. (2005). *New markets tax credits: Issues and opportunities.* New York: Pratt Institute Center for Community and Environmental Development, p. 9. Retrieved from http://ww.nyirn.org/sites/default/files/publications/PrattCenter_nmtc-report.pdf

Kelly, A. P. (2010). What the Republican surge means for education policy. *Teachers College Record.* Retrieved from www.tcrecord.org/content.asp?contentid=16225

Kelly, A. P. (2012, January 5). Don't blame for-profit colleges for the higher-ed lobbying epidemic. *The Atlantic.* Retrieved from http://www.theatlantic.com/business/archive/2012/01/dont-blame-for-profit-colleges-for-the-higher-ed-lobbying-epidemic/250921/

KIPP. (2013). Our schools. Retrieved from http://www.kipp.org/schools/

Kirp, D. (2007). *The sandbox investment: The preschool movement and kids-first politics.* Cambridge, MA: Harvard University Press.

Kluger, J. (2010). Astronauts Inc.: The private sector muscles out NASA. *Time.* Retrieved from http://www.time.com/time/health/article/0,8599,2037089,00.html

Koyama, J. P. (2010). *Making failure pay: For-profit tutoring, high-stakes testing, and public schools.* Chicago, IL: University of Chicago Press.

Krigman, E. (2010, June 8). Learning from charter schools. *National Journal.* Retrieved from http://www.highbeam.com/doc/1G1-228183515.html

Kunskapsskolan. (2010). Academic outcomes. Retrieved from http://www.kunskapsskolan.com/performance/academicoutcomes.4.52155b18128a87c7cfd80009598.html

Kutz, G. D. (2010, August 4). For-profit colleges: Undercover testing finds colleges encouraged fraud and engaged in deceptive and questionable marketing practices. Statement to the Senate Committee on Health, Education, Labor, and Pensions. Retrieved from www.gao.gov/new.items/d10948t.pdf

Lacy, S. (2010, May 19). Too cool for school: What the valley is missing in online education. *TechCrunch.* Retrieved from http://techcrunch.com/2010/05/19/too-cool-for-school-what-the-valley-is-missing-in-online-education/#ixzz0obMu0ksa

Lake, A. (1970). The day care business. *McCall's, 98*(2), 60–61, 96–97.

Lake Research Partners. (2009). *Research on American institutions of higher education.* Washington, DC: Lake Research Partners. Retrieved from www.adaction.org/media/09pres%20educationpoll%20d5.pdf

Lang, K., & Weinstein, R. (2012, June). *Evaluating student outcomes at for-profit colleges.* National Bureau of Economic Research Working Paper No. 18201. Retrieved from http://www.nber.org/papers/w18201

Lauerman, J. (2010, September 30). For-profit colleges singled out unfairly, Republicans say. *Bloomberg Businessweek.* Retrieved from www.businessweek.com\\news\\2010-09-30\\for-profit-colleges-singled-out-unfairly-republicans-say.html

Laughlin, L. (2010). Who's minding the kids? Childcare arrangements: Spring 2005/Summer 2006. *Household Economic Studies: U.S Census Bureau.* Washington, DC: U.S. Census Bureau. Retrieved from www.census.gov/prod/2010pubs/p70-121.pdf

Lederman, D. (2011, January 14). The House's new higher ed leader. *Inside Higher Ed*. Retrieved from www.insidehighered.com/news/2011/01/14/interview_with_virginia_foxx_new_head_of_house_higher_education_subcommittee.

Levitt, T. (1960, July–August). Marketing myopia. *Harvard Business Review, 38*, 24–47.

Lopez, S. J. (2010, August 25). Americans' views of public schools still far worse than parents'. *Gallup*. Retrieved from www.gallup.com/poll/142658/americans-views-public-schools-far-worse-parents.aspx

Lozier, C., & Rotherham, A. J. (2011). *Location, location, location: How would a high-performing charter school network fare in different states?* Washington, DC: Bellwether Education Partners.

Lyons, L. (2002, November 19). Can education be for kids and for-profit? *Gallup*. Retrieved from www.gallup.com/poll/7228/Can-Education-Kids-ForProfit.aspx

Lytle, R., Brinner, R., & Ross, C. (2010, February 24). *Private sector post-secondary schools: Do they deliver value to students and society?* Boston: Parthenon Group.

Mackey, K. (2009, October). Florida Virtual School: Building the first statewide, Internet-based public high school. *Innosight Institute*. Retrieved from http://www.innosight-stitute.org/innosight/wp-content/uploads /2010/02/FLVS.pdf

Marketdata Enterprises. (2010, May). *U.S. child day care services: An industry analysis* (7th ed.). Tampa, FL: Author.

Martinez, B. (2010, May 29). Charter-school advocates raise cap. *Wall Street Journal*. Retrieved from http://online.wsj.com/article/SB1000142405274870459650457527294271 6879192.html

Mathers, S., Sylva, K., & Joshi, H. (2007). *Quality of childcare in the millennium cohort study*. London, UK: Department of Educational Studies, University of Oxford and Centre for Longitudinal Studies, Institute of Education, University of London. Retrieved from www.education.gov.uk/publications/eOrderingDownload/SSU2007FR025.pdf

Mathews, J. (2011, November 27). 5 reasons for-profit colleges will survive. *Washington Post Class Struggle blog*. Retrieved from http://www.washingtonpost.com/blogs/class-struggle/post/5-reasons-for-profit-colleges-will-survive/2011/11/27/gIQApBvy2N_blog.html

Mathis, M. (2007). *Nonprofit non-marketing*. Bloomington, IN: Xlibris Corporation.

Matthews, H., & Ewen, D. (2011). Meeting the early learning challenge: Better child care subsidy policies. Washington, DC: Center for Law and Social Policy. Retrieved from www.clasp.org/admin/site/publications/files/subsidiesandelc.pdf

McKenna, C. (2010). Child care subsidies in the United States: Government funding to families. In *Sloan network encyclopedia*. Retrieved from https://workfamily.sas.upenn.edu/wfrn-repo/object/ad3j1t5wq2hm2h26

Medina, J. (2010, May 28). New York State votes to expand charter schools. Retrieved from http://www.nytimes.com/2010/05/29/nyregion/29charter.html

Meehan, W. F., Kilmer, D., & O'Flanagan, M. (2004). Investing in society: Why we need a more efficient social capital market—and how we can get there. *Stanford Social Innovation Review, 4*, 34-43.

Meier, D. (2011, September 15). Twitter @debmeier. Retrieved from https://twitter.com/#!/DebMeier/status/114466979934519296

Miller, B. (2010). *Are you gainfully employed? Setting standards for for-profit degrees.* Washington, DC: Education Sector.

Mishra, P., & Koelher, M. (2006). Technological pedagogical content knowledge: A framework for teacher knowledge. *Teachers College Record, 108*(6), 1017—1054. Retrieved from http://punya.educ.msu.edu/publications/journal_articles/mishra-koehler-tcr2006.pdf

Moe, M., & Quazzo, D. (2012, July). Fall of the wall: Capital flows to education innovation. *GSV Advisors.* Retrieved from http://gsvadvisors.com/wordpress/wp-content/themes/gsvadvisors/GSV%20Advisors_Fall%20of%20the%20Wall_2012-8-3.pdf

Molnar, A., Miron, G., & Urschel, J. L. (2010). *Profiles of for-profit education management organizations: Twelfth annual report, 2000–2010.* Boulder, CO: National Education Policy Center.

Morris, J. R., & Helburn, S. W. (2000). Child care center quality differences: The role of profit status, client preferences, and trust nonprofit. *Nonprofit and Voluntary Sector Quarterly, 29*(3), 377.

Naci Mocan, H. (2001). Can consumers detect lemons? Information asymmetry in the market for childcare. Working paper, NBER, Cambridge, MA. Retrieved from www.nber.org/papers/w8291.pdf

National Alliance for Public Charter Schools. Dashboard—Schools by management type, 2010–2011 data. Retrieved from http://dashboard.publiccharters.org/dashboard/schools/page/mgmt/year/2011

National Association of Childcare Resource and Referral Agencies. (2012a, August 14). Parents and the high cost of childcare. Retrieved from www.naccrra.org/publications/naccrra-publications/parents-and-high-cost-of-child-care-2011.php

National Association of Childcare Resource and Referral Agencies. (2012b). *We can do better: 2011 update: NACCRRA's ranking of state child care center regulation and oversight.* Washington, DC: Author.

National Center for Education Statistics. (2011). Condition of education 2011. Retrieved from http://nces.ed.gov/pubs2011/2011033_2.pdf

National Center for Education Statistics. (n.d). Fast facts. *U.S. Department of Education.* Retrieved from www.nces.ed.gov/fastfacts/display.asp?id=28

National Education Association. (2013). The case against privatizing school support services. Retrieved from http://hin.nea.org/home/29420.htm

National Institute for Early Education Research. (2003). *The state of preschool: 2003 state preschool yearbook.* New Brunswick, NJ: Rutgers University. Retrieved from www.pewtrusts.org/uploadedFiles/wwwpewtrustsorg/Reports/Pre-k_education/nieer_pre-school_2004.pdf

National Institute for Early Education Research. (2009). *The state of preschool: 2009 state of preschool yearbook.* New Brunswick, NJ: Rutgers University. Retrieved from http://nieer.org/publications/state-preschool-2009

National Institute for Early Education Research. (2010). *The state of preschool: 2010 state preschool yearbook*. New Brunswick, NJ: Rutgers University. Retrieved from http://nieer.org/sites/nieer/files/yearbook.pdf

National Nurse Emergency Preparedness Initiative. (2013.) *About NNEPI: History of NNEPI*. Retrieved from www.nnepi.org/about_nnepi.shtml .

Neugebauer, R. (2006). For profit childcare: Four decades of growth: Nineteenth annual status report on for profit childcare. *Exchange, 167*, 22–25.

Neugebauer, R. (2008). Challenges and opportunities in early childhood: Views of the CEOs of the big three: Twenty-first annual status report on for profit childcare. *Exchange, 179*, 32–37.

New Mexico Code. (2009). Section 22-8B-6. Retrieved from http://law.justia.com/codes/new-mexico/2009/chapter-22/article-8b/section-22-8b-6/

The New Teacher Project. (2010, December). *Resetting race to the top: Why the future of the competition depends on improving the scoring process*. [Policy brief.] Retrieved from http://tntp.org/assets/documents/Resetting_R2T_Dec6F.pdf

NewSchools Venture Fund. (2011). *NewSchools Summit 2011: Sal Khan and Joel Klein*. San Francisco, CA: NewSchools Venture Fund. Retrieved from http://www.newschools.org/blog/newschools-summit-2011-sal-khan-and joel-klein

Obama, B. (2009, March 23). Obama delivers remarks on clean energy and technology. *Washington Post*. Retrieved from http://www.washingtonpost.com/wp-dyn/content/article/2009/03/23/AR2009032301556.html

Office of Planning, Research & Evaluation. (2009). *The CCDF policies database book of tables: Key cross-state variations in CCDF policies as of October 1, 2009*. Washington, DC: Office of Planning, Research and Evaluation, Administration for Children and Families, U.S. Department of Health and Human Services. Retrieved from www.acf.hhs.gov/programs/opre/cc/ccdf_policies/key_cross.pdf

Office of the President, Arizona State University. (2012). ASU vision and goals. Retrieved from http://president.asu.edu/about/asuvision

Oracle Transcription. (2011, April 21). *Report on EHR growth from Kalorama information*. Retrieved from www.oracletranscription.com/blog/archives/report-ehr-growth-kalorama-information

Our president on energy and the environment. (2010). *Your community*. Retrieved from www.your-community.org/article.php?article_id=6&category_id=3

Patton, M. Q. (2002, January). *Utilization-Focused Evaluation (U-FE) checklist*. Retrieved from http://www.wmich.edu/evalctr/archive_checklists/ufe.pdf.

Patton, M. Q. (2008). *Utilization focused evaluation* (4th ed.). Thousand Oaks, CA: Sage Publications.

Pearson Education. (2008). Kids help Pearson design software.. Retrieved from www.pearson.com/about-us/feature/feature-archive/?i=97

Peterson, P. E. (2005). Making up the rules as you play the game. *Education Next 5*, 4: 42–48.

Petrilli, M. (2011, January 28). A new Washington consensus is born. *Education Next*. Retrieved from http://educationnext.org/a-new-washington-consensus-is-born

Phillips, D., Howes, C., & Whitebook, M. (1992). The social policy context of child care: Effects on quality. *American Journal of Community Psychology, 20*(1), 25–51.

Phi Delta Kappa International. (n.d.). PDK/Gallup past polls. Retrieved from www.pdkintl.org/kappan/pastpolls.htm.

Pianta, R., et al. (2005). Features of pre-kindergarten programs, classrooms, and teachers: Do they predict observed classroom quality and child–teacher interactions? *Applied Developmental Science, 9*(3), 144–159.

RAND Corporation. (2005, September 14). Rand study says computerizing medical records could save $81 billion annually and improve the quality of medical care. News release. Retrieved from www.rand.org/news/press/2005/09/14.html

Ravitch, D. (2011, November 29). Should schools be run for profit? *Bridging differences*. Retrieved from http://blogs.edweek.org/edweek/Bridging-Differences/2011/11/should_schools_be_run_for_prof.html

Rolnick, A., & Grunewald, R. (2003). Early childhood development: Economic development with a high public return. *Fed gazette*. Retrieved from www.minneapolisfed.org/publications_papers/pub_display.cfm?id=3832

Rose, E. (2010). *The promise of preschool: From Head Start to universal prekindergarten*. New York: Oxford University Press.

Rose, L. C., & Gallup, A. M. (2007, September). The 39th annual Phi Delta Kappa/Gallup poll of the public's attitudes toward the public schools. *Phi Delta Kappan*, 33–48. Retrieved from http://www.pdkmembers.org/members_online/publications/Gallup-Poll/kpoll_pdfs/pdkpoll39_2007.pdf

Rosen, A. S. (2011). *Change.edu: Rebooting for the new talent economy*. New York: Kaplan Publishing.

Samuelson, R. J. (2011, June 19). The great jobs mismatch. *The Washington Post*. Retrieved from http://www.washingtonpost.com/opinions/the-great-jobs-mismatch/2011/06/19/AGWdB3bH_story.html#TID=1656t2c10mhj8d&TData=99999|50213

Saul, S. (2011, December 12). Profits and questions at online charter schools. *New York Times*. Retrieved from http://www.nytimes.com/2011/12/13/education/online-schools-score-better-on-wall-street-than-in-classrooms.html?pagewanted=all

Schlesinger, M., Mitchell, S., & Gray, B. H. (2004). Public expectations of nonprofit and for-profit ownership in American medicine: Clarifications and implications. *Health Affairs* 23, 6: 181–191.

Schneider, M., & Klor de Alva, J. (2011, October). Cheap for whom: How much higher education costs taxpayers. *AEI Education Outlook*. Retrieved from www.aei.org/outlook/education/higher-education/cheap-for-whom/

Scholastic. (2011). *2011 Compendium of READ 180 Research*. New York: Author. Retrieved from http://read180.scholastic.com/reading-intervention-program/research/pages/313

Schrecker, E. (2010). *The lost soul of higher education: Corporatization, the assault on academic freedom, and the end of the American university*. New York: The New Press.

Schulman, K., & Blank, H. (2011). *State child care assistance policies: Reduced support for families in challenging times*. Washington, DC: National Women's Law Center. Retrieved from www.nwlc.org/sites/default/files/pdfs/state_child_care_assistance_poli cies_report2011_final.pdf

Scriven, M. (1991). Beyond formative and summative evaluation. In M. W. McLaughlin & D.C. Phillips (Eds.), *Evaluation and education: A quarter century* (p. 169). Chicago: University of Chicago Press.

Senate HELP Committee. (2011, June 3). Enzi says DOE rule is one more example of heavy handed regulation harming America's economy. Retrieved from http://help.senate. gov/newsroom/press/release/?id=9075d027-0a90-44da-93dd-8cbea94336e4

Sengupta, S. (2012, December 4). Online learning, personalized. *New York Times*. Retrieved from http://www.nytimes.com/2011/12/05/technology/khan-academy-blends-its-youtube-approach-with-classrooms.html?pagewanted=all&_r=0

Shonkoff, J., Boyce, W. T., & McEwen, B. (2009). Neuroscience, molecular biology, and the childhood roots of health disparities: Building a new framework for health promotion and disease prevention. *Journal of the American Medical Association, 301*(21), 2252–2259.

Shonkoff, J., & Phillips, D. D. (2000). *From neurons to neighborhoods: The science of early childhood development*. Washington, DC: National Academies Press.

Siry, D. (2009, December 1). In role as kingmaker, the energy department stifles innovation. *Wired*. Retrieved from http://www.wired.com/autopia/2009/12/ doe-loans-stifle-innovation/

Sperling, J. (2000). *Rebel with a cause: The entrepreneur who created the University of Phoenix and the for-profit revolution in higher education*. New York: John Wiley & Sons.

Stout Sosinsky, L., Lord, H., & Zigler, E. (2007). For-profit/nonprofit differences in center-based child care quality: Results from the National Institute of Child Health and Human Development Study of Early Child Care and Youth Development. *Journal of Applied Developmental Psychology* 28: 390–410.

Stuit, D. A. (2010). *Are bad schools immortal? The scarcity of turnarounds and shutdowns in both charter and district sectors*. Washington, DC: Thomas B. Fordham Institute.

Sumsion, J., & Goodfellow, J. (2009). Parents as consumers of early childhood education and care: The feasibility of demand-led improvements to quality. In D. King & G. Meagher (Eds.), *Paid care in Australia: Politics, profits, practices*. Sydney, Australia: Sydney University Press.

Thomas B. Fordham Institute. (2009). *The mad, mad world of textbook adoption*. Washington, DC: Author.

Tierney, W. G., & Hentschke, G. C. (2007). *New players, different game: Understanding the rise of for profit colleges and universities*. Baltimore, MD: The Johns Hopkins University Press.

Tom Harkin's Office. (2010, August 4). Statement of Chairman Tom Harkin (D-IA) at the HELP Committee hearing "For-profit schools: The student recruitment experience." News release. Retrieved from http://harkin.senate.gov/press/release.cfm?i=326942

Tomassini, J. (2012, February 21). K12 Inc.'s public status and growth attract scrutiny. *Education Week.* Retrieved from www.edweek.org/ew/articles/2012/02/22/21k12.h31.html

Tout, K., et al. (2010). *The child care quality rating system (QRS) assessment: Compendium of quality rating systems and evaluations.* Washington, DC: U.S. Department of Health and Human Services. Retrieved from www.acf.hhs.gov/programs/opre/cc/childcare_quality/compendium_qrs/qrs_compendium_final.pdf

Tuchman, G. (2011). *Wannabe U: Inside the corporate university.* Chicago, IL: University of Chicago Press.

Twombly, E. C., & Gantz, M. G. (2001). *Executive compensation in the nonprofit sector: New findings and policy implications.* Washington, DC: Urban Institute.

University of Phoenix. (2010). *2010 academic annual report.* Retrieved from http://cdn-static.phoenix.edu/content/dam/altcloud/doc/about_uopx/academic-annual-report-2010.pdf

University of Phoenix. (2013). Fact sheet. Retrieved from http://www.apollogrp.edu/sites/default/files/files/Apollo-Group-UOPX-Fact-Sheet.pdf

U.S. Bureau of Labor Statistics. (2011). *May 2011 national occupational employment and wage estimates.* Washington, DC: U.S. Bureau of Labor Statistics. Retrieved from www.bls.gov/oes/current/oes_nat.htm#00-0000

U.S. Department of Education. (2009, June 22). Turning around the bottom five percent: Secretary Arne Duncan's remarks at the National Alliance for Public Charter Schools Conference. News release. Retrieved from www.ed.gov/news/speeches/turning-around-bottom-five-percent

U.S. Department of Education. (2010a, April 29). ARPA-E project selections. Retrieved from http://arpa-e.energy.gov/LinkClick.aspx?fileticket=mK6vhQztzb4%3d&tabid=83

U.S. Department of Education. (2010b, January 21). Final requirements for school improvement grants, as amended in January 2010. Retrieved from www2.ed.gov/programs/sif/finalreq20100128.doc

U.S. Department of Education. (2010c, March 5). What's possible: Turning around America's lowest-achieving schools. *ED.gov* blog. Retrieved from www.ed.gov\\blog\\2010\\03\\whats-possible-turning-around-americas-lowest-achieving-schools

U.S. Department of Education. (2011). Charter schools program grants for replication and expansion of high-quality charter schools: Eligibility. Retrieved from www2.ed.gov/programs/charter-rehqcs/eligibility.html

U.S. Government Accountability Office. (2010, July). *Department of Education: Improved Dissemination and Timely Product Release Would Enhance the Usefulness of the What Works Clearinghouse.* Washington, DC: Author, Report 10-644.

U.S. House of Representatives, Office of the Clerk. (2011, February 18). *Final vote results for roll call 92.* Retrieved from http://clerk.house.gov/evs/2011/roll092.xml

U.S. Secretary of Education Duncan announce national competition to advance school reform. (n.d.). [News release.] Retrieved from http://www2.ed.gov/news/pressreleases/2009/07/07242009.html

Vandell, D., & Wolfe, B. (2000). *Childcare quality: Does it matter and does it need to be improved?* Institute for Research on Poverty Special Report, no. 78.

Vandell, D., et al. (2010). Do effects of early childcare extend to age 15 years? Results from the NICHD study of early childcare and youth development. *Child Development, 81*(3), 737–756.

Vander Ark, T. (2009). *Private capital and public education: Toward quality at scale.* Washington, DC: American Enterprise Institute.

Warner, J. (2004, July 27). Medical errors still plague U.S. hospitals. *WebMD Health News.* Retrieved from http://women.webmd.com/news/20040727/medical-errors-plague-us-hospitals

Watson, J., Murin, A., Vashaw, L., Gemin, B., & Rapp, C. (2011, November). *Keeping pace with K–12 online learning: An annual review of policy and practice 2011.* Durango, CO: Evergreen Education Group.

Webley, K. (2012, September 4). MOOC brigade: Will massive, open online courses revolutionize higher education? *Time.* Retrieved from http://nation.time.com/2012/09/04/mooc-brigade-will-massive-open-online-courses-revolutionize-higher-education/

Weiland, C. (2011). Preparing to succeed: The impact of a public preschool program on children's kindergarten literacy, math, executive functioning, and socio-emotional skills. Paper presented at the Universidad Diego Portales, Santiago, Chile.

White House Council of Economic Advisors. (2011, September). Unleashing the potential of educational technology. Retrieved from http://www.whitehouse.gov/sites/default/files/unleashing_the_potential_of_educational_technology.pdf

Whitebook, M., Howes, C., & Phillips, D. (1990). Who cares? Child care teachers and the quality of care in America. *Final Report: Child Care Staffing Study.* Oakland, CA: Child Care Employee Project.

Wikipedia. (2013a). History of the internet. Retrieved from http://en.wikipedia.org/wiki/History_of_internet#Transition_towards_the_Internet

Wikipedia. (2013b). Jimmy Wales. *Wikipedia, the Free Encyclopedia.* Retrieved from http://en.wikipedia.org/wiki/Jimmy_Wales

Wiley, D., & Barr, E. (2007) Health education textbook adoption in Texas: A lesson in politics and morality. *American Journal of Health Education, 38*(5), 295–300.

Wiseman, R. (2011, August 16). Enrollments plunge at many for-profit colleges. *The Chronicle of Higher Education.* Retrieved from http://chronicle.com/article/Enrollments-Plunge-at-Many/128711/

Youcha, G. (1995). *Minding the children: Childcare in America from colonial times to the present.* New York: Scribner.

Zagorin, A. (2011, June 13). Did education department officials leak market-sensitive info to stock traders? *Project on government oversight* (blog). Retrieved from http://pogoblog.typepad.com/pogo/2011/06/did-education-department-officials-leak-market-sensitive-info-to-stock-traders.html

Zigler, E., & Muenchow, S. (1994). *Head Start: The inside story of America's most successful educational experiment.* New York: Basic Books.

About the Contributors

John Bailey serves as the executive director of Digital Learning Now, a national initiative of the Foundation for Excellence in Education that works with policy-makers and innovators to accelerate the adoption of new models of education. John served in a number of positions in the Bush administration, working on domestic policy and innovation issues. He most recently served in the White House as part of the president's Domestic Policy Council, where he was responsible for coordinating education and labor issues. He coordinated the launch of three emergency programs to address nearly $200 billion in student loans, which saved the taxpayers over $10 billion and ensured that every student was able to secure a loan. He also served as deputy policy director for the U.S. secretary of commerce, where he worked on telecommunications and innovation issues. Mr. Bailey's experience also includes working at the Bill and Melinda Gates Foundation, where he built a portfolio of advocacy grants to advance college- and career-ready policies. He served as the nation's second director of educational technology, where he led several initiatives to expand online learning and improve the use of technology and data in education. He has been a formal or informal advisor to three presidential campaigns. He is on the board of directors for the Data Quality Campaign and serves on the regional board for the social innovation fund Indego Africa. He also serves as senior advisor to Whiteboard Advisors, which provides strategic consulting for investors, philanthropies, and entrepreneurs.

Tamara Butler Battaglino cofounded and coleads The Parthenon Group's Education Practice. She has advised clients on issues related to operational excellence, strategy development, and new venture creation. Her clients include a wide range of organizations from startups to Fortune 100 companies, government agencies, and some of the world's largest foundations. She has focused her time in the information and education sectors in the U.S and global markets, spanning early childhood, K–12, and higher education. Ms. Battaglino holds an AB in economics from Harvard College. She received her MBA from Harvard Business School and her M.Ed. from the Harvard Graduate School of Education.

Stacey Childress serves as deputy director of education at the Bill and Melinda Gates Foundation. She leads the Next Generation Models team, which supports the creation and growth of technology-enabled content, tools, and school models that support personalized paths to success for middle and high school students in the United States. Prior to joining the foundation, Ms. Childress was on the faculty of the Harvard Business School, where she wrote and taught about entrepreneurial activity in public education in the United States. Her work encompassed the behavior and strategies of leadership teams in urban public school districts, charter schools, and nonprofit and for-profit enterprises with missions to improve the public system. Before working in academia, Ms. Childress was a cofounder of an enterprise software company and spent 10 years in a Fortune 500 company in sales and general management. Early in her career, she taught in a Texas public high school. She is a graduate of Baylor University and Harvard Business School.

KC Deane is a research associate at the American Enterprise Institute. Her research focuses on financial aid and admission practices in higher education, charter school laws, and how state education policies can shape national education policy. She graduated from the University of Pennsylvania with her M.S.Ed. in education policy; her master's paper examined the impact of CMO growth on the composition of charter school operators. Prior to her studies at Penn, she worked for two years as an assistant dean of admissions at Reed College. Ms. Deane graduated from Reed with a BA in economics.

Whitney Downs is currently pursuing her JD at George Washington University. She is a former research assistant at American Enterprise Institute. Her research at AEI focused on school cost-cutting practices, the role of private enterprise and business engagement in public education, and the legal and structural barriers faced by education leaders. Her work has been published in *National Review Online* and *The Daily Caller*, and has been featured by the *Wall Street Journal*, *Huffington Post*, Policy Innovators in Education Network, and UT Austin's Institute for Public School Initiatives. Ms. Downs graduated magna cum laude with a BA in sociology from Princeton University, where she also captained the women's basketball team.

Todd Grindal is a doctoral candidate at the Harvard Graduate School of Education, where he studies the impact of public policies on young children and children with disabilities. Mr. Grindal was recently awarded a Julius B. Richmond Fellowship by the Harvard Center on the Developing Child in support of his dissertation research on the unionization of home child-care providers. He is also a recipient of the 2009 Meade Fellowship from the Institute for Educational Leadership and has been recognized as an Emerging Education Policy Scholar by the Fordham Foundation and American Enterprise Institute. Prior to beginning his doctoral studies, Mr. Grindal worked for 6 years as a teacher and school administrator at the high school level in Florida, and at the elementary school and preschool levels in the Washington, DC, metropolitan area. He earned a BA in history from The New College of Florida and an EdM in school leadership from the Harvard Graduate School of Education.

Frederick M. Hess, director of education policy studies at the American Enterprise Institute, studies a range of K–12 and higher education issues. He is the author of influential books on education, including *The Same Thing Over and Over, Education Unbound, Common Sense School Reform, Revolution at the Margins,* and *Spinning Wheels,* and he pens the *Education Week* blog *Rick Hess Straight Up.* His work has appeared in scholarly and popular outlets such as *Teachers College Record, Harvard Education Review, Social Science Quarterly, Urban Affairs Review, American Politics Quarterly, Chronicle of Higher Education, Phi Delta Kappan, Educational Leadership, U.S. News & World Report, National Affairs, The Washington Post, New York Times, The Atlantic,* and *National Review.* He serves as executive editor of *Education Next* and lead faculty member for the Rice Education Entrepreneurship Program. A former high school social studies teacher, he has taught at the University of Virginia, the University of Pennsylvania, Georgetown University, Rice University, and Harvard University. He holds an MA and PhD in government, as well as an MEd in teaching and curriculum from Harvard University.

Michael B. Horn is the co-founder and executive director of education of Innosight Institute, a not-for-profit think tank devoted to applying the theories of disruptive innovation to problems in the social sector. He is the coauthor of *Disrupting Class: How Disruptive Innovation Will Change the Way the World Learns* (2008) with Harvard Business School professor and bestselling author Clayton M. Christensen and Curtis W. Johnson. *BusinessWeek* named the book one of the 10 Best Innovation & Design Books of 2008, *Newsweek* named it as the 14th book on its list of "Fifty Books for Our Times," and the National Chamber Foundation named it first among its 10 "Books that Drive the Debate 2009." *Tech&Learning* magazine named Mr. Horn as one of the 100 most important people in the creation and advancement of the use of technology in education.

Andrew P. Kelly is a research fellow in education policy studies at AEI. His research focuses on higher education policy, innovation in education, the politics of education reform, and consumer choice in education. Previously, he was a research assistant at AEI, where his work focused on the preparation of school leaders, collective bargaining in public schools, and the politics of education. His research has appeared in *Teachers College Record, Educational Policy, Policy Studies Journal, Education Next,* and *Education Week,* as well as popular outlets such as *Inside Higher Education, Forbes, The Atlantic, National Review,* and *The Huffington Post.* He is coeditor of *Carrots, Sticks, and the Bully Pulpit: Lessons from a*

Half-Century of Federal Efforts to Improve America's Schools (2011) and *Reinventing Higher Education: The Promise of Innovation* (2011). In 2011, Mr. Kelly was named one of 16 "Next Generation Leaders" in education policy by the Policy Notebook blog on *Education Week*.

Mickey Muldoon is an MA candidate in computer science at Brooklyn College. Previously, he managed external affairs and online assessment delivery for the School of One initiative in New York City schools, was an assistant to Chester Finn at the Thomas B. Fordham Institute, worked as a field organizer for the 2008 Obama campaign in Ohio, and taught English in northeast Brazil. He attended Wilmette (IL) Public Schools, Evanston (IL) Township High School, and Harvard College.

Matthew Riggan is a senior researcher at the Consortium for Policy Research in Education at the University of Pennsylvania, and an adjunct assistant professor in Penn's Graduate School of Education. His current research focuses on formative assessment in elementary mathematics; assessing analytic and problem-solving skills for postsecondary readiness; systemic reform to support science, technology, engineering, and mathematics (STEM) education; and factors supporting or undermining the scale-up of promising reforms in urban school districts. He teaches courses in qualitative research design, data collection, and analysis, and has worked extensively on developing qualitative and mixed methods approaches to program theory evaluation and analysis of video data. Mr. Riggan holds a doctorate in anthropology and education from the University of Pennsylvania.

Chris Whittle is an entrepreneur with 4 decades of leadership experience in the fields of education and media. He is the chief executive officer of Avenues: The World School, a global network of schools to serve students in preschool, elementary, and secondary grades. Avenues opened its flagship campus in New York City in fall 2012. Mr. Whittle conceived and founded Edison Schools (now Edison Learning) in 1992 with Benno Schmidt and currently serves on its board of directors. Whittle is the author of *Crash Course—Imagining a Better Future for Public Education* and sits on the board of the Center for Education Reform in Washington, DC. Mr. Whittle began his career in publishing, building a single college magazine into Whittle Communications, one of America's top 100 media businesses in the 1980s. At the age of 32, his company bought *Esquire* magazine, where he served as chairman and publisher for many years. He founded Channel One, a national in-school television news program (first anchored by Anderson Cooper), which reached 8 million students daily in 12,000 schools.

Ben Wildavsky is a senior scholar in research and policy at the Kauffman Foundation and a guest scholar at the Brookings Institution. He is the author of *The*

Great Brain Race: How Global Universities Are Reshaping the World (Princeton University Press, 2010), which won the Frandson Award for Literature in the Field of Continuing Higher Education and is being translated into Chinese, Vietnamese, and Arabic. He is also coeditor of *Reinventing Higher Education: The Promise of Innovation* (Harvard Education Press, April 2011). Before joining the Kauffman Foundation in 2006, Mr. Wildavsky was the education editor of *U.S. News & World Report*, where he was the top editor of America's Best Colleges and America's Best Graduate Schools. Before joining *U.S. News*, he was a budget, tax, and trade correspondent for *National Journal*; a higher education reporter for the *San Francisco Chronicle;* and executive editor of the *Public Interest.* His writing has also appeared in *The Washington Post, The Wall Street Journal, Foreign Policy*, and *The New Republic*, among other publications. He is a guest blogger for *The Chronicle of Higher Education.* As a consultant to national education reformers, he has written several influential reports, including the secretary of education's Commission on the Future of Education's *A Test of Leadership.* He appears regularly in the media, including on CNN, in *The New York Times* and in *Marketplace.* He has spoken to dozens of audiences in the United States and abroad, including at Google, Harvard University, the London School of Economics, the Organisation for Economic Cooperation and Development, the *Economist's* Human Potential conference, the American College of Greece, and the University of Melbourne.

Index

Page numbers in italics refer to figures, tables, and charts.

2U, 33, *35,* 45

Aarons, D., 225
Abecedarian programs, 83
Abuses, 30–31, 209
Academy of Management, 61
Access
  to capital, 41, 43, 144, 146, 156, 198
  childcare and early education,
    81, 82, 85, 86, 91–92, 97
  for constituents, 19
  decline in, 17
  expansion of, 7, 12, 107–108,
    111, 117, 134, 143, 149
  nontraditional students, 57, 62
  and online education, 149–150
  and philanthropies, 33, 39, 40, 45, 47
  and SES, 29, 186
Accountability
  focus on, 11
  of foundations, 52
  increase in, 9, 185, 187, 191
  measures of, 5, 113
  outcome-based systems, 91, 151
  in public education, 186, 187, 188
  and regulations, 54, 186
  through evaluation, 9, 181
Accreditation requirements, 75, 90
Advanced Academics, 145

Advanced Research Projects Agency—
    Energy (ARPA-E), 127–128, 237
Advanced Technology Vehicles
    Manufacturing (ATVM) Loan
    Program, 127, 132, 135
African Americans, 12, 26
Altman, A., 225
Altwerger, B., 225
American Enterprise Institute,
    7, 49, 225, 231, 238
American Federation of
    Teachers (AFT), 194
American Hospital Association, 225
American Medical Association, 225
American Recovery and Reinvestment
    Act (ARRA) of 2009, 121,
    126, 128, 137, 208
Americans for Democratic
    Action, 18, 25, 225
Ánimo Watts Charter High School,
    131
Anthony, S., 227
Apple, Inc., 4, 196
Arizona State University, 143
ARPANET, 159, 160, 171
Asgedom, Mawi, *34,* 56
Aspire Public Schools, 147, *147*
Associate degrees program,
    29, 92, 114, 188

Associated Press and Stanford
    University, 25, 30, 225
Attainment, 11, 187, 204
Augustine, Norman, 129
Avenues: The World School,
    9, *38,* 43, 192, 196

Bachelor degree programs,
    29, 31, 60, 71, 72
Bailey, John, 3, 8, 208
Ball, Stephen, 7, 225
Baroody, K., 229
Barr, E., 238
Barth, Richard, *34,* 54, 207
Bassok, D., 225
Battaglino, Tamara, 9, 208
Battaglio, R. P. Jr., 225
Baumol, W. J., 225
Belfield, C., 22, 226
Bellwether Education
    Partners, *37,* 44, 232
Bennet, D. L., 226
Better Lesson, 49
Bias, 49, 98, 204
Bienen, Henry, 60–61,
    62, 66
Bill and Melinda Gates Foundation,
    9, *37, 38,* 39, 43, 155, 162,
    164–165, 172, 226
Bishop, Tim, 18–19
*The Blackboard and the Bottom
    Line* (Cuban), 6
Blackboard Solutions, *36*
Blank, H., 235
Blended learning, 60, 152,
    176, 183, 187, 188
Block, R., 226
Board leadership, 76
Bolden, Charles, 136

Boser, U., 226
Bowen, W. G., 225
Boyce, W. T., 236
Boyd, Thomas, 63, 64, 65, 69,
    70, 73, 77
Bradley, B., 226
Bright Horizons Family
    Solutions, 88, 99
Brin, Sergey, 124
Brinner, R., 232
The Broad Foundation, *35*
Brostek, M., 226
Bryant, P. R., 2
Buhl, S., 228
Bulkley, K. E., 226
Burch, P., 226
Bush, George W., 20, 125, 226
Bush administration
    community development entities
        (CDEs) support, 131
    regulatory efforts of, 5, 19–20
    support of electronic medical
        records, 125
Business Executives for
    National Security, 226

Cable, K. E., 226
Caldera, L., 227
California Master Plan for
    Higher Education, 113
California State University, 59
Campus Progress, 18, 226
Capella University, 58, 62, 63,
    65, 67, 68, 77, 185
Capitalism, 196, 201–202
Carey, Kevin, 188, 226
Carnegie Mellon University, 73
Carter, Samuel Casey, *34,* 54
Carter Research, *34*

Center for American Progress,
    18, 184, 226
Center for Global Prosperity, 227
Center for Non-Profits, 227
Center for Responsive Politics, 151, 227
Central Intelligence Agency (CIA), 129
Cerf, Chris, *34*, 46, 54
CfBT USA, *34*
Chamberlain College of Nursing, 60
Chancellor Beacon Academies, *35*
Change.edu (Rosen), 6
Charities Aid Foundation, 227
Charter management organization
    (CMO), 145, 157, 164, 165, 170
Charter School Growth Fund, *35*
Charter schools. *See also* K12
    Inc.; KIPP schools
  accountability of, 191
  contracting of services, 141
  and early childhood education, 81
  economies of scale, *146,* 146–147
  education reform, 204
  enrollment in, 145–146
  expansion of, 54, 176
  financing of, 31, 131
  founding of, 2, 199
  legislation, 3, 9, 146
  movement to, 40, 53–55, 192
  online, 141, 145
  per-pupil funding, 46
  and philanthropy, 198
  political support of, 11, 19, 46, 54
  privatization of, 1, 187
  use of metrics, 182
Charter Schools Program Grants for
    Replication and Expansion of
    High-Quality Charter Schools, 11
Child and Dependent Care Tax
    Credit (CDCTC), 80, 85, 98

Childcare and Development
    Act (CCDA), 85
Childcare and Development
    Fund (CCDF), 80, 84
Childcare Development Block Grant
    (CCDBG), 85, 87, 89–90, 98
Children's Discovery Center, 71
Childress, Stacey, 9, 208
Childs, D., 227
Christensen, Clayton, 58, 75, 227
Cigale, George, *34,* 41, 48, 50
City of Los Angeles, *38*
Clark, T., 227
Class size, 72, 90, 184, 195
Cleveland, Gordon, 94, 227
Clinton, Bill, 16, 44, 131
Clinton administration, 131
Coalition for Educational
    Success, 17, 20, 228
Collegiate Learning Assessment
    (CLA), 65
Commission on the Future of
    Higher Education, 112
Common Core State
    Standards, 164, 175
Community colleges, 17, 26, 31,
    61, 67, 74, 77, 78, 189
Community development
    entities (CDEs), 130–131
Community Development
    Financial Institutions
    (CDFI) Fund, 130, 228
Compensation, 19, 44, 59,
    68, 98, 184, 205
Congress, 11, 12, 13, 14, 17, 85, 110,
    122, 128, 129, 135, 137, 208
Congressional Black Caucus, 17
Connections Education, 118,
    145, 146, 149, 151

Cook, S., 227
Cook Political Report, 228
Council for American Medical
    Innovation, 228
CSU Fullerton, 70
Cuban, Larry, 6, 228
Curriculum
    design of, 63–64, 66, 75,
        148, 149
    online, 118, 119, 141
    standardization of, 6, 58, 63,
        64, 66, 70, 75, 77
Curriki, 36

Danner, John, 35, 46, 49
Debt
    debt-to-income ratio, 12,
        57, 108, 187, 190
    and gainful-employment
        regulation, 134, 137, 176
    high level of, 72, 107, 187, 200
    repayment expectations, 78
Deloitte, 228
Democrats
    and for-profit school
        management, 24, 25
    gainful-employment regulation,
        12, 17–19, 18, 20
    opposition to for-profits,
        11, 12, 13–14, 15, 31–32
    support of for-profits, 1, 24, 26, 40
    support of SES eligibility, 15–17
DeVry University, 58, 60, 66,
    67, 68, 69, 74, 76, 145
Diamandis, Peter, 124, 228
Digital Learning Now, 3
Disruptive innovation, 2, 6, 58, 75,
    100, 101, 103, 104–105, 106, 106,
    107, 110, 111–112, 123, 177, 227

Donations, 39, 41, 45, 47, 48, 52, 53,
    155. See also philanthropies
Donovan, J., 226
Duncan, Arne, 12, 14, 16, 62, 120,
    122, 137, 204, 229, 237
Durbin, Dick, 13, 228

E. L. Haynes Public Charter
    School, 131
Early childhood education (ECE). See
    also Early Head Start; Head Start
    access to, 90–91
    accountability of, 90–91
    business models, 87, 88–89
    center-based programs, 84
    classroom processes, 83
    economic benefit of, 83
    evaluation of, 97
    Florida model, 90–91
    and future academic success, 83
    growth in, 99
    history of, 84–86
    home-based programs, 84
    need for high-quality teachers, 98
    Oklahoma model, 91–92
    parental assessment of, 94–95, 96
    parental employment needs, 81
    parental involvement, 89
    participation, 82, 84, 86, 95
    program structure, 83
    public/private partnerships,
        80, 86, 88–89
    public-sector programs, 80–81
    quality of, 81–82, 83,
        93–94, 95–97, 98
    regulation of, 87–88, 97–98
    skill development, 80–81, 95–96
    staff-to-child ratio, 92, 97
    staff turnover, 93, 94

subsidizing of, 97, 98, 99
teachers' wages, 92
tuition costs, 81
types of, 83, 84
use of vouchers, 89–90
Early Head Start, 84, 86
Economies of scale, 144, 145,
    146, 146–147, 147, 153
EdisonLearning, 145
Edison Schools, 2, 34, 38,
    46, 49, 54, 55, 192
Education Impact, 36
Education management
    organizations (EMOs), 16, 17,
    30, 31, 141, 145, 179, 183
Education plc: Understanding Private
    Sector Participation in Public
    Sector Education (Ball), 7
Education Sector, 228
Educorp Consultants Corporation, 36
Elementary and Secondary
    Education Act (ESEA), 134
Else-Mitchell, Rose, 35
Emerging Risk?, 228
EMOs. See Education management
    organizations
EnCorps, 38
Energy Independence and
    Security Act of 2007, 127
Enrollment
    caps on, 149
    charter schools, 145–146, 147, 148
    cycles of, 71
    decline in, 3, 176
    evaluation findings, 180, 182
    funding model, 11, 191
    increase in, 2, 87, 144
    at K–12 level, 191
    nontraditional students, 72–73

online education, 73, 143, 145, 152
prekindergarten, 89
recruitment process, 14, 111
Enzi, Mike, 14, 15, 20, 228, 236
Epstein, J., 228
Equality Charter School, 35
eSpark, 38, 43
Evaluations
    accountability, 185
    availability of, 179
    customer feedback, 174–
        175, 189–190
    effectiveness of, 185, 189–191
    efficiency measures, 182–184,
        186, 189–191
    formative approach, 176, 177–178
    intellectual property, 184
    market as evaluator, 181–182
    need for, 175, 180–181, 186
    profit motive, 179–180, 185, 186, 189
    student outcomes, 174, 185
    summative approach, 177,
        178–179, 184
    third-party research, 174–175
    underused, 184, 185, 206–207
Ewen, Danielle, 98, 232
Executive MBA (EMBA), 69

Faculty
    adjunct, 63, 67
    compared to community college
        instructors, 67–68
    compensation, 68
    data-based evaluation of, 6
    evaluation of, 68–70
    full/part-time ratio, 67
    as practitioners, 67, 70–71, 77
    quality of, 74–75
    role of, 58

Faculty *(continued)*
  at teaching institutions, 66–67, 77
  tenure, 61–62, 69, 70, 77, 184
  training for, 68, 77
  turnover, 61–62, 69
Federal funding, 9, 26–27,
    27, 78, 124, 129
Federal policies
  Advanced Research Projects
      Agency—Energy
      (ARPA-E), 127–128
  Advanced Technology Vehicles
      Manufacturing (ATVM)
      Loan Program, 127
  barriers to, 9
  change in regulation, 110
  charter school, 9
  Clean School Bus USA, 128
  create incentives, 206
  and education innovation, 138–139
  eligibility of local education
      agencies (LEAs), 137
  encourage research and
      development, 133
  energy incentive programs, 127–128
  expansion of access, 107–108
  failure to incentivize, 210
  favors nonprofits, 103
  focus on outcomes, 103
  funding barriers, 122
  Hydrogen Fuel Excise
      Tax Credit, 128
  Improved Energy Technology
      Loans, 128
  incentives, 115
  legislative process, 110
  maintain status quo, 120
  need for, 4
  private-sector engagement, 121

  regulation, 115
  reward outcomes, 120
Federal student aid, 19–20, 26,
    65. *See also* Investing in
    Innovation Fund (i3)
Federal Way Public Schools, *38*
Fitzpatrick, M., 225
Florida Department of Education,
    228
Florida Kindergarten Readiness
    Screener (FLKRS), 90
Florida Universal Pre-Kindergarten
    (PreK) Amendment 8, 91
Florida Virtual School (FLVS),
    119, 141, 144, 149, 151,
    152, 227, 228, 232
Florida Voluntary Prekindergarten
    (VPK), 90–91
Flyvbjerg, B., 228
For-profit colleges and universities
  attracting educators/
      administrators, 58–62
  criticism of, 76
  degree programs, 58
  experimentation ability, 62–63, 77
  fixed revenue, 187
  growth in, 57, 78
  incentives for recruiters, 111
  learning outcomes, 58, 62–63
  mission of, 58
  program changes, 63
  quality of, 61, 62, 73–76, 111
  regulations, 57, 75, 111
  standardized curriculum, 58, 63
  tuition costs, 187
  value of education, 79, 187–188
For-Profit Colleges and Universities
    (Hentschke, Lechuga,
    & Tierney), 6–7

For-profit education. *See also* Charter
    schools; K–12 education;
    K–12 online education
    access to capital, 116–117, 132, 205
    advocacy for, 17, 140, 148,
        149–151, 152, 153, 201
    attracting talent, 4, 39, 40, 41,
        44, 45, 52, 100, 103, 117,
        138, 145, 155, 205, 207
    bias against, 49, 98, 204
    business model, 108–110, *109,*
        111, 112, 116, 156
    compared to nonprofits/public
        institutions, 1, 102, 187
    corporate structures, 102–103
    cost control, 2, 4, 100, 114,
        115, 116, 117, 206
    discrimination against, 9
    donor revenue, 52–53
    efficiencies of, 100, 206
    expands consumer choices,
        198–199, 203
    flexibility of, 132, 205
    funding formulas, 115
    good or evil belief, 101–102,
        119–120, 204
    growth, 2–3, 13, 26, 30
    intellectual property, 133, 168, 184
    investment in, 3, 195–197
    marketing viability, 118–119, 174
    motivation of, 112, 193–195
    non-U.S. countries, 201
    organizational culture, 108–109
    partnerships, 8
    perceptions of, 7, 100, 174,
        192–193, 202, 208, 209, 210
    politics of, 12, 28–30, 31–32
    and profit, 1–2, 100, 114,
        116, 118, 199

    quality of, 12, 25, *25,* 25–26,
        104, *105,* 107, 193, 194,
        195, 200, 206, 209
    regulation of, 3–4, 9, 11–12, 15, *42*
    reputation of, 1–2, 184
    research about, 5–7, 209
    research and development
        investment, 133, 155, 177–178
    responsibility to customers,
        112, 116, 118
    role in education, 10, 11, *29*
    scalability of, 204, 205–206
    and school management, 199
    stakeholders, 13, 17, 49, 140, 150
    success of, 103–104
    sustaining innovations, 104, *105*
    value networks, 110–111
For-profit status
    efficiency of, 56
    fundraising efficiency, 41, 43
    investment capital, 40, 43–44
    long-term value, 50
    moral equal to nonprofit, *42,* 48–49
    motivations, 51
    short-term profits, 50
    social impacts of, 40
Foundations, 9, 33, 43, 48, 73, 119.
    See also specific foundations
Foust, J., 229
Foxx, Virginia, 20
Franklin Montessori School, 88–89
Fuller, A., 229
Fuller, B., 229

Gainful-employment regulations
    affects, 112, 188
    declines in enrollment, 3, 176
    Democrat opposition to, 18–19
    Democrat support of, 12, 14, *18*

Gainful-employment
    regulations *(continued)*
    for-profit opposition to, 113
    Kline amendment, 15, 17–18, 18, 20
    managing student debt,
        134, 137, 138
    Republican opposition to, 14, 20
    sets low bar, 107
    and student performance, 187, 190
Gallup, A. M., 235
Gantz, M. G., 237
Garan, E. M., 229
Gayer, T., 229
General Social Survey, 28, 229
Gilroy, L., 229
Gleason, P., 229
Goes, Jim, 61, 68–69, 71, 74
Goin, L. I., 229
Gomez, L. M., 229
Goodfellow, Joy, 94, 236
Google, 4, 124, 130, 132
Gorman, S., 229
Gormley, Walter, 92, 229
Government Accountability
    Office (GAO), 14, 19, 74,
        131, 181, 226, 237
Government policies. *See*
    federal policies
Graduation rates, 74, 77, 78, 100,
        107, 108, 114, 173, 188
Gray, B. H., 235
Grindal, Todd, 8, 229
Grossman, J. H., 227
Grunewald, R., 235

Hall, Kevin, *35*
Hall, T., 227
Harber, Jonathan, *35*, 43, 48, 52–53
Harkin, Tom, 13, 14, 15, 229, 236

Harlem Children's Zone, 33
Harlem Success, 33
Hart, B. B., 229
Hartford Public Schools, *36*
Hasselbring, Ted, 177, 229
Hastings, Alcee, 18
Hawley Miles, K., 229
Head Start, 84, 85, 86, 87, 89,
        90, 91, 92, 96, 235, 238
Health Information Technology
        for Economic and Clinical
        Health Act, 126
Heckman, James, 83, 229
Heinrich, C. J., 229
Helburn, Suzanne, 95, 229, 233
HELP committee, 13, 14, 236
Henderson, Rebecca, 133, 229
Henig, Jeffrey, 15–16, 230
Hentschke, Guilbert C.,
        6, 7, 67, 78, 229, 230, 236
Hess, Frederick M., 49–50, 119, 230
Higher Learning Commission, 75
Hightower, A. M., 230
Hing, E., 230
Hispanic Caucus, 17
Hoey, Peg, *35*, 50
Horn, Michael B., 8, 9, 177,
        206, 227, 230
Houghton Mifflin Harcourt, 33, *34*
House Committee on Education
        and Labor, 17
House Committee on Education
        and the Workforce, 15
House Subcommittee on
        Higher Education and
        Workforce Training, 20
Howes, C., 238
Hsiao, C., 230
Hwang, J., 227

inBloom, Inc., 171
Incentives
    creation of, 7
    cut costs, 49–50, 114
    equity, 44
    federal funds, 30
    financial, 71, 78, 96, 97, 103, 110,
        121, 123, *158*, 159, 183, 186, 190
    for good behavior, 51, 107,
        108, 115, 116, 206
    in K–12 market, 158–159, 170–171
    long-term, 78, 162
    market, 164–171
    misaligned, 43, 47, 120, 156
    for nonprofits, 113, 114
    and quality, 50, 96, 97, 138, 190
    regulations, 19, 30, 102, 109, 111,
        115, 122, 127–128, 190
    rules on compensation, 19
    socially responsible, 78, 206
    strengthening of, 172
    tax, 130
    for teachers, 11
    to waste, 50, 184
    weakening of, 155, 157
In Defense of Our Children (Garan), 5
Innosight Institute, 8, 9
Innovations for Learning, *36*
Institute for Education Sciences, 178
Internet development, 159–160, *161*
Investing in Innovation Fund (i3),
    3, 11, 12, 13, 32, 101, 120,
    122, 128, 137, 151
Investors
    attracting, 138, 156, 157, 205
    and charter management
        organizations, 157
    collaboration with Department
        of Education, 15

discounted stock price, 117
    flexibility of, 44
    and K–12 education, 100
    and learning models, 183, 188
    in low-income communities, 131
    needs of, 117
    and performance analysis, 174, 183
    and philanthropy, 45, 164
    prioritized above students, 13, 195
    and regulations, 15
    return on investment, 2, 16,
        42, 46, 50, 104, 119, 130,
        154, 156, 159, 160
    risk level, 122, 136, 167

Jansen, P., 226
Jobs, Steve, 201
John and Laura Arnold
    Foundation, *38*, 41
Johnson, C. W., 227
Johnson, Lyndon B., 86
Johnson, M., 230
Joshi, H., 232

K12 Inc., *36*, 118, *146*, 146–147,
    148, 150–151, 177, 178, 230
K–12 education
    ban for-profits involvement, 3, 11
    competition between public
        and privates schools, 187
    contracted support services,
        2, 5, 136, 185
    government as customer, 55
    lack of for-profit analysis, 7
    learning models, 187
    local government management, 157
    market segments, 162–171,
        163, 170, *171*, 172
    and philanthropy, 137, 154, 198

K–12 education *(continued)*
  policy restrictions, 3, 150
  profiting in, 136–137
  public/private partnerships, 140, 154
  purchase decisions in, 20, 169–170
  reform, 32
  skepticism of for-profit
      management, 12, 21, 27, 29,
      31, 32, 136, 157, 176, 187
  test scores, 179
K–12 online education
  access to capital, 144
  advocacy for, 149–151, 153
  contracted support services, 145
  fixed capital, 144
  growth in, 143–144, 187
  philanthropic support, 145
  policy restrictions, 150–151
  quality of, 115
  regulations compared to
      nonprofits, 153
  research and development
      investment, 147–148, 153
Kagan, S. L., 230
Kamenetz, A., 230
Kaplan University, 6, 29, 58, 59,
      63, 64, 65, 67, 69, 72, 73,
      74, 75, 77, 78, 177, 235
Katzman, John, *35,* 41, 45, 51, 53
Kaufman, S. P., 227
KC Distance Learning, *38*
Keaton, P., 230
Keeney, Joseph, 137
Keller, Dennis, 60
Keller, Temp, *36,* 45, 47–48
Keller Graduate School of
      Management, 60
Kellogg, Cliff, 130, 231
Kelly, Andrew P., 7, 151, 208, 231

Kennedy, Ted, 16
Khan, Salman, 46
Khan Academy, 33, 45, 46,
      144, 145, 168, 236
Kickboard, *37,* 48
Kilmer, D., 232
KIPP schools, 1, 33, *34, 37,*
      54, 143, 144, 207, 231
Klein, Joe, 201
Kline, John, 14–15, 17
Klor de Alva, Jorge, 59–60, 61–62,
      64, 67, 70, 207, 235
Kluger, J., 231
Knowledge Universe, *36, 37,* 54, 89
Koelher, M., 233
Kopp, Wendy, 201
Koyama, J. P., 231
Krigman, E., 231
Kunskapsskolan USA, *35,* 50, 231
Kurshan, Bobbi, *36*
Kutz, G. D., 231

Lake, Alice, 98, 231
Lake Research Partners, 231
Lang, K., 231
Latinos, 12, 26
Lauerman, J., 231
Laughlin, L., 231
Learn Capital, *38,* 43
Learning models
  blended, 60, 152, 176, 183, 187, 188
  online, 133, 141, 146, 152,
      176, 187, 188
  student-centric, 6
Learning outcomes, 59, 62, 63–64, 65,
      66, 67, 77, 78, 155, 159, 162, 185
LearnNow, *37*
Lechuga, Vicente M., 6, 230
Lederman, D., 232

Legislation. *See also* federal policies
   charter schools, 9
   nondiscriminatory, 54
   prekindergarten, 91
   and public/private partnerships,
      123
   regulations against for-profits,
      12, 53, 103, 122
   restricted participation, 3
   vouchers, 177
Levitt, T., 232
Lieberman, Joe, 16
Liu, F., 230
Lobbying, 57, 111, 150, 151, 206
Lobbyists, 111, 150–151
Local education agencies (LEAs),
   137
Loeb, S., 225
Lopez, S. J., 232
Lord, H., 236
*The Lost Soul of Higher
   Education* (Schrecker), 6
Loyola University, 60
Lozier, C., 232
Lucchesi, A. R., 226
Lyons, L., 232
Lytle, R., 232

Mackey, K., 232
Making Failure Pay (Koyoma), 6
Malandra, Geri, 59, 63–64,
   65, 72, 73, 75
Marketdata Enterprises, 232
Markets
   distortion of, 135–136
   high incentives/high demand,
      163, 167–169
   high incentives/low demand,
      163, 164–165

K–12 fragmentation, *163,* 170, *171*
   low incentives/high demand,
      163, 169–171
   low incentives/low demand,
      163, 165–166
Market shares, 2, 160
Martinez, B., 232
Mathers, S., 232
Mathews, Jay, 49, 204
Mathis, M., 232
Matthews, Hannah, 98, 232
Mawi Learning, *34*
MBA programs, 3
McCain, John, 15
McEwen, B., 236
McKenna, C., 232
Medbery, Jennifer Schnidman,
   37, 48
Media, 27, 31, 57, 79, 115,
   167, 174, 192, 201
Medicaid, 126
Medicare, 126
Medina, J., 232
Meehan, W. F., 232
Meier, Deborah, 48, 233
Mental Karate, 56
Meyer, R. H., 229
Michigan Virtual University, 144
Miles, Karen Hawley, 184
Miller, B., 233
Minority groups, 12, 17, 31
Miron, Gary, 30, 233
Mishra, P., 233
Mitchell, S., 235
Moe, M., 233
Molnar, Alex, 30, 233
Mondo Publishing, *38*
Montessori schools, 8, 88
Morris, John, 95, 233

Mosaica, 33, *36,* 49, 54
Moskowitz, Eva, *36*
Muenchow, S., 238
Muldoon, Mickey, 8, 205, 207
Mulgrew, Michael, 48–49

Naci Mocan, H., 233
NASA, 4, 121, 123–125,
    133, 208
National Alliance for Public
    Charter Schools, *37,* 47
National Association of
    Childcare Resource and
    Referral Agencies, 233
National Center for Education
    Statistics, 233
National Education Association, 233
National Heritage Academies, *34,* 54
National Institute for Early Education
    Research (NIEER), 91, 233, 234
National Institute of Child Health
    and Development (NICHD), 93
National Nurse Emergency
    Preparedness Initiative, 234
National Press Club, 13
NetGravity, *35*
Neugebauer, Roger, 85–86, 234
Newell, Richard, 133, 229
New Jersey Department of
    Education, *34,* 39
New Mexico Code, 234
New Orleans Charter Science
    and Math Academy, *37*
New Players, Different Game
    (Tierney & Hentschke), 7
NewSchools Venture Fund,
    37, 39, 49, 52, 53, 54, 234
New Teacher Project, 33, 135, 234
New York City Council, *36*

New York City Department
    of Education, *34*
New York City Outward Bound, *35*
Next Generation Models (NGM), 164
Nexus Research and Policy Center, 59
Nixon, Richard, 85
No Child Left Behind, 1, 5,
    12, 15, 175, 186
Nonprofit organizations. *See
    also* philanthropies
    absence of market viability, 118–119
    business model, 113, 156, 168
    cost control, 114
    delayed organizational
        outcomes, 39, 45–46
    donation revenue, 45, 47–48
    foundations, 9, 43, 48, 73, 119
    fundraising ability, 33, 39, 43, 45
    incentives for, 113
    mission of, 51
    moral equal to for-profits,
        39–40, 48–49
    philanthropic capital, 197–198
    political pressure, 45, 46
    preference for, 55–56
    public perception, 39
    quality, 50
    restrictions of, 39
    salaries, 44
    tax exemption status, 39
    volunteer support, 45, 47
Nontraditional students
    enrollment, 72–73
    graduation rates, 114
    practical training programs
        for, 59–60
    risk factors, 72
    student loan default rate, 62
    target market, 58

Noodle, *35,* 45
Northwestern University, 60, 61, 66
NSFNET, 159, 160, 171

Obama, Barack, 11, 62,
     120, 121, 122, 234
Obama administration
  college completion goals, 122
  energy policy, 127
  Race to the Top initiative, 139, 175
  regulatory efforts of, 5, 13,
     18–19, 20, 137
  skepticism of for-profits, 11
  State of the Union address
     (2011), 11
  support of for-profits, 16
  support of public/private
     partnerships, 121, 123, 132
Oboler, Josh, 88–89
Offerman, Michael, 62–63,
     65, 67, 68, 73, 77
Office of Educational Research
  and Improvement, 178
Office of Planning, Research
  & Evaluation, 234
Office of Postsecondary Education, 20
Office of Science and
  Technology Policy, 123
Office of the President, Arizona
  State University, 234
O'Flanagan, M., 232
Online education
  availability of, 60
  enrollment, 73
  funding formula, 152
  growth of, 2–3, 9, 73, 140, 152
  incentives for, 107
  performance accountability, 152
  quality of, 152

regulation of, 9
scalability of, 140
Technology, Pedagogy,
     Assessment, and Content
     (TPAC), 141, *142,* 143
Oracle Transcription, 234
Oschman, S., 230

Packard, Ron, *36,* 151
Page, Larry, 124
Parker, Laura, 71, 72
Parsons, Ebbie, *36,* 54
The Parthenon Group, 9, 155, 232
Partisan Voting Index, 18
Party affiliation, K–12 school
     management, *24,* 24–25
Patton, M. Q., 234
Pay-for-performance systems, 132–133
Payne, Donald, 18
Pearson, 33, *35,* 52, 53, 137,
     145, 149, 178, 185, 234
Pell grants, 107
Pelosi, Nancy, 18
Performance-funding
     measures, 11, 126
Perry Preschool, 83
Personal Responsibility and Work
     Opportunity Reconciliation
     Act (PRWORA), 85
Peterson, P. E., 234
Petrilli, M., 234
Phi Delta Kappa International, 235
Phi Delta Kappa (PDK)/Gallup poll, 21
Philanthropies
  functional philanthropists, 158
  hamper for-profit companies,
     156–157
  influence on markets, 154–155, 208
  Internet development, 159–160, *161*

Philanthropies *(continued)*
  invest in for-profits, 52–43
  in K–12 education, 154,
      155, 162, 164
  and market conditions for
      investment, *163,* 164–165,
      167–168, 169–171
  scalability of, 198
  and social purposes, 154, 156
  unintentional outcomes of,
      171–172
  vaccine development, 160–162, *163*
Phillips, Deborah, 92, 229, 236, 238
Pianko, Daniel, 137
Pianta, R., 235
Plucker, J. A., 226
Policies. *See* federal policies
PowerMyLearning, 166
Princeton Review, 29, *34,*
      35, 41, 45, 51, 53
Princeton University, 60, 66, 207
Privatization, 1, 13, 15, 17,
      27–28, 30, 187
Privatizationwatch.org, 27
Productivity, 2, 11, 83, 88, 120, 206
Public education. *See also*
      K–12 education
  accountability pressures, 186
  budgets of, 183
  constrained resource allocations, 183
  constrained revenues, 118
  cost control, 102
  dropouts, 203
  efficiencies, 102
  flexibility of, 183, 207
  free enterprise in, 1, 4
  government as customers, 112
  privatization of, 13
  profitability of, 3

  public interest in, 16, 27–28, 101
  role in the sector, 3
  status quo, 203
  values of, 2
Public opinion
  contracting of non-instruction
      services, 21, 22–23, *23,* 24
  managing K–12 schools, 7,
      21–22, *22,* 23–24, *24*
  skepticism of for-profits, 7, 12
Public/private partnerships
  electronic health records
      (EHR), 121, 125–127
  energy advancements, 127–128, 132
  incentives for, 122
  and In-Q-Tel, 129–130
  Internet development, 159–160, *161*
  and NASA, 4, 121, 123–125, 133, 208
  and New Markets Tax Credit
      (NMTC), 130–131
  pay-for-performance
      systems, 132–133
  politically influenced
      decisions, 134–135
  vaccine development, 160–162, *163*

Quality rating systems (QRS), 96
Quazzo, D., 233

RAND Corporation, 235
Rasmussen College, 58, 60, 61, 62, 66
Ravitch, Diane, 3, 235
Raynor, M. E., 227
READ 180 program, 177
Reading Excellence Act (1998), 16
Reading for Profit (Altwerger), 5
Reason Foundation, 27, 229
Rebel with a Cause (Sperling), 6
Rees, Nina, *37,* 47, 54

Reform
  advocacy for, 151
  comprehensive, 175
  consensus for, 135
  effectiveness of, 178, 180
  in health care, 125, 139
  in K–12 education, 20
  need for, 204
  and philanthropy, 208
  postsecondary education, 113
  in relation to scale, 174
  state adoptions, 134
  student loan, 20
  sustainability of, 39
Regulations. *See also* Gainful-
    employment regulations
  balance of, 80, 133
  cap services demand, 4
  early childhood education
    (ECE), 87–88
  effects of, 112–113
  enforcement of, 153
  favoring nonprofits, 120, 137
  hindering for-profits, 12, 53, 103
  incentives, 19, 30, 102, 109, 111,
    115, 122, 127–128, 190
  and investors, 15
  need for flexibility, 139
  within online sector, 9, 151–152,
    153
  removal of barriers,
    121–122, 138, 139
  state reform of, 134
  stifling innovation, 133–134,
    135
REI, 4
Republicans
  gainful-employment
    regulation, 17–19, 20
  opposition to for-profit school
    management, 25
  support for-profits, 12, 13, 14–15,
    16, 19–20, 24, *24,* 26
Resources for Indispensable Schools
    and Educators (RISE), *36,* 45, 97
Revolution Foods, 49
Riggan, Matt, 9, 206
Rising above the Gathering Storm
    (National Academies), 129
Risley, T., 229
Riverside Community College, 72
Rocketship Education, *35,* 46
Rolnick, Arthur, 83, 235
Roper Center for Public
    Opinion Research, 21
Rose, E., 235
Rose, L. C., 235
Rosen, Andy, 6, 235
Ross, C., 232
Rotherham, Andy, *37,* 44, 232

Sable, J., 230
Salaries, 44–45, 59, 81, 83,
    154, 183, 195, 197
Samuelson, R. J., 235
Sangari, *34*
San Jose State University, 59
Saul, S., 235
Schein, Edgar, 108
Schlesinger, M., 235
Schneider, M., 235
Scholastic, *35,* 177, 178, 235
School Improvement Grants (SIG)
    program, 3, 12, 16, 17, 175
Schoolnet, *35,* 43, 48, 53
School of One, 8
Schorr, Jonathan, *37,* 49, 52, 53, 54
Schrecker, Ellen, 6, 236

Schulman, K., 235
Scott, Rick, 188
Scriven, M., 236
Securities and Exchange
    Commission, 15
Senate, 13, 16
Senate Committee on Health,
    Education, Labor, and Pensions
    (HELP), 13, 14, 236
Sengupta, S., 236
SES. *See* Supplemental education
    services (SES)
Shapiro, Harold, 60, 66, 67, 68,
    69, 73, 74, 76, 78, 207
Shared Learning Collaborative
    (SLC), 170–171
Shelton, Jim, 13, *37*, 43, 54
Shonkoff, J., 236
Shu, K., 227
SIG. *See* School Improvement
    Grants (SIG) program
Silverman, L., 226
Siry, D., 236
Skamris Holm, M., 228
Smith, Kim, *37*
Smith, Peter, 59, 67, 74, 78
Snell, L., 230
Soares, L., 227
Space Exploration Technologies
    Corporation (SpaceX), 124
Spellings Commission, 112–113
Sperling, John, 6, 59, 236
Spradlin, T. E., 226
St. Joseph's University, 60
Stake, Robert E., 176
Standardization, 6, 58, 63,
    64, 66, 70, 75, 77
State legislation, 3
Steinberg, M., 226
Stout Sosinsky, L., 236

Stratton, H. B., 2
Stroup, Sally, 20
Student convenience, 71–72
Student engagement, 72
Student loans
    debt-to-income ratio,
        12, 57, 108, 187, 190
    default rate, 57, 62, 128, 137
    eligibility for, 9, 137
    reform of, 20
Stuit, D. A., 236
Success Academy Charter Schools,
    36
Success rates, 63
Sumsion, Jennifer, 94, 236
Superintendents, 12, 22–23,
    194, 199, 226
Supplemental education services
    (SES), 7, 12, 15–17, 29,
    30, 175, 186, 229
Supply and demand
    characteristics, *158*
Sylva, K., 232
Sylvan Learning Centers, 29

Tax status, 7, 9, 49, 53, 54, 80, 84, 122,
    123, 138, 193, 194, 195, 205, 209
Teachers. *See also* Faculty
    autonomy of, 64
    curricula planning, 169–170, 178
    education of, 68, 83, 92, 93
    effectiveness of, 195
    for-profits' influence on, 5
    needs of, 4, 49
    as practitioners, 71
    quality of, 81, 83, 98
    wages, 83, 92, 145
Teacher unions, 46, 194
Teach For America, 1, 33, *35*, *37*, 201
Technology Crossover Ventures, 149

Temporary Assistance to Needy
    Families (TANF), 85, 87, 89–90, 98
Tennessee Charter School
    Association, *35*
Tenure, 61–62, 69, 70, 77, 184
Thinking of Forming A Non-
    Profi t? What to Consider
    Before You Begin, 39
Thomas B. Fordham Institute, 236
Thornton, Felicia, 89
Thrun, Sebastian, 143
Tierney, William G., 7, 230, 236
Time to Know, 119
Title I financing, 12, 16, 175
Title IV financing, 115–116, 153
TK Capital, *36*
Tomassini, J., 236
Tout, Kathryn, 96, 237
Towns, Edolphus, 18
Trail Blazers, *35*
Transparency, 2, 4, 167, 174
Tuchman, Gaye, 6, 237
Tuition costs, 81, 115, 176, 181,
    187, 195, 200–201
Tutor.com, *34,* 41, 48, 50
Tutoring
    for-profit management of, 28, 29
    incentives for, 30
    need for, 5, 175, 186
    online, 2, 141
    privatization, 16, 29
    and Reading Excellence
        Act of 1998, 16
    Title I funding, 16
Twombly, E. C., 237

Unions, 16, 17, 23, 46, 49, 110,
    150, 186, 187, 194, 203
United Federation of Teachers, 49
United Way, 102

University of Alaska, 61, 69
University of California, 113
University of Illinois, 73
University of Minnesota, 59, 61
University of Pennsylvania Graduate
    School of Education, 9
University of Phoenix, 2–3, 6,
    20, 46, 58, 59, 60, 61, 64, 71,
    78, 143, 151, 185, 237
University of Southern
    California, 67, 78
University of Texas, 65
University of Virginia, *36*
Urban Institute, 44
Urschel, Jessica L., 30, 233
U.S. Bureau of Labor Statistics, 237
U.S. Department of Commerce, 8
U.S. Department of Education, 3, 5,
    8, 13, 14, 15, 17, 19, 20, *37,* 39, 43,
    54, 128, 135, 137, 176, 178, 237
U.S. Department of Energy,
    124, 127, 128, 134
U.S. Department of Health and
    Human Services (HHS), 126
U.S. House of Representatives,
    Office of the Clerk, 237

Vaccine development, 160–162, *163*
Vandell, D., 237
Vander Ark, Tom, *38,* 43–44,
    45, 238
Vanderbilt University, 177
Vedder, R. K., 226
VHS Collaborative, 144
Vinca, David, *38,* 43
Vineis, Mark, *38*
Visibility, 30–31, 152
Voucher programs
    expansion of, 176, 177
    increased privatization, 187

Voucher programs *(continued)*
  infant and toddler care, 85, 89–90
  political support for, 12, 16, 19, 20
  in school choice, 4
  in Sweden, 201

Walden University, 58, 61,
  68, 69, 70, 71, 74, 75
Wales, Jimmy, *38,* 43, 47,
  49, 50, 51, 54, 238
Wannabe U (Tuchman), 6
Warner, J., 238
Web-based learning. *See*
  Online education
Webley, K., 238
Weiland, C., 238
Weinstein, R., 231
What Works Clearinghouse
  (WWC), 181
Whiteboard Advisors, 8, *37*

Whitebook, M., 238
White House Council of Economic
  Advisors, 132, 238
Whites, 26
Whitten, G., 229
Whittle, Chris, *38,* 43, 44, 49, 205
Wikia, *38,* 43
Wikimedia Foundation, *38*
Wikipedia, 33, 43, 46, 47, 54, 56, 238
Wildavsky, Ben, 8, 205, 207, 230
Wiley, D., 238
Wiseman, R., 238
Wolfe, B., 237
Wooten, A. L., 22, 226

Young, Caprice, *38,* 41, 49, 50, 51

Zagorin, A., 238
Zappos, 4
Zigler, E., 236, 238